Illman Brothers.

REV. JAS. W. HUNNICUTT.

THE

CONSPIRACY UNVEILED.

THE SOUTH SACRIFICED;

OR,

THE HORRORS OF SECESSION.

BY

REV. JAMES W. HUNNICUTT,

EDITOR OF THE FREDERICKSBURG (VA.) CHRISTIAN BANNER.

"THE UNION, NOW AND FOREVER, ONE AND INSEPARABLE."

PHILADELPHIA:
J. B. LIPPINCOTT & CO.
1863.

INTRODUCTORY REMARKS TO THE PUBLIC.

THE author of this *unpretending volume* being a Southern man by birth and education, by marriage and location, by every *sacred tie* and interest, political, religious, social, and domestic, which makes life desirable, but, by force of circumstances, driven from his *home* and all the endearing and hallowed associations of life, and thrown into communities in which all faces are strange and all eyes look with indifference on the *heart-crushed refugee* as he passes by in *sad*, silent, and lonely meditation, and presuming under circumstances so inauspicious to appear before his countrymen in the unenviable character of an author, it may be due to himself, as well as to a virtuous, intelligent, and patriotic public, to briefly give a few incidents connected with his past life.

He was born in Pendleton district, South Carolina, on the 16th day of October, 1814. His parents were pious and respectable, and both his father and mother, James and Nancy Hunnicutt, were natives of South Carolina.

In the month of February, 1834, he came as a student to Randolph Macon College, Virginia, at which institution he remained until the spring of 1836.

In the month of June, 1836, he married Miss Martha Frances Smith, the only surviving daughter of Dr. Charles Smith, *deceased*, of Lunenburg county, Virginia.

In the month of April, 1847, he moved to Fredericksburg, Virginia, and located in that city, in which he remained a resident up to the 29th of August, 1862, at which time the city was being evacuated by General Burnside.

On the 3d of April, 1850, his wife departed this life; and a *better woman* and a *more devoted Christian never lived nor died.* Her precious remains *lie* at rest in the Fredericksburg (Va.) Cemetery. She was the *mother* of six children: three are *in heaven,* and three were living last June.

In the month of August, 1854, he married Miss Elvira M. Samuel, of Fredericksburg, Va., his second and present wife. She has no child.

On the 4th of December, 1848, he commenced the publication of the "Fredericksburg (Va.) Christian Banner," and was the editor and proprietor of that journal until the 9th of May, 1861, at which time, by force of circumstances which he could not control, as the subsequent pages of this work will explain, he suspended its publication, and remained a quiet, but *anxious,* observer of passing events until the 18th of April, 1862, at which time Fredericksburg was delivered over to the military authorities of the United States Government by the civil authorities of that town.

On the 9th of May, 1862, he resumed the publication of the "Christian Banner;" but, owing to the scarcity of paper, and wanting other facilities, occasioned by the rebellion against the Government of the United States, the "Christian Banner," of necessity, was reduced to half its original size. When he closed his office in May, 1861, there was a small quantity of paper left on hand, which served for the first issue in May, 1862. There being at this time no facilities of transportation of goods by which citizens could obtain them from the North, and being unable to obtain white paper in Fredericksburg, he was advised to continue its publication on brown paper,—which he did.

Prior to the commencement of the publication of the

"Christian Banner" in 1848, he published several small works, principally, however, of a religious and controversial character, which, for the most part, were circulated in Virginia and the Southern States.

His prominent position before the public for the last thirteen years of his life as the editor and proprietor of a widely-circulating newspaper, and being a minister of the gospel for more than thirty years, should, in his *humble opinion*, entitle him to some share of public confidence, although a *stranger* and a *refugee* in the midst of strangers.

In politics, he has always been a *Constitutional* Democrat, according to the *true political* and *etymological* meaning of that term. He is *now* an *uncompromising Southern Union man*, which it is presumed no one will question after reading the subsequent pages of this volume. He is no office-seeker,—has never asked *for*, nor *held*, any office, either under the Government of the United States, in any individual State, county, corporation, or neighborhood. His highest aspirations are to serve his God and country and advance the cause of true Christianity and promote the happiness of his fellow-man. Prompted by a sense of duty, which he feels that he owes to his God and country, his wife and children, to his churches and to himself, has induced the publication of this volume.

On Friday, the 29th of August, 1862, about five o'clock P.M., a friend of the author came in full haste on horseback to his house, to advise him to leave Fredericksburg without a moment's delay, as the Confederate troops were supposed to be rapidly advancing in great numbers and were nearly in sight of the town. On receiving this intelligence, he hastened to take leave of his wife, who, on taking the parting hand, said, "*Farewell, my dear husband; take care of yourself, and I will pray constantly for you, and I will pray to the good Lord to watch over you and to take care of you. Farewell, farewell, my dear husband.*"

And with a spirit crushed to earth, and a heart overwhelmed with grief, the author was driven out from his house, his home, his wife, and from all that makes life desirable on earth, to wander in solitude and sorrow among strangers. And, to add to the poignancy of indescribable grief which already preyed upon his deeply-throbbing heart, he was insulted and treated with contempt by secessionists as he left his house and walked through the streets to the car-bridge across the Rappahannock River, over which he had to pass. And thus, after having been watched, suspicioned, persecuted, proscribed, ostracized, and having his very house *eavesdropped* by contemptible scoundrels and damnable traitors for more than twelve long months, was at last driven from his *home*, his *wife*, his *all* on earth, amidst the taunts, indignities, and insults of the worthless, the vile, the God-forsaken, and the hell-deserving.

On arriving at the head-quarters of General Burnside, which were on the north side of the Rappahannock River, as the author stood on the hill and looked over upon the devoted city, as the sun threw back his golden hues on the towering steeples, the tops of the beautiful houses, the lofty hill-tops in the far distance, and the lovely valley of the Rappahannock, and contrasted these with the awful grandeur of a mighty army with guns planted and all drawn up in battle-array, skirting the hills and bank of the beautiful Rappahannock River, as it *laved* the base of the hills on which the army was stationed,—as he stood and viewed the beautiful, sublime, but terrible melancholy scene before him, thoughts of the past, the present, and the horrible prospects of the future crowded his mind in such quick succession, that, for the first time in his life, he felt in *good earnest* as if he *wanted to taste the sweets of death.* His philosophy wellnigh forsook him. And for what was all this? Had he committed murder or larceny? Was he flying from justice? No: nothing of the kind. What then?

Because of his undying devotion to his country, his *detestation of secession, traitors*, and *treason*. This reflection *nerved* him to the resolve to meet the very worst *issue* that might be *forced* upon him.

On Saturday night, the 30th of August, 1862, he arrived in Washington City, where he remained, secluded from nearly all society except his dear friends and fellow-sufferers in tribulation, his fellow-refugees from Fredericksburg and its vicinity, of whom there were a goodly number, until the 5th of November, 1862, at which time he left Washington City, and on the night of the same day he arrived with his little son, in the city of Philadelphia, Pa., where he has remained in peaceful retirement up to the hour of writing this brief introductory sketch. *To say less than this, is hardly possible; to say* more than this, may be unnecessary.

In conclusion, the author would respectfully offer a few brief remarks in relation to the present volume which is now offered to the American people. In preparing this work for the press, the author has labored under the most unfavorable circumstances, as the intelligent reader may readily allow when he is informed that every word in this book has been written and copied by the author's own hand since he has been a refugee. Having no documents to aid him except the files of the "Christian Banner," he was forced to copy every extract which is introduced into this work. The deeply afflicting circumstances, also, under which the author has labored while preparing this volume for the press, will, no doubt, be taken into consideration by the intelligent reader.

This book, as the reader will observe, is divided into two parts. The first part contains sundry editorials which were published in the "Christian Banner," beginning as far back as the month of March, 1860, and continued until the 9th of May, 1861. From these editorials, and the matter contained in the first part of this book, the reader will learn some of the agencies, influences, intrigues, &c. &c. which were used by the arch-traitors of this rebellion to consummate their plot of damnable treason against the Government of the United States. These editorials having been published during the time of the great national excitement, and in the very heart of the rebellion, entitle them to more than ordinary consideration, as they were written and published while the scenes were being acted out, and, therefore, are certainly more accurate and correct than if written simply from memory. From March, 1860, to May, 1861, the certainty of a dissolution of the Union, in the event of certain contingencies, and the horrors of secession, revolution, and civil war, were kept prominently before the readers of the "Christian Banner," to deter them from committing the *suicidal* act which the author *knew*, if committed, would inevitably plunge the whole country into ruin. Writing so repeatedly on the same subjects—the Union, secession, the intrigues of politicians, the certainty of a dissolution, and the horrors of civil war, &c. &c.—of necessity causes a sameness of language and ideas in some articles, which it is hoped by the author will be excused by the patriotic and intelligent reader. During the time these editorials were being published in the "Banner," some said they would "lock them up, and keep them," for the purpose in after-years "to prove the editor a false prophet." Let them now do it.

The circumstances connected with this deep, dark, and damnable conspiracy against the United States Government are gradually unfolded to the mind of the reader, until he reaches the culminating-point, the *sacrifice of Virginia*, when the testimony becomes overwhelming, and every doubt is irresistibly swept from the mind, however skeptical that mind may be.

The second part of this work embraces all the leading

editorials of the "Christian Banner" during its publication from the time of the occupancy of Fredericksburg by the United States troops to the time of the evacuation of the town by General Burnside in August, 1862. From these editorials the reader will learn something of the condition of affairs in and about Fredericksburg during the time that *that ill-fated* city was held by the Federals.

There is one fact connected with this subject which is of great and vital importance to the author, and one which the intelligent reader cannot fail at once to appreciate. It is the following. The editorials of the "Christian Banner" before the war, and the editorials of the "Christian Banner" since the war, which are published in this book, were published in the same town, in the same office, by the same hands, and circulated in the same community: if, therefore, the author had written falsely, every man, woman, and child in that community could and would have risen up and denounced his editorials as falsehoods and a base imposition on the public. This fact alone is sufficient to carry conviction to the mind of the intelligent reader as to the truth and correctness of the statements of the author. Moreover, the author hopes to be able to secure for this work a large circulation among the *people* of the South, believing as he does that the facts and truths contained in it would be heartily endorsed by thousands of the Southern *people,* if they could only throw off the iron yoke which the arch-traitors of this diabolical conspiracy have forced upon their necks. We join *issue* with the *leaders* in this rebellion, and not with the *people.* The *leaders forced* the war upon the *people,* and then have the unblushing impudence to say, "It's the people's war;" "the people got it up, and the people must fight it out." It is an *infamous libel* upon the *people.* The *people* never wanted war; the *people* never got it up: the accursed leaders got it up, and *make* the *people* fight it out. Just as if a tyrant, with a loaded pistol pointed at the head of his servant, says, "Thrust your hand into the fire, or I'll blow your brains out;" when in goes the hand; and when it is burned to a crisp, the demon tyrant says, "You did it; it was your own act; you have no one to blame but yourself." But we must close these remarks.

That this unpretending volume may serve some humble part in helping to put down this ungodly rebellion, and in restoring peace, order, prosperity, and happiness to the country; that the leaders in this rebellion may receive punishment commensurate with their crimes; that the people who have been deceived by them and led into ruin may see their error, renounce their leaders, and return to their former loyalty to the Union; that refugees everywhere may be blessed of God and cared for by their fellow-citizens; that their wives and children may be provided for and protected by Heaven from all harm; that the time may speedily come when the "Star-Spangled Banner" shall be thrown to the breeze from the top of every Capitol and State-House in the Union; that tyrants and despots may be crushed; that liberty and freedom may triumph over slavery and despotism; that secession, with all its horrible train of curses, may be *eternally damned;* that the Union may continue "one and inseparable, now and forever;" that God in mercy may overrule all things for the ultimate good of the whole people; that the reader may be blessed, the country redeemed, and the world saved,—is the sincere wish and constant prayer of the

AUTHOR.

CONTENTS.

PART I.

PAGE

CHAPTER I.—The Author's Devotion to the Union—Terrible Results of a Dissolution foreshadowed—Editorial of March 8, 1860........... 13

CHAPTER II.—Signs of Dissolution—Charleston Convention—Seceders jubilant—Corruption of Politicians, etc. etc...................... 15

CHAPTER III.—Political Changes—The Author Democratic—War Spirit, etc. etc.. 19

CHAPTER IV.—Extract from "Christian Banner" of June 28, 1860... 25

CHAPTER V.—Extract from "Christian Banner" of July 26, 1860...... 27

CHAPTER VI.—Fusion of Political Parties urged—If they do not, they are reprehensible—Peaceable Secession impossible—Separation of the Democratic Party—Separation of the M. E. Church..... 30

CHAPTER VII.—The "Nigger!" "Nigger!" "Nigger!"—War-Cry for Political Purposes—Politicians Great Knaves, etc. etc............. 37

CHAPTER VIII.—Terrible Revolution predicted—Fusion of Political Parties urged—Why the Author attends Political Meetings—Infernal Plot of Treason—Are Wise, Smith, Seddon, etc., Traitors, etc.?—Servile Insurrections predicted, etc. etc........................... 42

CHAPTER IX.—The Election of Abraham Lincoln no Just Cause for the Secession of any State, etc... 58

CHAPTER X.—Political Parties in North Carolina—The State for the Union—Certainty and Horrors of Civil War predicted, etc. etc....... 59

CHAPTER XI.—The "Banner's" Fidelity to the South and the Union —Importance of Preserving the Union, etc. etc......................... 65

CHAPTER XII.—Shall the former Glories of a Nation's Greatness be annihilated?—Dissolution of the Union cannot better the Condition of the Country—Property depreciating—Confidence destroyed, etc. etc... 74

CHAPTER XIII.—Horrors of a Dissolution of the Union—South Carolina passes an Ordinance of Secession—The Secessionists jubilant —General Remarks, etc.. 86

PAGE

CHAPTER XIV.—Extract from "Christian Banner" of January 3, 1861 ... 95

CHAPTER XV.—Extract from "Christian Banner" of January 10, 1861 ... 100

CHAPTER XVI.—Extract from "Christian Banner" of January 24, 1861 ... 105

CHAPTER XVII.—Extract from "Christian Banner" of January 31, 1861 ... 115

CHAPTER XVIII.—There's Hope for the Union—Union Candidates elected to the State Convention by a Large Majority—General Remarks, etc. etc. ... 140

CHAPTER XIX.—Extract from "Christian Banner" of February 14, 1861 ... 145

CHAPTER XX.—Hope for the Union wanes—Jeff Davis's Speech in Montgomery—General Remarks, etc. etc. ... 151

CHAPTER XXI.—Secesh Caucus Cliques—Great Secesh Meeting and Union Meeting in Fredericksburg—Imposition of Secesh Orators—Secesh Remarks, etc. etc. ... 163

CHAPTER XXII.—Extract from "Christian Banner" of March 21, 1861 ... 178

CHAPTER XXIII.—Saint Paul and the Gospel, and the Rev. Dr. George W. Carter and Secession—a Contrast ... 186

CHAPTER XXIV.—Extract from "Christian Banner" of March 28, 1861 ... 203

CHAPTER XXV.—Extract from "Christian Banner" of March 28, 1861 ... 213

CHAPTER XXVI.—Extract from "Christian Banner" of April 4, 1861. 216

CHAPTER XXVII.—Everybody in a Fog—Stampede—Raising Secession Flags—Petition of R. Thom, Esq., for Post-Office—What then?—Let the North and South be heard—Secession Convention ... 233

CHAPTER XXVIII.—The Conspiracy Unveiled—Virginia Sacrificed. 241

CHAPTER XXIX.—Extract from "Christian Banner" of April 25, 1861 ... 289

CHAPTER XXX.—The Last Editorials of the "Christian Banner" of 1861—General and Closing Remarks ... 291

PART II.

PAGE

Chapter I.—Extract from "Christian Banner" of May 9, 1862...... 301

Chapter II.—"The Crisis on us"...... 303

Chapter III.—Heart-Rending Thought...... 306

Chapter IV.—Secession like the Devil...... 307

Chapter V.—Why dethrone Reason?...... 311

Chapter VI.—Reflections...... 312

Chapter VII.—A Word of Admonition to the Citizens of Fredericksburg...... 314

Chapter VIII.—The Confederate Army leave Fredericksburg...... 316

Chapter IX.—Federal Troops take Possession of Fredericksburg.... 319

Chapter X.—Federal Troops landing on the Wharf of Fredericksburg...... 320

Chapter XI.—Extract from "Christian Banner" of May 17, 1862... 321

Chapter XII.—Extract from "Christian Banner" of May 27, 1862.. 332

Chapter XIII.—Extract from "Christian Banner" of May 27, 1862. 339

Chapter XIV.—Extract from "Christian Banner" of May 27, 1862. 342

Chapter XV.—President Lincoln and Hon. E. M. Stanton visit Fredericksburg...... 343

Chapter XVI.—Extract from "Christian Banner" of May 20, 1862. 344

Chapter XVII.—Extract from "Christian Banner" of May 31, 1862. 349

Chapter XVIII.—Extract from "Christian Banner" of June 7, 1862...... 351

Chapter XIX.—Colored Population of Fredericksburg...... 354

Chapter XX.—Extract from "Christian Banner" of June 14, 1862... 355

Chapter XXI.—Then and Now...... 357

Chapter XXII.—The Great Battles near Richmond...... 360

Chapter XXIII.—Getting our Rights...... 361

Chapter XXIV.—God will prosper the Right...... 362

Chapter XXV.—A New Era will dawn upon the Old Dominion..... 363

Chapter XXVI.—Extract from "Christian Banner" of June 18, 1862...... 363

Chapter XXVII.—Negro Stampede...... 369

Chapter XXVIII.—Ring-Leaders of Secession...... 370

PAGE

CHAPTER XXIX.—Extract from "Christian Banner" of June 26, 1862 ... 370

CHAPTER XXX.—Practical Secessionists ... 375

CHAPTER XXXI.—Extract from "Christian Banner" of July 2, 1862 ... 376

CHAPTER XXXII.—Won't Patronize You ... 383

CHAPTER XXXIII.—Extract from "Christian Banner" of July 5, 1862 ... 383

CHAPTER XXXIV.—Extract from "Christian Banner" of July 14, 1862 ... 387

CHAPTER XXXV.—Secession ... 396

CHAPTER XXXVI.—True to One's Own Section of Country ... 405

CHAPTER XXXVII.—Lying ... 406

CHAPTER XXXVIII.—Extract from "Christian Banner" of July 30, 1862 ... 407

CHAPTER XXXIX.—Extract from "Christian Banner" of July 30, 1862 ... 416

CHAPTER XL.—Extract from "Christian Banner" of July 30, 1862 ... 418

CHAPTER XLI.—Privileges Abused.—Sundries ... 421

CHAPTER XLII.—Guerrilla Bands ... 422

CHAPTER XLIII.—Examine the Logic ... 423

CHAPTER XLIV.—"Can't disgrace Ourselves and our Children by taking the Oath of Allegiance" ... 424

CHAPTER XLV.—Fredericksburg Three Years ago, and Fredericksburg now ... 426

CHAPTER XLVI.—Virginians, Prepare for the Worst! ... 427

CHAPTER XLVII.—Wonderful to Tell ... 430

CHAPTER XLVIII.—"I never expected it would come to this" ... 432

CHAPTER XLIX.—Respectability ... 435

CHAPTER L.—Poor Whites Loyal ... 436

CHAPTER LI.—The Union as it was ... 437

CHAPTER LII.—Order in Fredericksburg during the Time the Town was occupied by our Troops ... 439

CHAPTER LIII.—Slaves Seeking Freedom ... 444

CHAPTER LIV.—Union Element of the South ... 448

THE CONSPIRACY UNVEILED.

CHAPTER I.

THE AUTHOR'S DEVOTION TO THE UNION—TERRIBLE RESULTS OF A DISSOLUTION FORESHADOWED—EDITORIAL OF MARCH 8, 1860.

DISSOLVE THE UNION.

Of all the terribly wild and wicked infatuations that has ever befallen any nation since the creation of man, surely the most awfully reckless and ruinous has seized the American people.

To dissolve the Union in thought is wicked, in word it is treason, in act would be to damn a nation wholly. *Dissolve* the Union! And then, what? Then may holy angels weep, and all the sainted patriots who fell in freedom's cause on American soil veil their faces at the departed glory of the happiest and most highly-favored people to be found on the pages of the world's great history! Then may devils damned laugh at the finished folly of man, and chant in fiendish anthems the utter annihilation of the purest form of government the world has ever known! Dissolve the Union, and civil war begins; fire and sword, carnage, blood, death, pestilence, and woe, like a fearful, desolating *avalanche* from heaven, would sweep over "the land of the free, and the home of the brave," involving all in the common ruin.

Dissolve the Union, and the Constitution is gone! lost! lost! forever lost!

The "Star-Spangled Banner" would wave no longer, inspiring American hearts with confidence of the freedom of speech, the freedom of the press, and the rights of conscience! No: the liberty of speech, the liberty of the press, and the rights of conscience would all be crushed to earth,—trampled into dust beneath the unhallowed feet of wicked tyrants and bloodthirsty despots!

Dissolve the Union, and the South is dissolved, and the North is dissolved, and the whole Confederacy is dissolved! It is vanity—the consummation of folly—to talk about North and South, if the Union be dissolved! All confidence, not only between North and South, but between man and man, would be destroyed. Brother would meet brother, sword and bayonet in hand,—brother against brother, father against son, and son against father. A man's enemies would be everywhere, and his friends nowhere. Enemies abroad and enemies at home, without a Constitution, without a Congress, without a country, and—may we not say?—without a God. For how could such a people look unto and call upon a God of justice, love, and mercy, having spurned all his blessings and dashed their blood-bought privileges into the dust?

The Constitution of these United States should be as sacred to the American people as was the *Ark of the Covenant* to God's ancient Israel. Let no polluted hand touch the Constitution. It is the legacy—the great national legacy—left us by our ancestors. It is the price of blood,—the blood of brave men,—the blood of patriots, who loved liberty, fought for liberty, bled for liberty, died for liberty. Let every true-hearted patriot, every American citizen, lay his hands on the altar of his God and the Constitution of his country, and swear by the God of Abraham, Isaac, and Jacob,—by the God of all the holy apostles,—by the God of Washington and the signers of the "Declaration of Independence," and by the God of our patriotic ancestors,—to live or die, stand or fall, by the Constitution of these United States.

It is supreme nonsense to talk of a "peaceable dissolution" of the Union. It is just as reasonable to talk of concord between God and Satan, or of harmonizing the laws of heaven and hell. The fact is, dissolve the Union, and all is lost,—irrevocably lost! Who is prepared to meet the issue? Let him speak.

CHAPTER II.

SIGNS OF DISSOLUTION—CHARLESTON CONVENTION—SECEDERS JUBILANT—CORRUPTION OF POLITICIANS, ETC., ETC.

For a number of years we had been fearfully impressed with the idea of an eruption in the Federal Government, produced by the officious intermeddling of the ultra Abolitionists of the North, and the reckless, hot-headed "fire-eaters" of the South. We were convinced that, if ever these two extremes should meet, revolution and civil war would be the result. Hence, we anxiously watched the course of political events more critically than many of our friends had supposed. Having witnessed, when a boy, the unhappy state of excitement in South Carolina on the question of "Nullification and Union," we dreaded to pass through another scene so exciting, unpleasant, and destructive to the social and religious privileges and enjoyments of the people.

Prior to the assembling of the "National Democratic Convention" in Charleston, South Carolina, on the 23d of April, 1860, we were constantly troubled with a strange presentiment that some terrible catastrophe was about to befall our happy country. It will be remembered that great confusion and excitement commenced with the organization of that Convention, occasioned by Mr. Fisher's insisting upon his right to present a letter from the Wood delegation, with a resolution attached. The Chairman, Francis B. Flournoy, deciding that the subject was out of order, a spirited debate took place upon the resolution providing for the appointment of a committee upon permanent organization. Without entering into the details of that ever-memorable Convention, suffice it to say that the delegates from South Carolina, Mississippi, Arkansas, Louisiana, Texas, Florida, &c. &c., withdrew from the Convention; whereupon the wildest enthusiastic excitement prevailed among the friends of the seceding party, and salutes were given in honor of the seceders. Why was all this? And what was it but the strongest demonstration the people could give of their delight at the prospective downfall of the Republic? In scanning the proceedings of that Convention, and the final result, together with the manifest jubilant spirit of the seceding party, and that of their adherents all over the South, our heart sickened, and our spirit was stirred within us, and in the number of the "Christian Banner" of May the 3d, 1860, we wrote the following editorial:—

"CHARLESTON DEMOCRATIC CONVENTION.

"We had thought at one time to say nothing about the Charleston Democratic Convention. But what friend to his God and country can forbear? Who can look into the awful future and with almost a prophetic eye behold the destiny of this great republic, and hold his peace? What true, patriotic American citizen can be an indifferent looker-on? *None.*

"Our country has reached a fearful crisis. The whole political *sea* is in a state of universal commotion, while awful storms are looming up from every point of the compass, all rapidly converging to a single result, *the overthrow of the republic.* Political corruption will prove the downfall of our once happy country. Deny it who may, political corruption is doing its *hellish* work.

"Does the secession of Alabama, Mississippi, Louisiana, South Carolina, Florida, Arkansas, Delaware, and Texas from the Charleston Convention, prognosticate nothing? Who will say so? They quarrel about *platforms,* and fight ghosts and phantoms, when, in fact, it is men, money, and fame that absorbs their mind, consumes their time, and is working the ruin of the Union. The whole body politic is corrupt to the very *core.* From the crowns of their heads even unto their feet they are naught but one great mass of political corruption. The loaves and fishes, the spoils of government, to occupy high places, to fill important offices, and fatten and revel off of the sweat and toil of the *people,* is the *ultimatum* of the ambition of most modern politicians. We scorn to advocate any such course of reckless, wicked, traitorous conduct in any man, or set of men.

"What patriotic soul would hold connection with a party of men who are sapping the foundation of our Government? Let party men and party measures sink into the deepest and darkest shades of political *damnation!* Our country has been duped, gulled, swindled, oppressed, and crushed too long already by sycophantic knaves, turn-coat politicians, and contemptible demagogues, who stoop lower than the *devil* would to get into office, and, after being promoted by the *dear people,* are totally unfit, for want of principle and good sense, to manage the affairs of Government. Despite all the men on earth and devils damned, we will stand by the Constitution and the flag of the Union until we die."

From the time of the publication of the above article we became a *marked man* by many of the party-leaders contemplating secession. We knew it not at the time, so gradual and cautious were the means used to crush our influence. We were advised to "write nothing on political subjects." "The 'Banner' was a literary and religious journal," and the "organ of a religious denomination," and should, therefore, refrain from entering into political discussions, for fear of doing "injury to the cause of Christianity," "the denomination," and, forsooth, for fear the editor should lose "popularity and patronage"!

For ministers to dabble in the muddy, filthy waters of politics, we always regarded as a leap from the truly sublime to the supremely ridiculous. But for ministers to write and talk in defence of their country, is patriotic, commendable, honorable, Christian, Godlike; and we now deeply regret that we had not devoted every column of our paper to the cause of our beloved country. And we also regret, and feel partially condemned, that we did not travel all over the State of Virginia and deliver speeches in behalf of the Union, in behalf of our country. Now we have no home, no church, and no permanent abiding-place,—a *refugee* and an exile from our quiet, peaceful, happy home, because we loved our country and tried to save her from ruin.

CHAPTER III.

POLITICAL CHANGES—THE AUTHOR DEMOCRATIC—WAR SPIRIT, ETC. ETC.

"Eye nature's walks, shoot folly as it flies,
And catch the manners living as they rise."

STEADILY watching the current of events, in the number of the 'Christian Banner' of June the 7th, 1860, we wrote the following:—

"Just think how easily politicians *slide* out of the minority into the majority party, in their respective counties, districts, &c. &c., and how easily they can *slip* back when the popular current turns. To-day, a fellow is fighting for life and death in one place to raise high the standard of Know-Nothingism, &c., and to crush out Democracy; and to-morrow he is in some other section, fighting like a tiger to crush Know-Nothingism, &c., and to raise the Democratic standard.

"Since the failure of the Whig organization and administration, thousands upon thousands who were once rampant Whigs have taken shelter in the Democratic ranks and fattened under the Democratic administration. Should the Democratic administration fail, thousands who belong to that party now will wheel right round and join in with the popular administration party, whatever it may be, and *swear* they were right all the time and acting perfectly consistent, but the *dear people* were such *dolts* as not to be able to understand and comprehend them and their principles.

"Look round and think a moment. How many of the blustering, wrathy, frothy, sycophantic, disgusting Democratic demagogues who are now cutting up fantastic tricks sufficient to excite the scorn and contempt of all *gentlemen* and true patriots, were once as brainless, unprincipled, and uncompromising Whigs? The popular current turned, and they turned in with it. Yes; and let the popular current turn again, and again they will turn *in* with it,—they'll *slide in*. They've 'slid' in, and they've 'slid' out; and they'll slide-in, and they'll slide out, just as often as there are great national political evolutions and they find it to their interest to keep on sliding and changing.

"The people of these United States are gulled, duped, and led on to the very brink of political ruin by this *avalanche* of unprincipled political *harpies*, and seem to be reckless and perfectly indifferent as to the impending danger. When unprincipled men hold the reins of government, farewell to liberty, happiness, country, and *all!* Nor is this all. If a man of the party have the moral courage, the political honesty, the national patriotism, to expose the corruption and political intrigues of the leaders, he is *branded* as a traitor and politically *damned* by the party.

"Our country has approached a terrible crisis, and fallen on evil times. Jackson, Clay, Webster, and a host of others, who formed the mighty galaxy of our national glory, have passed away, and with them the happiness, tranquillity, and prosperity of our country; and we fear it will not be long until our national liberty shall pass away also.

"*Democracy!* This is a *powerful word.* We *love* it. We heartily endorse the principle contained in it. Did you ever think of its true meaning, reader? It comes from two beautiful Greek words, *demos, the people,* and *kratos,* power, *sovereignty,* and simply means power lodged in the people. *Demokratia, a popular,* or *republican, government,*—absolute power in, or belonging to, the people.

"What true, patriotic American citizen can object to *democracy* when properly understood? Let the sovereign people rise up in all the majesty of their glory, and crush and crumble to atoms every system and platform that conflicts with the Constitution, harmony, prosperity, and perpetuity of our glorious country, and hurl all opposing *isms* into the whirlpool of deep, dark, and eternal oblivion."

It is impossible for any lover of his country to conceive how very annoying it was to see the constant preparations for war, and to have the war-cry forever ringing in his ears, unless he were actually to realize it. And this, too, in time of peace and quietness. We constantly witnessed this state of things in Fredericksburg during the year 1860, and the reader can form some faint idea of the state of affairs by reading the following brief editorial published in the "Christian Banner," June 7, 1860:—

"WAR SPIRIT.

"The atmosphere, the very element in which we live, seems to be pregnant with the spirit of war. All the elementary principles of war, death, and carnage appear to be in lively exercise all over the world. Our exchanges come teeming in upon us filled with notices of riots and murders of every kind, and perpetrated by all classes of men, and women too.

"The very devil seems to be turned loose among the people. Battalions are being formed all through the South, and sublime and costly preparations for war are being made everywhere. The signs of the times indicate that the country is bent and determined on war at any and all hazards. Every political move points directly to war. Like a desolating pestilence, the disease has infused itself into all classes, male and female, old and young. Even the *little* boys in our town, who have scarcely doffed their infant strings, have caught the war spirit and formed themselves into *military* companies, and perambulate the streets dressed out in uniform, with their banners floating before the breeze, their mock drums beating, and their imitation guns on their shoulders. All this they are permitted to do, to the great annoyance of the quiet, business part of the men of our town. Surely no people were ever more completely under the wild, wicked, and reckless infatuation of the *devil* than what the American people appear to be at the present time. Our country is *demented;* we fear it is *doomed.*

"The people seem to have taken it into their heads that there will be war, there must be war, and there shall be war. Well, if they *will* have it, and nothing but war will satisfy them, then let them have it and enjoy it to their hearts' content. No doubt but that many of those *brave* souls in time of peace who are so much bent and determined on war, when it actually comes, will be the first to *dodge* and *hide* in the bushes and brier-hedges, drop into gully-holes, or *sneak* off as deserters and traitors. Many of those fellows who are now so active in instigating war, if it come, will either have to fight or run; and in either case they will be very apt to get killed. Poor laboring-men are not going to do all the fighting. *Gentlemen* will have to lend a helping hand, and perform some active part in the drama, before the scene winds up. 'Tis right and just that those who provoke and *force* war should *die* in the fight.

"It may be that war is absolutely necessary at the present time, to purify the political and religious atmosphere of our country. Both state and church have become so corrupt that war, as an instrument to sweep off the *agents* of evil, may prove in the end the salvation of our country. A remnant of *patriots* and *Christians*, good and true, may survive the wreck and ruin, *by* and *through whom* our country and the church, in the good providence of God, may become regenerated and ultimately saved. The people must be taught humility and yield obedience to the statutes of Jehovah. War and pestilence may sometimes be as essential to the purification and salvation of a country as medicine is to the recovering of health and the salvation of diseased bodies. In the midst of all our present and approaching calamities, whatever they may be, or however severe, let us look unto God, and confide in his wisdom, goodness, and power. The Lord God omnipotent reigneth: let all the people rejoice in their King."

Notwithstanding war-preparations were being made all over the South, the cry in Virginia was, "There is no danger of war,"—while many confidently and constantly affirmed that there would be "*no* war,"—the thing was impossible,—but still it was "well enough in time of peace to prepare for war." Companies were formed and drilled as a sort of pastime, and to give an air of *military* dignity and bearing to young men. We told them, and that, too, honestly, constantly, and faithfully, that they would get their satisfaction of it before they were done with it; but they laughed at our "wild notions," and scorned our kind admonitions, and mocked at our solemn warnings. We were sorry for the men, because we saw that a trap was laid to catch them, and we were convinced that the leaders would prove but too successful in their mighty efforts to ensnare the unwary youth and ignorant classes of the country. The noose of damnable treason was thrown around the necks of the poor, credulous men of the South, and the ropes were drawn tighter and tighter, until strangulation and death have ended the sufferings of unknown thousands. The Southern heart was "fired up," and men were drawn gradually into the horrible vortex of ruin before they had even suspected danger. The uniform, with all its *pretty* buttons, shoulder-straps, and stripes, was bewitching, and thousands became wildly infatuated with the charm. The women, and especially the young girls, were wonderfully delighted with the "beautiful uniforms," and the young men *donned* in uniform were much more popular with the girls than young men dressed out in plain citizen's clothing. This stimulated others to join companies and *don* the uniform also. Thus the work went on gradually,—every thing tending to a sure and certain rebellion against the Federal Government.

CHAPTER IV.

In the number of the "Christian Banner" of June the 28th, 1860, we wrote the following article:—

"*Quos Deus vult perdere, prius dementat.*

"Whom God wishes to destroy, he first makes mad, or deprives of reason.

"Reader, is not this peculiarly applicable to the delegates of the late Charleston and Baltimore Democratic Conventions? Men delegated by the *sovereign people* to meet and deliberate on a nation's destiny, to cut up such fantastic tricks as not only to prove themselves *demented*, but to create disgust and loathing in the hearts of all patriotic outsiders! We have been gravely asked where the 'burst up' of the Democratic Convention at Baltimore has left us. So far as the actions of the factionists are concerned, we are left just *nowhere*. So far as our own conviction of principles is concerned, we are just where we have always been,—*a firm, uncompromising, Constitutional Democrat.* We have, however, always been convinced of the absolute importance, for the perpetuity and prosperity of our Government, that there should exist at least two great political parties, who shall alternately wield the affairs of state. And we do devoutly hope that two such parties will now be created.

"That secession is the grand stepping-stone to disunion, or rather disunion itself, we presume none will deny. If gentlemen are determined on dividing the Union, let them do it. The sooner the better, if it *must* be done. But the sword of retributive justice will fall heavily on their own heads. If this Union be dissolved, and civil war comes,—and come it will, and come it must,—these gentlemen will have to do some tall fighting, as certainly as God rules the universe. Remember this, will you?"

That the leaders in the Breckinridge party at the South had resolved on the overthrow of the Government, in the event that they could not rule it, we suppose, has long since become a settled fact in the minds of most of the American people. Their whole course of action since their defeat proves that this was their original determination.

CHAPTER V.

In the number of the "Christian Banner" of July the 26th, 1860, we wrote the following:—

"The whole political and ecclesiastical world is, at this moment, in a state of wild commotion. The waters are troubled; the dark waves of mighty revolutions are rolling heaven-high and spreading the wide world over; political associations and parties are everywhere being disbanded; governments are already being overturned, producing great revolutions and undergoing ominous mutations.

"Our own happy country has passed through her palmiest days; her glory is departing, and will soon be gone, and gone forever, unless God in mercy stays the impending ruin. The Constitution is holy, just, and good, but politicians are corrupt, base, and vile, and, beneath the weight of accumulated guilt, they blindly seek their own destruction and the ruin of us all. To carry out their own *malevolent* designs, they would sever the Union, fill our country with blood and flame, and reckon their own promotion, their own glory, a sufficient atonement for all the common ruin.

"Will *freemen*—American citizens, over whose heads the banner of freedom has waved so long—now submit to the *will and ambition of petty tyrants*, and passively receive upon their necks the yoke of worse than British despotism? Think, reader, for God's sake think, and, while you think, swear in your heart that, upon the altar of your God and country, you will yield your life a sacrifice rather than this thing shall be! Our country,—our whole country,—thank God, is yet in the hands of the *people!* Let not petty tyrants wrest it from them; let the devil take the man, or men, who shall ever be the instruments in the downfall and *ruin* of this glorious Republic."

"Let the devil take the man, or men," &c. &c. This expression was caught at by our enemies and handled very ingeniously to our injury. Some said it was right down swearing,—absolutely wicked and profane. What do men now think of it? Look at all the horrors with which secession has cursed our whole country, and then say it is wicked and profane for the sufferers to say, "let the devil take the man, or men," who have been directly instrumental in bringing all these curses upon us. This war has sent thousands of souls in an unprepared state into eternity; it is to a very great extent demoralizing the people of the whole nation, both in and out of the armies. It has filled a nation with mourning, lamentation, deep, heart-felt sorrow and woe; it has made and will make thousands of widows and millions of orphans. It has blasted and blighted the hopes and fairest prospects of millions of men and women; it has paralyzed the influence of the Bible and Christianity all over the country. In a word, it has *damned* a nation, at least for the time being. And yet it is wicked and profane for a minister to say, "let the devil take the man, or men," who have caused a nation to weep, a nation's heart to bleed!

Men who are incapable of reasoning from cause to effect, and never once suspicioned the game of deep villany and unparalleled rascality that was about being played out upon them, could readily see a world of sin in the simple but emphatic expression, "Let the devil take the man, or men," who would sacrifice the lives of thousands and the happiness of millions on the altar of their own wicked, ungodly ambition. We said this long before the war commenced, and we said it, because, reasoning from cause to effect, we knew what would certainly come to pass "in the event of certain contingencies," which was a very common saying with a certain class of politicians about the time we made the remark. We positively knew that secession would produce revolution; that revolution would inaugurate civil war; that civil war would ultimately annihilate the institution of African slavery, and dissolve society, and introduce infinities of curses and evils upon the whole nation and the civilized world. We saw all these evils in the distant future, and tried to save our country from them; for the doing of which, we received in turn for our kindness the reproaches of many and curses of some of our fellow-citizens, and are now in the midst of strangers, a refugee from our home and from those whom we love and with whom we have lived, and for whom we would die, if the sacrificing of our life would convince them of their error and save them from ruin.

3*

CHAPTER VI.

FUSION OF POLITICAL PARTIES URGED—IF THEY DO NOT, THEY ARE REPREHENSIBLE—PEACEABLE SECESSION IMPOSSIBLE—SEPARATION OF THE DEMOCRATIC PARTY—SEPARATION OF THE M. E. CHURCH.

HAVING been urged by a number of correspondents to give our views on the subject of the political affairs of our country, in the number of the "Christian Banner" of August 23, 1860, under the head of "Random Thoughts Shot at a Venture," we wrote and published the following leading editorial, which we give entire:—

"Dear reader, if you have learned to think like a man, we are not afraid to write. We are willing to abide your verdict. Correspondents solicit us to write on a number of subjects. Courtesy demands that we shall notice them. This we must do under the head of 'Random Thoughts.' Our answers to inquiries will be brief.

"How or where to begin, we scarcely know. As the salvation of our country, however, is paramount to any and all other subjects which call in requisition the thinking faculties of our fellow-citizens, we will notice it first. We shall express our views fearlessly, let results be what they may.

"We think it highly probable that there will be a speedy dissolution of this Union. A large portion of the South is fully committed on the question of secession, in the event that Lincoln is elected President of these United States. We think that chances at present are altogether favorable to his election. If the Democratic parties would *coalesce* and centre on one man, Lincoln's defeat would be almost certain. This, however, we can hardly hope for, as matters now stand.

"If the Democratic parties and the Unionists would unite on one man, the Black Republicans would certainly be defeated, and the salvation of our country would be preserved, at least for the present. If all the candidates remain in the field, it is reduced to almost a mathematical certainty that neither Bell nor any one of the Democratic candidates can be elected. They mutually weaken the force of each other, and strengthen the Black Republican party. Is this wisdom? Is it patriotic? It is neither.

"Would not the Government be safe, and the Union preserved, in the event of the election either of Bell or of any one of the Democratic candidates? We firmly believe they would. Then, the salvation of our country is *now* in the hands of these parties. They can save the Union, if they will. All must admit this. If they can save it, and will not, then let them be *anathema maranatha.*

"They are like those bigoted religionists who would rather blow up all heaven, and let the devil take the whole, than that men should go to heaven in any other way than that which they prescribe. Are they not? Is this the spirit by which the leaders of these parties are influenced? From present appearances, it would seem so. No one can question the happy results of a *fusion* of all these political parties,—*the preservation of the Union, and the salvation of our country.* On the other hand, if they remain antagonistic, as they now are, the results are *inevitable,—a dissolution of the Union, the destruction of our country, and civil war.* It cannot be otherwise, if gentlemen are earnest and sincere in their declarations, and carry out what they say they will if a Black Republican be elected.

"'Suppose Lincoln shall be elected, and the Union should dissolve: can there not be an amicable secession and a peaceable separation?' 'Amicable secession and a peaceable separation!' Heavens! what an idea! What man of sense can for a moment believe it?

"Was it an amicable secession and a peaceable separation when the colonies of these United States seceded from the usurpation of British tyranny? Was it an amicable secession and a peaceable separation when the Southern Methodist Conferences seceded from the Northern Conferences? Was it peaceable between these two great ecclesiastical bodies? Was it peaceable all along the border line? Was it peaceable in Fredericksburg? Let their belligerent records answer the question. Let their pugnacious editors, the belligerent effusions of their newspapers, the incendiary harangues of their clerical stump-speakers, their criminations and recriminations, and their long and malignant litigations, answer the question.

"If bishops, elders, deacons, and sanctified Christians cannot secede and separate peaceably, in the name of heaven, how can it be supposed that any portion of this great Confederacy of States, with its thousands of *totally* corrupt politicians at its head, can secede and separate peaceably? Blot out the sun from the firmament of heaven, and then tell us that we still enjoy light and heat! Annihilate the Constitution of these

United States, dissolve this glorious Union, riddle the 'Star-Spangled Banner' of our liberty, peace, and safety into infinite fragments, and then, O madman! point us to the goal of peace and safety!

"Was there an amicable secession and a peaceable separation of the National Democratic Convention at Charleston? Was there an amicable secession and a peaceable separation at the adjourned Democratic Convention in Baltimore? Do the parties manifest an amicable and pacific spirit towards each other now? If there has ever been a time since the organization of this Government when the element of brotherly love and patriotism should do its work in cementing the hearts of brethren and uniting all to the Constitution of our blessed country, now is the time. Yes, now, when the storm is gathering, and the awful cloud looms up in terrible grandeur, threatening sudden and universal destruction to us all, to be divided among ourselves and act with hostility the one to the other is an awful sin against God, our country, our families, our wives and children, the whole world, and ourselves.

"That civil war will be the necessary, legitimate, and unconditional result of a dissolution of this Union, no reflecting, well-informed mind can question for a moment. Nor is this all. The work of war and death once commenced, the spirit will diffuse itself *everywhere* and into all classes. Kindle the fire, and from ten thousand sources fuel will be gathered, to increase the raging conflagration, until the smoke and flames in awful volumes shall roll heaven-high, desolating every thing in its onward course. And, moreover, it should be borne in mind that, in the event of a dissolution of the Union and civil war, thousands upon thousands will naturally ask themselves the all-important question, 'For what are we fighting. For our country?' No: we have no country: it is lost in the deep, dark vortex of political corruption. 'For what are we fighting? For liberty?' No: the *canvas* of our *Stars* and *Stripes* is torn into a thousand fragments and wafted to the four winds of heaven, and our liberty is wrested from us. 'Whom are we fighting? A foreign enemy?' No: our brothers, our sons, our fathers, our own countrymen. 'What shall we gain if we achieve the victory? Liberty, peace, prosperity, and happiness?' No: these have all been violently and basely wrested from us by despotic politicians, who, as soon as we have fought their battles and gained the victory, will place the *iron heel of petty despotism* on our *necks* and will grind us into dust.

"Are these considerations calculated to nerve the arm of the warrior to strike down the father, the son, the brother, and the citizen? Answer us, will you? In the Revolutionary struggle our fathers fought for their country and for liberty. In a struggle such as we have been anticipating, no such motives can fire up the soul and inspire courage in the actors. Traitors and deserters by thousands will spring up everywhere, and those who are permanently located and have property to defend and interests at stake will find themselves surrounded by enemies on every hand, when it will be too late to avert the awful ruin. Remember this, *you* who would *damn* the purest form of government that has ever existed, and the happiest country the world has ever known.

"If the Democratic parties will not unite with each other and defeat the Black Republican party, we would then advise the Unionists and any one of the Democratic parties to unite on one man, and, if possible, move heaven and earth to secure his election, and thus defeat the Black Republicans.

"We are asked if under any circumstances we would vote for Bell. We answer *yes*. If there shall be one chance in nine hundred and ninety-nine thousand of his election over Lincoln, we will go our whole soul for him. 'But he is not a Democrat.' No matter whether he has the name of Democrat or not. Is he a *sound constitutional man?* Will his election calm the boiling whirlpool of political agitation and strife, and secure the salvation of the Union? What citizen, we ask, who loves his country, would refuse to vote for such a man simply because he has not the name *Democrat?*

"Democrat! Who are Democrats? And where are they? Suppose we vote for Breckinridge? He is a *Democrat*. Then the Douglas party would denounce us as a disunionist. Suppose we vote for Douglas? He is a *Democrat*. Then the Breckinridge party would denounce us as an Abolitionist. So, under such circumstances, what are we to do? 'What are we to do?' We shall do just as we please, and ask no man any odds: that's the 'upshot' of the whole affair. Our country first, last, and forever! And may laurels, imperishable as the duration of eternity, wreathe the brow of *him* who shall be instrumental in its salvation! May God in mercy lend a helping hand to the party that is working for the peace, prosperity, and salvation of our country, the blessed nursing mother of us all!

"Finally, 'suppose Lincoln shall be elected: what then?' Let him take his seat, and, if he act well his part, continue until his term expires. If he shall violate his constitutional rights, let him be dealt with accordingly. What else can be done?"

And now, reader, we must close this chapter, having extended our remarks on this subject far beyond what we intended; but it is a subject which fires up our whole soul. What is life without a happy, peaceful home? And how can this be enjoyed without a happy, peaceful country? It cannot. But we must close, and leave other questions for future chapters.

We urged a *fusion* of the Bell and Douglas parties because there was no material issue of any important character between them so far as we could observe. They seemed to harmonize throughout. The Douglas electors argued that he was an uncompromising Union man,—that he was the regular nominee of the National Democratic party,—that he had done more, suffered more, and had been more reviled for the support he had given to the South than any other living man. The only objection to his political principles appeared to be his devotion to what was termed "Squatter Sovereignty." He was eulogized by the Bell electors, and Bell was lauded by the Douglas electors. Hence it seemed strange to us that these two parties would not *coalesce* for the sake of saving the Union; especially when the electors of both these parties denounced the Breckinridge party as disunionists.

The electors of the Breckinridge party in Virginia indignantly repelled the charge of being disunionists, unless "in the event of certain contingencies," which, in plain English, simply meant, If Lincoln is elected then we will secede; or, unless *we* are successful, *we* will break up the Government. They were exceedingly cautious on this question, for fear the party might lose influence. Yancey and Newton had already avowed themselves as being disunionists, but they were "isolated exceptions;" they were by no means the proper and fair "exponents" of the party. It was our devotion to the Union, and our very soul's desire that our country might be saved, that influenced us to urge a *fusion* of any two or of all three of these parties. We felt that we were willing to make any sacrifice for the salvation of the country, and we thought that others ought to do the same. They think so, too, now.

CHAPTER VII.

THE "NIGGER!" "NIGGER!" "NIGGER!"—WAR-CRY FOR POLITICAL PURPOSES—POLITICIANS GREAT KNAVES, ETC. ETC.

IN the number of the "Christian Banner" of September 13, 1860, under the head of "Random Thoughts," we wrote and published the following:—

"We are tired, disgusted, and sickened out with this 'nigger' question. In every political speech, in every newspaper, at the corner of every street, in social circles, at churches, in prayer-meetings, in parlors, in kitchens, in workshops, and barber-shops, and everywhere else where two or three are met together, the 'nigger' topic is first, last, and forever. We want a stop put to it. Can it be done? We trust in God that this question will soon be settled and silenced forever. Men talk about it; boys talk about it; women talk about it; girls talk about it; negroes talk about it; and everybody talks about it; and they talk everywhere, without prudence or any sort of discretion whatever.

"If we had talked, when a boy, as everybody talks now on this subject, if our voice could not have been silenced in any other way, we verily believe our tongue would have been pulled out of our mouth. The times have changed, and the people have changed, and it seems that the very seasons themselves have changed, and the whole world appears to be undergoing changes.

"Some say that all the noise that has been made and is now being made about dissolving the Union is 'child's talk,'—that there is no danger of a dissolution of the Union,—that the cry of dissolution of the Union has been gotten up for political purposes. Is it possible? Can it be possible that all this strife, and war, and noise, and excitement all over the country is gotten up by politicians for political ends? If this be true, politicians are a set of greater knaves and scoundrels than we had even supposed. Whether they design the dissolution of the Union or not, or whether the Union will be dissolved or not, their course of conduct is working fearful results all over our country.

"If there be no danger of a dissolution of the Union, then great men and statesmen, the leaders of the masses of the people, have made a long, loud, terrible, and thundering fuss, simply to ignore their claim to public confidence in all time to come. They merit the execrations of a brave, intelligent, free, and patriotic people.

"Was the John Brown raid a political stratagem? Is the Texas excitement a political trick? Are all the insurrectionary moves, all the rebellions and murders, which have taken place all over the South, political *manœuvrings* to dupe and deceive the good and quiet citizens of our country? Who believes it? Who can believe it? Be not deceived, fellow-citizens. That there is danger,—imminent danger,—no man of sense can deny! Yes, there is danger, and a fearful danger, of precipitating *this* country, *this whole* country, *this* country of our forefathers, *this* country of *ours*, *this* country which we had hoped to bequeath to our children, into one of the most terribly awful revolutions the world has ever witnessed! Yes: and the sin of it all will fall on the heads of corrupt politicians and designing preachers, who have been, and now are, leading the great masses of the people captive at their will! Is not this so? Think! will you?

"Some say the design of the cotton States is to dissolve the Union at all hazards, and reopen the African slave-trade. Now, reader, mark what we say. If this Union be dissolved and a Southern Confederacy formed, the cotton States will soon find that they have already as many negroes as they want,—as many as they can safely manage. Remember this, will you? The institution of African slavery and the prosperity and glory of the South are destined to fall together: they are *doomed!*

"We are gravely told by politicians that this whole question of *intervention* and *non-intervention* by Congress is simply a political abstraction,—a mere political dogma. Is it possible that pure, honest-hearted, patriotic politicians will plunge their whole country into fatal revolution on a mere political abstraction,—a worthless, political dogma? Is it possible that they will *even hazard* their country's welfare—her final destiny—on an abstraction, a useless dogma? Of what practical importance is tho Congressional intervention and non-intervention questiion at present? If this whole question be nothing more than an abstraction, a mere political *dogma*, why so much fuss about nothing?

"If there be, in fact, the danger of a dissolution of the Union, as anticipated by many in the event of the election of Mr. Lincoln, would it not be patriotic in two of the three candidates to withdraw their names from the contest, entirely? Would not such a course immortalize them through all time in the hearts of the American people? Suppose Douglas was to withdraw his name from the contest, and say, 'Fellow-citizens, I fear that by having so many candidates in the field we shall all defeat ourselves and elect a common enemy, and thereby hazard the safety and salvation of the Union. Therefore I withdraw my name, and shall throw all my influence on the strongest candidate, —whether he be Bell or Breckinridge,—and thus try to defeat our common enemy.' An act so magnanimous and patriotic, at such a crisis as the present, would immortalize Douglas, and make the *people love* him, whether they had wished to do so or not. If Mr. Douglas, Breckinridge, or Bell were to act thus, their election in 1864 and 1868—first the one and then the other—would be almost certain, should they live and run for the Presidency. It would not be necessary for them to make electioneering speeches. The *people* would *speak* for them at the polls.

"No matter who is elected President of these United States, it is not necessary that the Union shall be divided. In the event of the election of Mr. Lincoln, suppose the Representatives of any of the States were to say, 'We won't serve.' Then, what? Then, let the people elect others who will serve. True, it might throw things into a state of temporary confusion. But what of that? It would be nothing in comparison to a dissolution of the Union. One thing is reduced to a certainty: if all three of the candidates—Bell, Breckinridge, and Douglas—remain in the field, neither one of the three can be elected by the people. Therefore, all the stump-speaking and time and labor lost by them and their friends are just so much thrown away."

The result of the election is well known to the American people, and the fate of the three opposing candidates—Bell, Breckinridge, and Douglas—is also well known to the American people. Poor Douglas—with all his natural and acquired abilities, with all his devoted patriotism and fidelity to the South—has fallen. His country has lost one of her most talented and patriotic sons. *Peace to his ashes, and glory to his memory!*

Bell and Breckinridge have both turned traitors to their country; and their names will go down to posterity steeped in national treason and covered with political infamy.

CHAPTER VIII.

TERRIBLE REVOLUTION PREDICTED—FUSION OF POLITICAL PARTIES URGED—WHY THE AUTHOR ATTENDS POLITICAL MEETINGS—INFERNAL PLOT OF TREASON—ARE WISE, SMITH, SEDDON, ETC., TRAITORS, ETC.?—SERVILE INSURRECTIONS PREDICTED, ETC. ETC.

IN the number of the "Christian Banner" of September 27, 1860, under the head of "Random Thoughts Shot at a Venture," we wrote the following leading editorial:—

"Great God, reader, we are astonished beyond measure! The whole world is rolling on through immeasurable space, and all nature, animate and inanimate, rational and irrational, the whole body politic, and every particle, separately and singly, seem convulsed from centre to circumference.

"That the whole world is on the fearful brink of a terribly sublime revolution, we do not entertain a doubt. As to the results of the maddening question which is now agitating every heart in this great and grand country of ours, the least we can do is simply to give our opinion, as many of our readers have earnestly solicited us to do. This, in part, is our apology for the matter contained in this chapter of 'Random Thoughts.'

"To begin:—There are now four candidates before the American people begging popular suffrage for the

Presidency of these United States. The friends of Lincoln, the Black Republican candidate, are moving heaven and earth to secure his election. We think it more than probable, unless a *fusion* of other parties take place, that Lincoln will be elected by the popular vote of the people. Neither Bell, Breckinridge, nor Douglas can be elected by the popular vote of the people, if all three candidates remain in the field. This is a *fixed* fact, which the most obtuse intellect cannot mistake. If, therefore, neither Bell, Douglas, nor Breckinridge can be elected by the people if all three continue candidates, and if these parties actually believe that the election of Lincoln will consummate a dissolution of the Union, why, as patriots and friends of the Union, do they not unite their influence on one man, and thus defeat Lincoln and save the Union? They remind us of certain stubborn, refractory persons who would break up and destroy the peace and harmony of heaven itself, unless they can have things their own way. What pleasure can it be to all three of these parties simply to defeat one another? They'll 'cut off their noses to spite their faces.' They'll achieve great victories and win immortal honors, will they? Mark what we say. If they persist in their reckless, ruinous course, the career of their political glory will wind up at the close of the present Presidential canvass,—and that, too, with the election of Mr. Lincoln! Who will hereafter trust men who, without any just cause, will jeopardize the peace, harmony, and salvation of a whole nation? None but madmen!

"'Why,' we are asked, 'do we attend political meetings?' First, because we feel deeply interested in the final result of this political struggle, and wish to thoroughly understand the principles and true positions of the parties. Secondly, because we wish to be able to advise our readers correctly, which we cannot do if we are ignorant on these subjects ourself. Thirdly, because we love to hear 'smart' men 'talk,' whether we agree with them or not.

"'Well, what's the difference between them? What's the great bone of contention?' What? Why, the almost invisible shade of a shadow,—*intervention*, or *non-intervention!*

"Congress cannot constitutionally legislate slavery into a State or Territory, nor can she legislate it out. She can only protect it where it exists by the organic law of the State or Territory. Congress cannot legislate slavery into the State of Ohio, nor can she legislate it out of Virginia. It is all a 'fuss kicked up' about nothing. There is not a single Federal question or principle of any importance introduced into the canvass by any one of the parties as an issue between them.

"The great question is this:—Shall the South continue her 'social existence' or not? In other words, shall the institution of slavery be perpetuated, and shall slave territory be extended, or not? We have listened to able addresses from Douglas, Breckinridge, and Bell electors, and have tried to analyze the specific difference between them all. The Bell and Douglas men seem to harmonize throughout. Bell electors eulogize Douglas to the very heavens, but charge the Breckinridge party with the awful sin of being disunionists, bent and determined on breaking up and dissolving this glorious Confederacy of States. Douglas electors charge on the Breckinridge party the same design.

"Do the Douglas and Bell parties actually *believe in their hearts*, or do they *honestly believe*, that the Breckinridge party is composed of disunionists? Or is this a political stratagem to widen the breach between the Douglas and Breckinridge parties for the purpose of so far weakening the Breckinridge party as to defeat Breckinridge in Virginia and to secure the State for Bell? Every vote that shall be cast for Douglas will weaken the Breckinridge party, and give strength to Bell. Why? Because there is no *possible* chance for Douglas to gain Virginia. Why, then, throw away votes on him?

"Why will not the Douglas men, if they are so fearful of a dissolution of the Union and believe that the object and aim of the Breckinridge party is to break up and dissolve the Union, unite with the Bell party at once, and make sure of his election so far as the vote of Virginia is concerned? And, again, why will not the Bell party unite with the Douglas party, if they have the exalted opinion of Douglas which they say they have? In either case, the vote of Virginia would be cast for a sound conservative, constitutional candidate, according to the acknowledgments of each one of these parties.

"Why is it, then, in fearful and critical times like the present, that these two parties, harmonizing as they do, will not *fuse* at once, and set the noble example for other sister States to follow?

"Look at it, reader, will you? If the Bell and Douglas parties throughout the United States would unite either on Bell or Douglas, they could and certainly would defeat the 'disunionists' of the South and the Black Republicans of the North. Will they do it?

"If they see the deep, dark, 'hellish' plot to dissolve the Union, and can defeat the 'infernal' design of these 'black-hearted traitors,' and will not do it, are they any better than the disunionists themselves? An enemy has our infant child in his hands, preparing to precipitate it down an awful precipice; we have the power to arrest the enemy and save our child from ruin, but refuse to do it: are we any better than he who actually commits the deed?

"Look at it, will you? Here are two large political parties, each avowing that they believe a third political party in their very midst is plotting and scheming a conspiracy against our common country, which, if consummated, will inevitably involve all parties and our whole country in irretrievable ruin, and these two parties by uniting their undivided forces and influence can defeat the whole scheme and save all parties and the whole country from ruin; and still they refuse to do it! Can they be sincere in what they say? If so, can they be regarded as patriots?

"Think, will you? This is a grave subject,—one with which no man can trifle with impunity. We say nothing against either of these two parties. We look at the whole subject impartially, *free* from *all* prejudice, and we earnestly hope our readers will do the same. However much we may admire either Bell or Douglas, or both, as statesmen, we *love* and admire our country *more*.

"But is it a *fixed* fact, is the case clearly made out, that the Breckinridge party are determined on dissolving the Union? If so, can it be *possible* that such men as Governor Wise, Governor Smith, Hunter, Sedden, and a host of others whom we could name, are ignorant of the deep-laid scheme to dissolve the Union? If they are not ignorant of the 'infernal' plot, and know it to exist, can it be *possible* that they will become accomplices in a work which, if accomplished, will *damn* them politically, ruin them financially, and annihilate their social existence? Is it *possible* that they are such consummate fools as not to be able to see the results? and, if they see them, can they be so wicked and reckless as to persist in a course which must inevitably end in death, and the common ruin of us all, and the ruin of our whole country?

"Look at it, will you? If the cotton States are so blind and infatuated as to believe it would be to their financial interest to dissolve the Union and establish a Southern Confederacy and reopen the African slave-trade, it cannot possibly be to the interest of Virginia. So far from it, it would involve her in universal and irretrievable bankruptcy. If cotton-planters could obtain laboring-hands from Africa for one hundred dollars per head, they would never think of paying Virginians from five hundred to two thousand dollars per head for laborers! Think of that, will you? Virginians have no large cotton, rice, and sugar plantations to cultivate. What then becomes of her negroes? And they increase like rabbits! Where will you send them? Nowhere; for there will be no market for them. What can you get for them? Comparatively nothing. They shall be sold, and, in fact, no man shall buy them. The insignificant sum which they would command would not be regarded as any price at all.

"Think, will you? In case of insubordination, rebellion, and insurrection, what would be the result? The whole of the cotton States would be flooded with transported Africans and native negroes, and there would be, in all probability, in many sections fifty, if not one hundred, negroes for every white man. Then, what? Is the reader so blind as not to see, *what?* 'Send for help.' Where? To the North? Think you that the North would come to the rescue of the South in such emergencies to suppress negro insurrections? No: there would be no help obtained from any of the *free* States. This is a *fixed* fact. 'Send to Virginia.' The idea is ludicrous! Send to Virginia for help, when she is crowded with like enemies and subject to like dangers? What man of sense and feeling would leave his own wife and children unprotected to go to the rescue of strangers abroad? Pause and think, reader! This is a terribly fearful subject to contemplate!

"Nor is this all. Men living in the same counties and adjacent counties would not leave their own houses willingly to go to aid others, knowing that their own families were unprotected and in danger every hour. We are giving no fancy sketch, nor false coloring to this subject. We are only stating facts, which will certainly be realized in the event of a dissolution of the Union.

"'But we have the fullest confidence in our negroes.' You have! Well, then, we are frank to confess that we have not. 'Oh,' say some, 'our negroes are loyal: they would die by us and for us.' Yes: think, will you? Jones's negroes would not kill Jones, but they despise Smith, and will murder him; and Smith's negroes would not take Smith's life, but they despise

Jones, and will murder him and his family, and burn up his property. Do you not see? These horrible tragedies will be acted out if the Union be dissolved.

"'But this is all fancy-work.' Dissolve the Union, and you will soon see whether it is fancy or reality. The fact is, there is no confidence to be placed in the negroes at such times and under such circumstances. And the South, instead of bringing more and more negroes into her territories, would be very willing to have them all back in Africa under any circumstances. Remember this!

"Think, will you? Precisely in proportion to the increase of negroes and their decline in value would the labor of white men decrease. Who would give a white man one hundred dollars per annum to work his farm, if he could get a negro man for fifty dollars per annum to do the same work? No one. As the country would become glutted with negroes, the laboring class of white men would be forced to seek new homes.

"Again, much reliance seems by many to be placed in laboring white men, in case of danger, who never have been, and who never expect to be, the owners of slaves. So far as the fidelity to the South (or to the institution of slavery) is concerned of this class of men, we are bold to confess that we have but little faith in them when it comes to fighting about negroes. They will be for taking care of themselves, and will leave slave-holders to defend themselves as best they can, in the hour of danger. We have but little confidence in the great majority of this class of the people of the South in a war for the perpetuity of slavery and the extension of slave territory. Men who have neither land nor negroes, and are treated and looked down on with contempt by these lordly cotton, rice, and sugar planters, will hardly put their own lives in danger to protect those who have never treated them with even common respect. Reader, think, will you? This is a practical article. No theory about it.

"In view of all these facts, can it be possible that there are slave-holders in Virginia, and in our very midst, who are working for a dissolution of this Union? If they wish such a result, they certainly cannot be sane. If, therefore, Breckinridge men in Virginia are disunionists, for God's sake let them openly avow themselves. We say nothing against either the Bell, Douglas, or Breckinridge party, nor shall we, until we perceive their ultimate designs. And we would advise all our readers not to be too hasty in jumping to conclusions and committing themselves too soon in this canvass.

"Our own opinion may be very different to-morrow, a week, or a month hence, from what it is to-day. We have neither declared ourself for Bell, Douglas, nor for Breckinridge. We have thrown out these hints for the benefit of our readers, who are not blessed with the facilities of reading many of the newspapers of the day. As we have said before, we now repeat, that, if we vote at all, we shall cast our vote for the man whom we think most likely to carry the State of Virginia, and thus far defeat the election of Mr. Lincoln.

"As to our opinion about Lincoln's administration if elected, we can only say that he may, or he may not, discharge the duties of his office to the satisfaction of the people of the United States. A nation's eye will be upon him and thoroughly scan his every official act. Should he discharge his duties, maintain and enforce the Constitution, it will be the duty of all parties to respect his administration, although they may have but little respect for the man.

"And now, reader, we will close this article by earnestly entreating you to ponder this subject thoroughly. Let passion and prejudice find no resting-place either in your mind or heart. Remember, this is a subject in which your happiness and that of our whole country are involved. Say not that you will support either Bell, Breckinridge, or Douglas, under any and all circumstances. Remain open to conviction until the very day before the election. Learn all you can, and, when you cast your vote, let it be done rationally, conscientiously, patriotically, fearlessly, and manly, and then if things do not turn out well you will have the peaceful assurance that you acted as you thought for the best. If you are a Douglas or a Breckinridge Democrat, and find that neither of these men can carry the State, and that chances are strong for Bell, then secure his election by casting your vote for him. If, however, you find that chances are strong against him, vote for the next strongest man. And so we would advise the Union or Bell party. This is the course on which we have determined, and we, therefore, advise our friends to do likewise. May God bless all the people, and save our country forever!"

It will be observed that the one great idea and grand object with us was the preservation of the Union. That being paramount to any and all other considerations, we thought every thing should bend and yield to that. All the electors of Bell, Douglas, and Breckinridge denounced Lincoln as a "black-hearted, uncompromising Abolitionist," whose object and aim was, if elected, to make war on the institutions of the South,—that his long-cherished object was to abolish slavery in the South. Hence our uncompromising opposition to his election. The disunionists of some of the Southern States, particularly South Carolina, had avowed their determination to secede from the Union in the event of the election of Mr. Lincoln. This the Douglas and Bell parties seemed perfectly to understand, and they charged this design upon the Breckinridge party in Virginia during the Presidential canvass. But the Breckinridge electors repelled the charge as a political slander, gotten up by the other parties out of which to make political capital. To us the idea seemed so preposterously absurd and *suicidal* for Virginia to secede, that we could not believe that such men as Hunter, Wise, Smith, Sedden, &c. &c., would lend their influence to accomplish a work so *ruinous*, so *damnable* to Virginia and every interest which she held near and dear on earth. Hence we asked, "Can it be possible that such men as Governor Wise, Governor Smith, Hunter, Sedden, and a host of others whom we could name, are ignorant of the deep-laid scheme to dissolve the Union? If they are not ignorant of the 'infernal' plot, and know it to exist, can it be possible that they will become accomplices in a work which, if accomplished, will *damn them politically, ruin them financially*, and *annihilate their social existence?* Is it possible that they are such consummate fools as not to be able to see the results? And, if they see them, can they be so wicked and reckless as to persist in a course which must inevitably end in death, and the common ruin of us all, and that of our whole country?"

Subsequent developments convince us that all the leading politicians of the Breckinridge party at the South were privy to the "infernal" plot of conspiracy against the Republic, and had leagued together to break up the Government in the event that they were defeated in the election of Breckinridge. Had Breckinridge been elected, and they remained in office, which they certainly would, then would there have been no secession, no revolution, and no civil war at the present time. Their motto was, *Rule or ruin.*

What object had Floyd in view when sending such vast quantities of munitions of war all through the Southern States? Was he not preparing the South for war in the event of "certain contingencies"? And were not the leading politicians of the Breckinridge party at the South privy to the object and designs of his actions? Had Floyd no advisers, aiders, nor abettors in this vast and responsible undertaking? Did he assume the whole responsibility himself, having no specific object in view but simply to scatter broadcast the munitions of war all over the South? Who can admit an idea so supremely absurd?

The "infernal" plot of treason against the Republic was long meditated, maturely digested, systematically planned, ingeniously infused into the minds and hearts of the people, and simultaneously acted out by the arch-leaders of the Gulf States. We look back upon the past, and analyze this whole subject, with loathing and disgust. Oh, the depth of wickedness developed in this infernal plot of treason against the Republic!

Strange as it may seem to the reader, because of our

devotion to the Union we were already *marked* by some as being a traitor to our own *native*, our own *beloved* South. Because of our devotion to the South, and the undying love we had for Virginia, the State of our adoption, we so earnestly and constantly opposed disunion, and the damnable political heresy, *secession*. We knew that to destroy the whole was to destroy all its parts. The South was a part, and, with us, a very material part, of the Union; and we knew that to destroy the whole Union was to destroy our part of the Union. And hence it was that we so earnestly and constantly plead against the destruction of the Union. If to oppose traitors, and expose treason against our beloved country, constitute one a traitor to the South, then we plead guilty to the charge. It is useless to say that our devotion to the Union, and our untiring efforts to save the South, and especially Virginia, from ruin, cost us much. Patronage went from us like drifted snow beneath the rays of a vertical sun. But we heeded it not. We felt willing to sacrifice every thing, and life itself, if necessary, so that our country might be saved. And, so help us God, we had rather be a refugee, as we now are, from every local interest on earth, with all the *odium* of traitors heaped upon us, than to be Jeff Davis, with all the laurels that shall ever wreath his brow, and all the wealth of the whole Southern Confederacy. We love our country, our whole country, and the South in particular; and for our country, and our particular part of it, we are now writing.

"Much reliance seems by many to be placed in laboring white men, in case of danger, who never have been and never expect to be the owners of slaves. So far as the fidelity to the South (or the institution of slavery) is concerned, of this class of men, we are bold to confess that we have but little faith in them when it comes to fighting about negroes. They will be for taking care of themselves, and will leave slave-holders to defend themselves as best they can, in the hour of danger. We have but little confidence in the great majority of this class of the people of the South in a war for the perpetuity of slavery and the extension of slave territory. Men who have neither land nor negroes, and are treated and looked down on with contempt by these lordly cotton, rice, and sugar planters, will hardly put their own lives in danger to protect those who have never treated them with even common respect."

We deem it necessary to make a few remarks in explanation of the above, lest our views should be misconstrued by the reader. We have never questioned the loyalty and patriotism of the poor class of white men in the South, nor their devotion to their section of country. That they are as true patriots, and are as much devoted to their country, as the richer class of citizens, we suppose none will deny. But to fight and die for one's country, is one thing; and to fight and die for the institution of African slavery, is quite another thing, and especially with those who have but little or no interest in its perpetuity, or the extension of its territory.

In our calculations, above stated, we were not mistaken.

"How is it, then, that so many poor men are in the

Southern army?" Thousands of them are not there of choice. In the commencement of the making up of and the organizing of the Southern army, men were told that their services would only be required for a few months; that, in fact, there would be no war, and, to make the most of it, it would be nothing more than a holiday-frolic. Others were organized as Home-Guards, with assurances given to them that they should never leave their own neighborhoods or counties, and, in the event of war in reality, they would not be pressed into service, being already members of companies for home-protection. Thousands had no employment, and, as a matter of necessity, were forced into the army to keep from starvation. Others were told that, if they had to leave their homes at all, it would only be for a short period; that they should not go out of their States, and that they should have the privilege of visiting their homes every few weeks, and that the travel would be at Government expense and would cost them nothing.

At length, when the appearances of war in the spring of 1861 became more and more palpable, and the militia were ordered out in Virginia, thousands were persuaded to volunteer to escape being drafted; as volunteers stood higher, were better treated and better paid than the militia. Every sort of means were resorted to in order to induce and force men to volunteer. Whenever Government wanted to raise troops, "Drafting! drafting! drafting!" was the cry. "The militia are called out!" "The militia are called out!" And men everywhere were frightened, for fear they would be drafted. Fredericksburg was one of the important places of *rendezvous* for the militia. There they met, and remained for more than a week, early in the summer of 1861. We heard the men talk, learned their views, and *know* that they did not go willingly into the service, notwithstanding they volunteered. Of two great evils—to be drafted or volunteer—they chose, as they thought, the least, and volunteered. Matters worked—or rather *dragged*—on in this way until the *Conscript Act* was passed by the Confederate Congress, and then there was no redress—no escape. All had to go. Did they go willingly? Ask their suffering wives and starving children. Ask the scouts who hunted them up and hurried them away from their homes at all hours of the night. And when this war shall have ended, and these poor men return home,—if they shall be so fortunate as to do so,—they will answer for themselves, and will tell stories of woe and sufferings that will almost chill the blood of the listeners. And, finally, liquor had much to do in making up companies for the war. When sober, men would swear they would never join the army, but, so soon as they were put under the influence of liquor, they would "enlist." And all this for what? To aid a set of traitors in establishing an infernal negro oligarchy down in the Gulf States, who would have no more respect nor regard for the poor soldiers who had suffered and fought their battles for them, than they would for their negroes in their cotton, rice, and cane plantations.

CHAPTER IX.

THE ELECTION OF ABRAHAM LINCOLN NO JUST CAUSE FOR THE SECESSION OF ANY STATE, ETC.

IN the number of the "Christian Banner" of October 11, 1860, we wrote the following paragraph, in answer to correspondents requesting us to give our opinion as to the result of the Presidential election:—

"We are asked how we think Virginia will go in the Presidential election. Of course, we cannot tell. Our opinion, however, is, that the contest lies between Breckinridge and Bell, and that Breckinridge will carry the State. This is our honest conviction, from the facts now before us.

"As to the final result of the Presidential election, there is but little doubt in our mind, but that Lincoln will be the next President of these United States. If he should be, we again say to our readers, prepare to discharge your duties as loyal citizens to your country, and firmly supporting the Constitution of the Federal Government.

"The election of Abraham Lincoln, by the people of these United States, to the Presidency, is no just cause for the secession of any State or States. If Lincoln should be elected, we hope the Southern people will act with that prudence and discretion which shall secure to our country as much peace and quietness as possible.

That this is to their interest, and to the interest of our common country, all sensible men must allow. We make these remarks because we feel it to be our duty to prepare the minds of our readers for the worst that may come. Should Lincoln act well his part, and the people act well their part, all will be well."

Because we constantly advocated the Union and the strict observance of the Constitution of the Federal Government, and wrote in the conciliatory style which we uniformly did, it was an easy matter to associate our name and principles, and those of Union men generally, with "Old Abe Lincoln and the Black Republicans" of the North. This infamously slanderous work our enemies engaged in and executed with a zeal and ardor worthy a better cause. To all their indignities, however, we submitted for the sake of our common country.

CHAPTER X.

POLITICAL PARTIES IN NORTH CAROLINA—THE STATE FOR THE UNION—CERTAINTY AND HORRORS OF CIVIL WAR PREDICTED, ETC. ETC.

In the month of October, 1860, we were sent as a delegate to the Grand Council of the Union Baptist denomination of Christians, which met at Bethel meeting-house, Lenoir county, North Carolina, some ten or twelve miles east of Kinston. In our editorial correspondence from that place, we wrote, in the "Christian

Banner" of November 1, 1860, the following remarks, under the head of "Random Thoughts Shot at a Venture:"—

"*The Greatest Study of Mankind is Man.*"

"The country here is in a state of general excitement. Fairs, pole-raisings, barbecues, political meetings, and religious meetings, all help to keep up the whirl, and roll on the tide of general excitement.

"Here they have the Douglas party, the Bell party, and the Breckinridge party, just as the people have them in the *Old Dominion.* The Douglas party is comparatively small in this State; but the Bell party hope it will be sufficiently large to defeat Breckinridge, and thus give the State to Bell. The facts in the case, however, will soon be demonstrated. As yet, we have heard no one express himself as being a disunionist. Our opinion is, that the State is *conservative,* and will go for protecting and saving the Union even if Lincoln should be elected. God save our country! should be the wish, fervent and constant prayer, of every American citizen. Without the blessings of our God and our country, we are all just *nothing* and *nobody.* Think of that, will you?

"Be the result what it may, before God, we feel that we have constantly and faithfully discharged our duty to our readers. We have earnestly urged a *union* of the Bell, Breckinridge, and Douglas parties, and have feebly and imperfectly foreshadowed the awful evils which must inevitably result and befall our country if precipitated into a revolution. The horrors of such an event will be far more indescribable than were the joys of the third heaven by the venerable apostle of God.

Mark this, reader; and when it actually comes to pass, then say if we predicted falsely!

"The Southern and border States will be the stage on which the most tragical scenes will be acted out, while the whole civilized world will realize the terribly paralyzing effects of the awful convulsion. Aspiring would-be despots may now think that they will rise and shine on petty thrones, and sway infernal sceptres over a crushed and ruined people; but, in the stead of this, they will sink so *deep into* the whirlpool of political, national, and eternal infamy, that the long and strong arm of Omnipotence can never, never reach them more; while the woes and wails of the dead and dying, and a nation's curse, will follow their *anathematized* ghosts to the lowest depths of the profoundest hell, there to haunt them as long as God *shall* be and eternity shall roll her ample sweep.

"Is there—can there be—any redemption or salvation for him who, to effect his own demoniacal, ambitious aspirations, would establish his throne on the blood and bones and ashes of his fellow-citizens, and the downfall and eternal ruin of his whole country? Think, reader! God bless you, think of the awfully terrible results which will follow secession and a dissolution of the Union!"

In the number of the "Christian Banner" of November 15, we wrote the following paragraphs. They were written and sent to the publisher before the Presidential election, but were not published until after the election:—

"Since writing our last article, we have conversed with a gentleman,—a citizen of North Carolina, who has just returned from a visit to South Carolina. He was in Columbia, S.C., and says that the people there are unanimously for Breckinridge, and are in favor of secession. His testimony can be relied on, for he is himself a Breckinridge man and an avowed disunionist. But, reader, before this article goes to press, the destiny of our nation will be sealed.

"We still hope that, in the providence of God, Lincoln will not be elected. But, in the event that he is, we would candidly advise our readers to act with the profoundest deliberation and the greatest prudence. The present and future happiness of us all is involved in this matter. Don't act rashly. Theory and practice are widely different. To *talk* of war and fighting is one thing; *actual war* and *hard fighting* is quite another thing. If possible, let us ward off the evil; but if nothing else will do, and war must come, then let every one prepare for the very worst."

We learned during our visit to North Carolina that, while the South Carolinians were for Breckinridge and in favor of secession, they actually wanted Lincoln to be elected. This may appear strange to one who does not understand the "infernal" plot of *treason* laid by these *arch-traitors* to destroy the Republic. The leaders of this treasonable plot wanted some pretext to justify them in their worse than *hellish* work in the eyes of the people and of the world. They wanted something to thoroughly "fire up the Southern heart," and to prepare the masses of the people in the slave States to fall into their "infernal" plot to destroy the Republic and effectually and forever break up the Government. The election of Mr. Lincoln they supposed would do this. The Breckinridge electors throughout the South had been careful to prepare the minds and hearts of that party, by teaching them what to do and how to act in the event of "certain contingencies;" that is to say, "if Abe Lincoln is elected, we, the Breckinridge party, will secede from the Union, and will *drag* all the slave States along with us." "We will *rule* if we can, but *ruin* if we cannot."

That the whole plot was *preconceived* and *predetermined* by the leaders needs no stronger evidence than the simultaneous action of the whole party, turning, as they did, right over to the *damnable* doctrine of secession immediately after the election of Mr. Lincoln.

In less than one month from the day of the Presidential election, the contemptible "secesh" flag was floating from the top of a tall pole in the town of Goldsboro', North Carolina. We saw it there early in the month of December, 1860, even before South Carolina had seceded. This we were told by a citizen was the work of the Breckinridge party. Our heart pained us as we gazed upon what we then considered and remarked at the time to our friend to be the *abomination of the desolation* of our own native, dearly-beloved South.

In returning to Fredericksburg early in the month of December, 1860, from North Carolina, we learned in Richmond that the doctrine of secession was becoming popular, and men everywhere were avowing disunion sentiments. On entering the cars in Richmond city, we fell in with an acquaintance—an able member of the *bar*—who immediately introduced to us the question of secession, and, Breckinridge lawyer-like, warmly and most enthusiastically argued to convince us of the correctness of his disunion sentiments. We reasoned the subject with him, and, finally, in a summary manner, summed up a few of the many horrible results of his principles, if carried into effect, at all of which he seemed to be perfectly astonished. We closed our remarks to him in the presence of others by simply remarking, "Time will prove who is correct on this subject." Subsequent facts speak for themselves. Come and see.

On our arrival in Fredericksburg we were utterly surprised to learn that the subject of uncompromising, unconditional secession was advocated by many, mostly, however, by men of the Breckinridge party. One of our citizens had gone so far as to put a star on his hat, determined that all who saw him might know him to be a disunionist,—a rampant, hot-headed, brainless South Carolina secessionist. We began to tremble for the fate not only of the Gulf States, but also for good old Virginia. We say uncompromising, unconditional secession, because the leaders of the secession party had determined to accept of no compromise whatever. They were unconditional secessionists,—disunionists for the sake of disunion.

CHAPTER XI.

THE "BANNER'S" FIDELITY TO THE SOUTH AND THE UNION—IMPORTANCE OF PRESERVING THE UNION, ETC.

In the number of the "Christian Banner" of November 29, 1860, under the head of "Random Thoughts Shot at a Venture," we wrote and published the following:—

"Dear reader, this number closes the twelfth volume of the 'Christian Banner.' While we reflect on the *ups* and *downs*, the trials and afflictions, the crosses and losses, the incidents and accidents, the sorrows and troubles, the privations and pleasures, of the last twelve years of our eventful life, the emotions of our heart are indescribable. We can't crush back the rising tear of mournful sadness. Our feelings are inexpressible,—known to none but God, our heavenly Father. The waters of affliction run deep, and roll heavily over our troubled breast. We trust in God's promises.

"Dear reader, permit us to say in this chapter of 'Random Thoughts' that, in our editorial of the first number of the 'Christian Banner,' which was published the 4th of December, A.D. 1848, we distinctly and most emphatically stated that we were with the South first, last, and forever. That by the South, and with the South, we'd stand or fall, sink or swim, live or die. That with her destiny our own is inseparably connected. Come weal or woe, peace or war, famine or plenty, victory or death, it shall be our pride and boast while living, and our honor and glory when dying, to yield up to God the blessed, Southern, vital air which we first breathed when we came into this grand, glorious, and sublime world.

"We love the South, and we can't help it, and we don't want to help it, and we shall not try to help it. The farther we get into the South, the more and more we feel like staying in the South. We *were born* and *cradled* in the South, we were *educated* in the South, *embraced* Christianity in the South, were *ordained to preach* the gospel of Jesus Christ in the South, *married* in the South, *settled* in the South, *have lived* all our life in the South, and intend to *die* in the South.

"The companion of our early manhood, the idol of our heart, three of our children, our parents and ancestors, are buried and sleeping beneath the sacred soil of the South. If we must fight, and nothing will do but fight, let us fight where our noble ancestors fought, and bled, and died,—so that, when the fight is over, should we fall on the battle-field, and have no friends left to lay us low in the ground by the side of our ancestors, companion, children, and relatives,—we may at least be blessed and honored with the divine privilege to lie and repose on the surface of Southern soil over their sacred graves.

"Were we to turn traitor to the South, the very ghosts of our ancestors would haunt us through all time; and our sainted parents, companion, and children would never meet and welcome us to the heaven and home of the redeemed. What! wake up in the general resurrection among Black Republicans! No, *never, never, never!* Our prayer to God is, that, when we wake up in the general judgment, we may appear there a *white* man, an *honest* man, a *gentleman,* and a *Christian.* This Black Republicans do not believe can be possible, for they '*do not fellowship slave-holders or their apologists as Christians.*' We hope that in eternity our individuality will be retained, and that we shall be our *identical self*, and nothing more nor less.

"Reader, you begin to think, perhaps, that we have turned disunionist, secessionist; but we have not. We are *decidedly, constantly,* and *wholly* opposed to a dissolution of the Union, if it can by *any possible, honorable means* be avoided.

"'But how can we defend the South by staying *in* the Union?' *Ay*, that's the question,—the problem to be solved! How, we answer, can we the better defend the South by going *out* of the Union?

"We will fight for the South, but we will fight for her *in* the Union; then, if we gain the victory, we shall have preserved both the South and the Union, for the South can only be saved by remaining in the Union; then, if we gain the victory, we shall retain a prize worthy the battle, however long, hard, and bloody that battle may be.

"If we go out of the Union, whom shall we fight? Black Republicans? They are the only ones of whom fears seem to be entertained. What! voluntarily surrender the Union, the *boon* of our ancestors, which cost them their fortunes, their blood and lives, into the hands of our sworn enemies, and then wage war upon them and try to whip them because we have yielded up to them the Federal Government?

"Let us stay *in* the Union, and fight for our rights *in* the Union, and, if we cannot get our rights by fighting Black Republicans in the Union, let us drive *them* out of the Union, and have things our own way, and the right and constitutional way.

"Do we not virtually acknowledge our inability to contend against the Black Republicans by going voluntarily out of the Union and giving up all into their hands? If we are not able to contend with them in the Union, how shall we be able to do it out of the Union? If they can whip us while we are in the Union, they can whip us after we get out of the Union; so that we shall be no safer out of the Union than we are in the Union.

"Again, while we remain in the Union we shall have the aid and influence of all conservative, constitutional, and law-abiding citizens at the North on our side; but if we go out of the Union, *by force of circumstances* they will be compelled to yield to the Black Republicans, and must, consequently, finally become enemies, or at least inefficient friends, to the South. So that, by going out of the Union, it seems to us that the South has every thing to lose and nothing to gain: hence, in advocating the perpetuity of the Union, we feel that we are advocating the peace, prosperity, and future glory of the South.

"We were opposed to any sectional man being brought out as a candidate for the Presidency of these United States. The result is just what we fearfully anticipated. But, seeing that a sectional President is about to be forced upon us, let us by every possible means influence him to do his duty, and crush out sectionalism, annihilate Black Republicanism, and thus restore peace, good order, and harmony once more to the whole country. If he shall fail to carry out in good faith the provisions embraced in the Federal Constitution, and his *Black* Republican constituents should sustain him in the violation of the Federal Constitution and his solemn oath, then let all constitutional and Union-loving citizens in the United States rise up in all the strength of their awful majesty and level all their united forces against him and his wicked accomplices in crime, and make a full, clean, and clear sweep of the whole party.

"We heartily repudiate the summary manner of individuals, little communities, counties, and States running out of the Union by themselves before the time comes, and before the word is authoritatively and officially given, by dragging down the glorious *flag* of the Union and running up little 'one-star' banners, to be gazed at by the prudent, the wise and patriotic citizens of our once happy country. No such demonstrations should be made over the downfall of our glorious Republic.

"The 'American flag' has been the pride and boast of every true-hearted American citizen. It has been the safeguard of all our rights at home and abroad, on land, and on the waters of the deep, blue seas. In the protection of our persons, our wives, our sons and daughters, our property, our political, social, and religious privileges, we have always looked to the American flag; nor have we looked in vain. Should we not now mourn to see it *trailing* in the dust,—the sport and plaything of the rash, the unwise, the imprudent, the profane, the wicked traitors of our country?

"Had any one dared to perpetrate an act so sacrilegious six months ago, he would have been regarded as being either a traitor or a madman, and would either have been hung for treason, or else sent to a lunatic asylum.

"Great God! Is the Republic lost! Canst thou not, O Lord, raise up another Washington to save the sinking Republic? A Jackson? A Webster? A Clay? Is our country ruined,—the mother of so many thousand sainted followers of the Adorable Redeemer,—the nursing mother and home of the Church, the Word, and the Truth of the living God, and of the gospel of the Lord Jesus Christ? Is our country gone, lost, and ruined, and has her glory departed forever? Save, Lord, by thine own almighty power, and save now!

"Reader, think, will you? This is no time to criminate and recriminate. Evil has fallen upon us. Destruction is at our very door. We cannot shun the consequences. To ask who has done the wrong—who has done the evil—will do no good now. The house is on fire. It is nonsense to stop to ask who set it on fire. Take it for granted that an incendiary did it, and let us go to work and try and extinguish the flames before the building is entirely consumed. If we cannot save the whole, let us be united in saving all we possibly can. If we fail in saving the whole Union, let us save every inch we can. Let there be a united South. Let us plant our standards all along Mason and Dixon's line, and say to every Black Republican, Hitherto shalt thou come, and no further, and here shall thy insolent march be stayed; and let every Black Republican who may dare to set his foot south of that line, to wage an unprovoked war upon the South and her institutions, pay the penalty by the loss of his head. The safety of the South now depends on the unity of the South. If the secession of any two, three, or four of the cotton States takes place, then let the whole scope of territory south of Mason and Dixon's line roll off in one united body, and leave the Black Republicans to fight it out, and to take care of themselves, away over on the other side. This seems to us to be the best course to pursue to secure present and future safety to the South, and to prevent war and bloodshed. Let us be calm, cool, collected, deliberate, and determined, and when the word is officially given, and the time comes to act, if action must be taken, let the mighty blow be given as if made by one man. Then will it produce the desired effect, and in no other way, nor at any other time.

"Let us wait patiently, until we learn the result of the deliberations of all the Southern Legislatures and Conventions, and trust that God, in his wisdom and mercy, may yet devise a remedy for the salvation of the Union. We trust our Legislators, Congressmen, Senators, and President will all act wisely and prudently. This is the time when all should invoke the aid of an all-wise, all-merciful, and all-powerful Arm to save. Every one should think and act promptly. Let there be no division in the South. If there should be, there is fearful danger that the South and the Union will both be inevitably ruined. Reader, think, will you? May God grant us wisdom to do right, and to act in conformity to his will in all things."

Convinced, as we were, and as events have proven, that the South could only be saved by remaining in the Union, and all our sympathies, ties, and interests being in the South, it was unnatural and impossible that we could be any thing other than a Southern man with Southern principles and sympathies. From the reading of the Abolition journals of the North, we feared that their object was, under the Administration of Mr. Lincoln, to make war on the South for the avowed purpose of abolishing African slavery in the South; and, from the character given Mr. Lincoln, during the Presidential canvass, by all the Breckinridge, Bell, and Douglas electors, we feared that when he came into power he would aid and abet the Abolitionists in carrying out their purposes and plans against the South. The only way, therefore, that we saw, by which the South could save herself, in the event of any of the States seceding, was for the whole of the slave States to unite for the purpose of repelling the threatened invasion of the Northern Abolitionists.

Subsequent developments, however, convinced us that the South was not, and never could be, a unit. The Breckinridge party—the leaders, we mean—were as bitter in their denunciations of the Union men of the South as they were against the most *ultra* Abolitionists of the North, and, if any thing, more so. The degrading epithets which were constantly heaped upon the Union men of the South, by the leading Breckinridge or secession journals and orators, were only calculated, and that continually, to alienate the parties more and more. And, instead of becoming united, we saw that they never could and never would *coalesce* and harmonize, and that, if the rebellion were to succeed, Union men, by force of circumstances, would be crushed to earth. A man might just as well make a lumping business of it, and give a *bill of sale* of himself to the devil at once, as to have the iron yoke of secession unconditionally placed upon his neck. But we shall notice this subject more particularly in a subsequent chapter.

There is one consideration that has always been a source of deep mortification to our feelings. It is this: our friends and fellow-citizens either cannot, or will not, comprehend and understand our true position. With the most of them, every man who opposes secession is an enemy to the South and a friend to the Abolitionists of the North,—when, in fact, it is exactly the contrary. Every secessionist is an *actual, practical* enemy to the South, and to the institutions and interests of the South, whether he knows it and believes it, or not. This requires no argument: facts which are now constantly being developed prove it true beyond any and all contradiction. Secessionists are the traitors and enemies to the South and to all her long and warmly cherished institutions, as well as traitors to their whole country and to all the free, high, and holy privileges and institutions of this great Republic, —this grand and glorious country. Because of our heart-felt devotion to the South, our own dear South, and because we loved the people of the South, we opposed secession. And because of our continued devotion to the South, we are now a *refugee*, homeless, and almost penniless, among strangers. But, we glory in it, we love the South, and shall until we die,—but we love the Union more.

CHAPTER XII.

SHALL THE FORMER GLORIES OF A NATION'S GREATNESS BE ANNIHILATED?—DISSOLUTION OF THE UNION CANNOT BETTER THE CONDITION OF THE COUNTRY—PROPERTY DEPRECIATING—CONFIDENCE DESTROYED, ETC. ETC.

In the number of the "Christian Banner" of December 13, 1860, we wrote and published the following article under the head of "Random Thoughts Shot at a Venture:"—

"Great God! Reader, has the fatal hour come? Has the golden age of peace, happiness, safety, plenty, and liberty, fled forever? Has the 'Iron Age,' the reign of terror, commenced? Is the problem, 'Is man capable of self-government?' solved? Has the experiment been made, and has the result proved an awfully-sublime failure?

"Shall the 'Stars and Stripes' of this once honored and revered Republic—the token of American *freedom*, the pledge of security at home and abroad, by land and by sea—henceforth and forever trail in the dust, and become a proverb, a by-word, and a hissing among all the despotic nations of the earth?

"Shall the American Flag of Liberty stand out through all coming time as a fearful *beacon*, to which all future despots will point, warning all future adventurers of liberty of the fearful and fatal American experiment? Shall this signal failure bear down and sweep into the vortex of deep and dark oblivion all future attempts for national liberty?

"Shall the greatness, the honor, the glory, and the freedom of this grand and sublime Republic be trampled into dust beneath the unhallowed feet of traitors, tyrants, demagogues, despots, and demons?

"Shall the names of Washington, of Franklin, and of the fathers of American Independence be honored and revered no more forever? Shall future generations, our children and our children's children, never learn to lisp their names and talk of their moral greatness? Shall there be no heart, in all coming time, to love them? Shall their statues be broken down and crumbled into dust, and their graves desecrated? Shall a tyrant's sceptre wave over their ashes?

"Shall all the glorious memories which cluster around the Fourth of July be forever forgotten? In a word, shall the American people—American greatness, American glory and honor, American liberty, and proud, happy *America—all, all* be *crushed,—crushed,—lost, and lost forever?*

"Reader, think! God bless you, think! Can the condition of the American people be bettered in any wise by a dissolution of the Union? Let us suppose, what is absolutely impossible, that the Union will be peaceably dissolved. Then what? Will produce be any higher? Will the prices of negroes be higher than they have been and now are? Will the people generally be more prosperous and happy than they have been for years past? If so, how? And why? Answer us, will you?

"Twelve months ago, there was confidence between all the commercial interests of America and of the other nations of the civilized world. There was commercial confidence between all the States of the Union. There was commercial confidence between the North and South. There was confidence among our fellow-citizens generally. Produce of all kinds was bringing fine prices. Real estate was constantly advancing everywhere. Negroes commanded enormously high prices. Within the memory of our oldest citizens, the country was never in a more prosperous and happy condition. Religion seemed to be shedding and spreading its benign influence all over our happy country. But hark, reader!

"Within the last six weeks the small *caps* have shot up above the lofty mountains, portending the distant, gathering storm, and men everywhere are beginning to prepare against the desolation of the whirlwind, which threatens universal ruin. Already the ominous rumbling of the awful thunder is heard in the far distance, and the hearts of the bravest men are beginning to quail as the heavens gather with blackness and darkness, the tempest and the storm. Men are sobered into thoughtfulness. They look serious, solemn, and care-worn. They think, and wonder *where*, and *how*, and *when* the scene will end. A nation stands trembling on the thin surface beneath which the furious volcano burns!

"The final results of this awfully-alarming state of things are too deep and obscure to be fathomed by the profoundest intellects of the nation. The President, Senators, Congressmen, Legislators, and people are all shorn of their intellectual strength, and are brought to almost a perfect stand-still point. How to shun the fearful consequences, all seem to be at a loss.

In the mean time, confidence is everywhere on the wane. Produce has fallen; negroes have depreciated in value at least thirty-three and a third per cent.; real estate has also diminished in value to an alarming extent, and still the tendency is downward.

"The general commotion and the awful financial pressure are being felt by all classes throughout the whole Union. Nobody knows *where* to go, *what* to do, or *how* to act. Universal bankruptcy threatens our whole country. This—yes, all this—is but the fitful glimmering, the deep-toned whispering, of the lurid lightnings and awful thunders which shall soon play at our feet, and roll in terrible grandeur over our heads, while the majestic storm is raging on. Will the people submit to be engulfed in one common ruin by demagogues?

"As yet, we say, all is peace. The Union is not yet officially dissolved. The first blow has not yet been given. The American soil is yet unstained by the blood of her citizens spilt in civil war. If such be the effects at the first appearance of the gathering storm before the Union is officially dissolved, to what port shall we be drifted when the dreadful storm shall have passed away? For God's sake, think! Dissolve the Union, and then what?

"Universal anarchy, for a time at least, will reign rampant everywhere. Divide the country! By whom? Where shall the dividing-line be fixed? Who shall decide? Divide the property of the Federal Government! By whom shall the division be made? And how? Appoint standing armies all along the border lines for the safe protection of the slave States? Where are all the soldiers to come from? And by whom are they to be equipped, fed, clothed, and paid? They will all have to be taken out of the slave States to protect slavery, and will have to be equipped, fed, clothed, and paid by this prospective Southern Confederate Government. Money must be raised, and onerous taxation must fall upon the people, to support this newly-constructed Southern Confederacy! What next?

"Prepare the Constitution for the Southern Confederacy! By whom shall this important document be prepared? And how shall it be presented to the people of the several States who are to ratify it? And who are to form the Constitution of this Southern Confederacy? When prepared and presented to the people of the several States, suppose some States will not endorse certain articles contained in it? As South Carolina is to prepare the document, suppose that when it is presented to North Carolina she rejects one point, Virginia objects to another clause, Maryland to a third, Delaware to a fourth, Kentucky to a fifth, and so on? That which may be greatly to the interest of some States may be wholly ruinous to others. Then what? Try it over again? Why, there will have to be more concessions and compromises to complete the Constitution and permanent organization of this Southern Confederacy than now exist under the Federal Government, or the Government of these United States!

"But what States will concede, yield, or compromise? Some of these Southern States will have it all their own way and to their own interest, or they won't have it at all. What then becomes of this anticipated strong Southern Confederacy? South Carolina, Georgia, Alabama, Florida, &c. &c., may confederate, because their interests, for the most part, are the same;

but is it certain that all the slave States can confederate and move on harmoniously together? This is a fearful experiment, yet to be made,—a dark and mysterious problem *to be solved.*

"What a deplorable and humiliating condition, we fear, awaits our happy country in the future! Before the Federal Government is entirely and eternally broken up, we think it just and due to each and every citizen in the Southern States to have the chance of either voting themselves out of the Union or to remain in it. If we are to go out of the Union, we want to go out of our own accord, and not be thrust out against our wishes.

"If the cotton States have determined to go out, this is no reason why the border States shall be forced out. And, before we consent to go out of the Union, we want to know where we can and shall go after we get out. Before we take ourself from under the protection of the Federal Government, we wish to know something about the government and laws by which we shall be governed in our new relation. This the people have the right to demand, and it is their imperative duty to demand it, before they madly and blindly rush into irretrievable ruin. This is no trifling subject. Our political and religious liberties are at stake. Our peace, our happiness, our fortunes, and that of our families,—in a word, every thing,—all, all is at stake. Shall we therefore rush on, in our madness and blindness, to universal and eternal ruin? Think, will you?

"War-preparations are being made in all directions. Whom are we going to fight? For what are we going to fight? How are we going to fight? Where are we going to fight? When are we going to fight? When the Federal Government is broken up, who can officially and authoritatively issue a war-proclamation? Reader, for God's sake, think! Surely blindness and darkness and madness have seized the people! To destroy the purest and best form of government the world has ever known,—a Government formed by the clearest heads and purest hearts our country ever produced, or perhaps ever will again, and rear up a new order of things in a few days, weeks, months, or even years! How preposterous the idea! The wisest sages and purest patriots would become paralyzed at the threshold, and shrink from sacrilege so great.

"Reader, we urge you to stop and think. Consider well before you unconditionally resolve to take the fearful leap into the awfully mysterious future. Once gone, all is gone!—lost! lost! forever lost! Do not allow passion to drive you to ruin. Let us not act too hastily in so momentous a cause as the present one. One false step may destroy every thing.

"Let us force our enemies to do their duty. Let every friend to God and his country frown them into obedience. Withhold from them your influence and patronage; perish them into the path of duty, or starve them out of the Union and out of the world. This can be done, and it ought to be done. After all is said and done, however, that can be said and done to reclaim them, if they then take up the sword of rebellion, let the South and the conservative element of the North slay them, hip and thigh, one and all, good and forever. Save the Union,—save the Constitution,—save our country,—at all hazards. Our duty is, to save our country. This we can do, and this we ought to do; and every true heart should exclaim,

'By the God of our fathers, *this we will do.—The country shall be saved.*' Think, reader, think! And may God order your thoughts in the right direction."

While Abolitionism was culminating in the North, Secessionism was culminating in the South, and, these two extremes meeting, the work of ruin is completed. And we now say that upon the souls of the leading Abolitionists of the North and the leading secessionists of the South rests the whole responsibility of *all* the *horrors* and *bloodshed* of this awful civil war. The Abolitionists were constantly goading and irritating the passions of the Southern people by meddling with the institutions of the South, especially that of African slavery,—an institution which they neither understood, nor in which they were in any wise interested, nor for which they were held responsible either before the tribunal of God or man, of heaven or earth,—an institution which was recognized and protected by the Constitution of the United States.

The disunionists of the South eagerly seized upon the meddling and intermeddling of Abolitionists as a fit and justifiable excuse and cause for dissolving the Union. Every little aggression of Abolitionists was magnified into a mountain, while the strongest appeals were made to the passions of the people to "fire up their hearts," and to prepare and fit them for the perpetrating of the most unchristian acts upon strangers travelling through the South and upon citizens who had emigrated to the South from the North. Hence almost every man who was not a blatant disunionist was eyed with suspicion: some were fined and imprisoned, others were tied to posts and whipped, others were *tarred* and *feathered* and ridden on fence-rails,—while others, again, were actually hung; and in one case a man was fastened up in a hogshead and rolled down a deep precipice into the Mississippi River. In a word, it had become both difficult and dangerous for strangers to travel through the South unless they had recommendations from the very highest authorities of slave-holding States. Spiritualism had already by law been suppressed in some of the Southern States; and all teachers, male and female, from the North, were becoming more and more suspected, and many of them had been discharged and ordered to leave the South,—all which was calculated to irritate and stir up the worst passions of the people of the North.

The leading editors and orators of the Abolitionists of the North, and the leading editors and orators of the secession, disunion "fire-eaters" of the South, seemed to vie with each other as to who should be the most successful in effectually and speedily breaking up the Federal Government. Hence we repeat that all the horrors of this horrible civil war rest on their guilty souls; and they will have to atone for their abominable black-hearted wickedness through all time and eternity, and to the people of these United States, and to God, the Judge of all. This may be considered by the very sanctimonious religionists, Abolitionists, and Secessionists, as rather severe language to be applied to *mock-philanthropists* and *traitors*, or to *Abolitionists* and *Secessionists;* but if, according to the teachings of the Bible, no liar nor murderer can enter into life everlasting, in the name of Heaven, what must be the punishment in eternity of men who have been instrumental in bringing about a state of affairs by which a nation of men, women, and children have been murdered and ruined? We have no apology to offer for, nothing to retract in the opinion advanced above.

In the number of the "Christian Banner" of December 13, 1860, we wrote the following:—

"In this hour of our country's gloom and deep distress, where is the peace *conservative* spirit of the Christian Churches? Ay, reader! there has been a deep, dark, successful, ecclesiastical under-current at work, of which the great body of the people have remained in darkness.

"The ecclesiastical parties that have agitated the *institution* which has brought our country to the present fearful crisis should feel responsibilities resting on their sinful souls, weighty and lasting as eternity. *Beware* of them; for within the folds of the white robes of the Church lie hid the keys of empire and an iron sceptre.

"Why do not *the* ministers and religious editors who have worked long and hard to bring about the ruin of our country now hold ecclesiastical conventions, and resolve to act as peace-makers between the antagonistic parties? Why fold their arms, close their eyes, and remain as dumb as death, when sudden destruction is at our very doors? Because the work of ruin and death is going on too finely to be obstructed now!

"They may think to offer up their long prayers and *fool* the people into the belief that God will listen to their folly! Know, reader, that, if our country is saved, it will not be in consideration of the prayers of men who have helped to do the mischief. Trust not to the prayers of vain and foolish men, neither to the schemes and intrigues of ambitious politicians. Let *the people*—all the people—put their trust in God,—take their country's cause into their own hands,—and the God of Abraham, Isaac, and Jacob, the God of Washington, the God of our fathers, will stretch out his strong arm of deliverance, and our country *shall be saved. Lord,* help, or we perish!

"Think, reader! The atheist takes from us all the consolations of the gospel,—all hope of future being and future bliss,—and for the hope of immortality and eternal life offers the boon of eternal annihilation!

"Destroy the Constitution of this happy country, this grand Republic, and what boon is promised to us for the relinquishment of all we hold so dear, so sacred? Bankruptcy, anarchy, civil war, starvation, death, and national annihilation! Reader, we stand on the brink of an awful chasm, deep, dark, and terrible! Let us think before we take the fatal leap!"

It will be remembered that, for many years past, there have been a number of professed gospel ministers at the South who have toiled with as much untiring zeal to infuse the spirit of rebellion into the hearts of the Southern people, and to prepare them for the terrible work of dissolving the Union, as ever did the *ultra* Abolitionists of the North. To this heaven-daring, God-forsaken, traitorous, ignorant, ambitious class of *preachers* we allude, who offer up long, loud, and hypocritical prayers for God to save the South,—that is, the institution of *African slavery!* For, with this unhallowed class of white-washed *devils*, *negroism* is the *South*, and the *South* is *negroism*. *With* this set of *demons*, (and their name is legion,) *negroism* and *treason* constitute the standard of respectability, and give to traitors office, respectability, and position in society. But we shall speak more of this class of scoundrels in a future chapter. The reader who has never felt nor realized the severities of secession may think we use strong language. But when history, in coming time, shall unfold the horrors of this unnecessary and ungodly war, and the stories of suffering millions shall be rehearsed among themselves, men will be astonished at the mildness of the language and terms used by us. It is not necessary in order to murder a man to pierce a bayonet to his heart: to be continually persecuted, threatened, goaded, slandered, ostracized, to be treated with continual contempt by old and young, by males and females, at home and abroad, by day and by night, at all times, in all places, and under all circumstances, is a death to die which no feeling, sensitive man will ever covet but once. To live in a community, and be watched and suspected, and to have one's house eaves-dropped by traitors and traitoresses, is a living hell on earth, to be more dreaded and shunned by all honest men, gentlemen, and true patriots than Homer's *hell* of ice and fire.

CHAPTER XIII.

HORRORS OF A DISSOLUTION OF THE UNION—SOUTH CAROLINA PASSES AN ORDINANCE OF SECESSION—THE SECESSIONISTS JUBILANT—GENERAL REMARKS, ETC. ETC.

IN the number of the "Christian Banner" of December 20, 1860, under the head of "Random Thoughts Shot at a Venture," we wrote the following,—which was the last article we wrote during the year 1860. At the time we wrote it, we had not learned of the passage of an *ordinance* of secession by the Convention of South Carolina.

"Thank God, reader, this is the last chapter of 'Random Thoughts' which we shall write in the ever-memorable and eventful year of our Lord one thousand eight hundred and sixty. This will ever be memorable in the history of America as a year of resolutions, legislatures, conventions, resignations, secessions, and of the breaking up and the downfall and utter ruin of this great American Republic.

"The seeds of national ruin are sown, and the germ lives, grows, and thrives. The leaven of discord is doing its mighty work with unparalleled swiftness and accuracy. We have acted the part of a faithful sentinel ever since we assumed the high responsibilities of the *editorial chair*. Some have mocked, others have become offended, while others, again, have professed to admire the bold, fearless, and independent course of the 'Banner.' Fools may mock and laugh at the voice of wisdom now; but at the last they will weep over their own folly, and cry for mercy when it will be too late forever.

"We have from time to time expressed our views relative to the present crisis of our common country. We could write volumes, if it would do any good or save our country. We fear, however, that the *die is cast*, and can only now warn our fellow-citizens to prepare for one of the most awful and terribly-sublime revolutions to be found in the world's history,—the result of all which, we fear, will be a *military despotism*. Let us not close our eyes to the fearful dangers which surround us on every side. Let us be watchful, prayerful, looking unto, and constantly trusting in, the mercy and goodness of God to save us and our country from one common ruin.

"To our female readers of the 'Banner' we would say, Be calm. Be not unnecessarily alarmed. The God who has always protected his people can protect them still. Look to the Bible, the cross, and up to the *throne* of your Father in heaven. Remember, a sparrow falls not to the ground without his notice, and that even the hairs of our head are all numbered. The reins of universal empire are in his almighty hand, and the rise and downfall of kingdoms, empires, and republics are all at his command.

"Nations, as well as individuals, have repented and obtained forgiveness from him. As a people, we have grown great and proud; and, although nominally Christians, we have been unmindful of God our creator, and neglectful of our duties. If, therefore, our kind heavenly Father is about to lay on us the chastening rod, let us neither murmur nor repine. It may all be for our eternal good. Remember, also, that you will be constantly watched and cared for by every brave son of this declining Republic. Be strong, therefore, and fear not.

"Never have we felt more cool, calm, collected, and determined. We have passed through many storms of infinitely more importance to ourself, individually, than a great national revolution can be, so far as the dangers of simply passing through a revolution are concerned. The after-consequences are more to be dreaded than the revolution itself. *To die* is a small matter, provided the work of death be quickly executed; but the idea of becoming the *vassal* of a *petty despot* is intolerable.

"Remember what we say:—If this Republic be broken up, in process of time, we doubt not, every State in the Union will become a separate, independent sovereignty, with a contemptible despot at its head, and that church and state will coalesce. In each little monarchy the religious party that is most popular, wealthy, and influential will be protected and supported by Government, to the neglect of all others. Reader, you may laugh now; but you, your children, and your grandchildren may weep and lament when too late.

"Some even yet talk of a peaceable dissolution of the Union. What wild and strange infatuation! Do South Carolina, Georgia, Florida, Alabama, North Carolina, and Virginia think there will be a peaceable dissolution? Why, then, are they arming themselves and making such heavy outlays in preparing for war? What mean these 'Minute-Men' at the South and

'Wide-Awakes' at the North, if there be no danger of war? 'Tis folly, absurd, downright madness, to think of revolution without war. The thing is impossible.

"We think it is an outrage for the Union to be broken up by extreme sectionalists. Let the South and the conservative men at the North resolve that the Union shall not be destroyed. Annihilate the champion Abolition leaders at the North and the leading secession traitors at the South, first. If they cannot be conquered in the Union and by the Union, how in the name of Heaven can they be after the whole South goes out of the Union? Let us have our rights, and have them *where* we ought to have them,—*in* the Union, not *out* of the Union. Let us never be driven out of the 'big house into the kitchen,' or (should we not rather say?) out-of-doors into the wide world, when all our rights are in the 'big house,'—and that, too, by a set of fanatical Black Republicans and secession demagogues! Think of that, will you?

"We are for the preservation of the Union, though American soil should be *steeped in the blood* of her brave, warm-hearted, patriotic sons. This will be the result if we go out of the Union. Therefore, before we would voluntarily surrender up the Federal Government to Black Republicans, and go out of the Union, we would fight them and secession leaders, the arch-traitors in this rebellion, until the judgment of the great day, and run all risks of servile insurrections. We would either conquer them, or they should conquer us. Never, for God's sake, for honor's sake, for our country's sake, for our children's sake, for humanity's sake, and for liberty's sake, never, never let us act the cowardly and dastardly part of acknowledging ourselves whipped before we fight, and surrendering all to our enemies before we make an effort to save all. Cæsar did not act in this way, nor did our forefathers, nor will we. Never surrender. Cling on to the Union. Cleave to the 'Stars and Stripes,' come weal or woe, victory or death. This is the way in which brave, patriotic Americans should talk and act. Stand up for your rights, fellow-citizens; and nothing less than this Federal Government, this blessed Union, are our rights."

In the same number of the "Christian Banner" we wrote the following brief paragraph:—

"The South Carolina Secession Convention organized in Columbia on the 17th inst., and were driven by a small-pox panic to Charleston, where they arrived on the 18th instant. They had not entirely passed the Secession Ordinance when last heard from. But, in all probability, they will be out of the Union before this paragraph meets the reader's eye; rather a bad start."

Before our paper went to press, we received the following news from Charleston, which we published in the same number of the "Banner:"—

"The Union dissolved! Late and important from South Carolina! Fourth day's proceedings. Secession Ordinance passed unanimously! Great excitement throughout Charleston! The news received all over the city with loud cheers.

"CHARLESTON, *Dec.* 20.—The Convention was opened

with prayer to-day, after which the roll was called and the journal read.

"A resolution was offered inviting the Mayor of Charleston to a seat on the floor of the Convention. It was amended by including the Governor of the State, the President of the Senate, and the Speaker of the House. In this form it was passed.

"The chair announced the appointment of a committee to draw up a summary of the causes for the secession of South Carolina, and also for standing committees.

"Mr. Rhett offered a resolution for the appointment of a committee of thirteen for the purpose of providing for the assemblage of a convention of the seceding States, and to form a Constitution. Adopted.

"Mr. Inglis made a report from the committee to prepare and draft an ordinance proper to be adopted by the Convention. The ordinance is as follows:—

"'An ordinance to dissolve the union between the State of South Carolina and the other States united with her under the compact entitled "The Constitution of the United States of America."

"'We, the people of the State of South Carolina, in Convention assembled, do declare and ordain, and it is hereby declared and ordained, that the ordinance adopted by us in convention, on the 23d day of May, in the year of our Lord one thousand seven hundred and eighty-eight, whereby the Constitution of the United States of America was ratified, and also all acts and parts of acts of the General Assembly of this State and amendments of the said Constitution, are hereby repealed, and that the union now subsisting between South Carolina and the other States, under the name of the United States of America, is hereby dissolved.'

"PASSAGE OF THE ORDINANCE.

"The ordinance was taken up and passed by a unanimous vote of 169,—all the members voting.

"*The passage took place at precisely a quarter-past one o'clock*, P.M.

"The news spreads over the city. Great cheering.

"As soon as the passage of the ordinance was known outside the doors of the Convention, the tidings spread rapidly all over the city, and a great crowd collected in the vicinity of Secession Hall. Immense cheering ensued.

"Mr. Miles moved that the clerk telegraph to members of Congress at Washington that the ordinance had passed, and the motion was unanimously carried.

"Mr. Dessausue offered the following:—

"'*Resolved*, That the Secession Ordinance be engrossed on parchment, under the direction of the Attorney-General, and signed by the President and members, this evening, at Institute Hall, and that it be placed among the archives of the State.'

"Half-past six o'clock was agreed upon as the hour to proceed to Institute Hall for the purpose of signing the document."

The reader will bear in mind that "at precisely a quarter-past one o'clock, P.M., on the 20th day of December, one thousand eight hundred and sixty, South Carolina committed the *suicidal* act, which action influenced all the other seceding States to perpetrate the same acts of self-destruction. Notwithstanding we had long anticipated the course which South Carolina would take, yet when the intelligence was received that the ordinance of Secession was actually passed, and that South Carolina, *our native State*, had declared herself dissolved from all connection with the United States of America, the news fell upon our ear like the deafening thunder of heaven at noonday from a clear sky. To us it sounded like the *death-knell* of a nation's glory. The cheering and dancing of ungrateful, wicked children over the grave of of a kind and affectionate mother would have seemed no more unnatural to us than did the great cheering of the citizens of Charleston over the downfall of their State and country. Oh, what blindness! What madness!

South Carolina had suffered less from the aggressions of Northern Abolitionists than any other State, perhaps, in the Union. Her geographical position effectually secured her slaves from the aggressions of the Abolitionists of the North. But she was not satisfied. Secession and the reopening of the African slave-trade and free trade were long-cherished *idols* and *hopes* of South Carolina. Charleston was to be a London, or Liverpool, and the leaders in this rebellion were to be despots and tyrants over thousands of the suffering, benighted sons and daughters of Africa's unhappy race.

We venture the assertion that Virginia alone had lost more negroes up to the time of this rebellion than all the Gulf States together; and yet Virginia was willing and anxious to remain in the Union, while the Gulf States, with scarcely the pretext of the shade of a shadow of cause for their rash act, thrust themselves out of the Union, and declared they would drag the border States with them. We have often said, and it has ever been the honest conviction of our mind and heart, that if South Carolina had been geographically located as Virginia is, she would never have seceded.

But Virginia was made a "cat's paw" for South Carolina and the other cotton States, and she has paid but too dearly for her credulity and imbecility. However much we detested the course pursued by Northern Abolitionists, the rash act of South Carolina in seceding from the "United States of America" was far more reprehensible than any thing the Abolitionists had ever done.

It may be well to remark *here,* for the satisfaction of the reader, that the impression was made upon the minds of the people of the South that the fixed purpose of the Black Republican party, of which Mr. Lincoln was represented as being the head, was to make war upon the South, for the purpose of abolishing slavery, and that they intended to stir up the negro population to *servile* insurrections, to murder the whites indiscriminately, and turn loose all the negroes upon the whole South to do as they pleased. In a word, that there was to be a general "John Brown raid" upon a magnificent scale, which, with all the aids and Government facilities, would secure almost certain success. Hence it was that the whole South was considered a unit to drive back any such diabolical, aggressive party. The Abolition journals of the North went very far to confirm the minds of the Southern people in this belief. But South Carolina was too fast for the Abolitionists, even if their purpose was as above suggested. The *honor,* the *imperishable glory,* of *secession* and *inaugurating civil war* was reserved for South Carolina! Shame on the State, and infamy on the leaders!

CHAPTER XIV.

In the number of the "Christian Banner" of January 3, 1861, we wrote the following paragraphs:—

"*New Year.*—We enter upon the New Year with feelings quite different from any in the past history of our eventful life. This is the last New Year's day we ever expect to be worthy of being accounted a citizen of the United States of America. We have resolved to take all things calmly and coolly, and wait the final result, whatever that result may be.

"Before the next New Year our country will either be flooded with blood and carnage, or else settled down upon terms which will secure peace and harmony for generations yet to come. 'Tis awful to be held in a state of everlasting suspense. If war is to come, and come it will, we care not how soon. The sooner this question is settled the better it will be for the whole country. We fear nothing, so far as we are individually concerned. All we care for is the thought that our happy country is to be broken up; that the 'Stars and Stripes' of this glorious Union are to trail in the dust; that so many lives of our fellow-citizens are to be sacrificed; that our whole country for the time being is to become bankrupt; that all our social, political, and religious blessings, for the time being at least, are to become paralyzed. When, however, the storm shall have passed away, and this question is forever and permanently settled, we may bless God that we passed through the storm to the end, that we and our children may forever thereafter enjoy the calm and the sunshine.

"Our readers must pardon us for writing no more editorials. Our opinions now are not what the excited people want. They want to know what is going on. They want facts, not opinions; and these we will continue to give until the battles are all fought and the victory won.

"We say to the South, for God's sake, for one another's sake, for the sake of our country, let us all at the South be a unit. As long as there was any hope of the Union, we were for it, but, now that all hope is gone, we earnestly urge the necessity that the whole South stand shoulder to shoulder; come weal or woe, let us all live or die together. We confidently say to all our readers that they need not be surprised at any moment to hear that war has commenced. We read the papers from all sections of the country, and have a fair opportunity of forming tolerably correct opinions upon the future result of affairs.

"In the event of civil war, the North has decidedly the advantage over the South. The Northern people have war-implements, and all necessary facilities for manufacturing them. They outnumber the people of the South by thousands and millions. When they leave their families and property to march to the battle-field, they leave all safe behind them. They have provisions and means to carry on and keep up a war of extermination. All these things should be well considered by the Southern people. And it should be remembered, likewise, that the Northern people are fighting at *home*, as well as the Southern people. The old Revolutionary War and the Revolution of France will not be a comparison to the scenes which will be acted out during the American *internecine* war.

"We should not be surprised at any moment to hear of a collision between the secessionists and the troops of the Federal Government. That a peaceable secession is impossible, and that civil war is inevitable, are facts which we suppose no sensible man will for a moment question. We have again and again warned our fellow-citizens of the fearful and terrible results of secession, and the breaking up of this great and glorious Government. Men will now be *forced to fight* and *defend their rights,* whether they wish to do so or not. Think of that, will you?

"If Virginia secedes from the Union, she will, by the force of circumstances, be a free State in less than a quarter of a century; and, as soon as she secedes, her slave property will become comparatively valueless. The actual depreciation of the value of servants in the slave States since the election of Mr. Lincoln is more than every negro in the State of South Carolina would sell for, at the enormous prices they would have brought twelve months ago. This is only one of the small blessings of blessed *secession.* Think of that, will you?"

At the time of writing the above, there was but little to hope for. South Carolina had already seceded, and the Governor of that State had been tendered the services of troops from Georgia, Alabama, and different portions of South Carolina. A committee had been sent from Wilmington, North Carolina, to consult with Governor Ellis upon the propriety of taking

Fort Johnson, a Revolutionary fortress, situated on Cape Fear River, about two miles from its mouth, and near the town of Smithville. Governor Ellis did not advise the taking possession of the fort, but the committee returned home resolved upon taking care of the entire Cape Fear section,—which clearly and fully demonstrated the fact that Governor Ellis would not oppose the action of the committee, thus tacitly consenting to the capturing of the fort.

The Cabinet of the Congress of the United States at Washington was divided, and in a state of the most deplorable and ridiculous disorder and confusion, in relation to the course to be pursued in reference to Major Anderson,—the commissioners from South Carolina peremptorily demanding that he should be ordered back to Fort Moultrie. Messrs. Floyd, Thomas, and Thompson were in favor of his being ordered back, while Messrs. Holt, Black, and Stanton opposed it. Toucey and the President were non-committal. The commissioners from South Carolina affirmed that unless Major Anderson was dealt with according to their demands, they should consider a non-compliance on the part of the Administration an act of coercion, which the State of South Carolina would not tolerate. Senator Wigfall, of Texas, and Senator Davis, of Mississippi, urged President Buchanan to send Anderson back to Fort Moultrie immediately, as the only way of preventing a collision between the United States troops and those of South Carolina. It was stated that Buchanan determined to shirk the responsibility of ordering Major Anderson back, and throw it on some one else.

At this time, also, great war-preparations were being

made at the North. It was said that Massachusetts was ready to respond promptly to any demand made upon her for troops to sustain the Union and the laws; that seven thousand troops could be put in marching order at twenty-four hours' notice; that one hundred and forty-five thousand were enrolled in the militia of the State, and of that number twenty thousand could be easily mustered. If the reader is at all acquainted with the history of the proceedings of our country from the meeting of Congress in 1860 up to the time that it adjourned in 1861, he will not be at all surprised that men should have despaired of all hope of any amicable settlement of our national difficulties. South Carolina in arms at the one extreme, and Massachusetts in arms at the other extreme, what were men in the border States to expect, but to be overwhelmed, annihilated, in the common ruin?

We saw no possible chance of avoiding collision between the United States troops and those of South Carolina, unless Virginia could step in between the two belligerent parties as a *pacificator*, and devise some compromise by which to reconcile them. Of this, however, we had but little hope, owing to the fact that all the secession journals and orators of Virginia were moving heaven and earth, as it were, to force secession upon the people of Virginia. Already had the secession party begun openly and boldly, and, we may add, impudently and insolently, to upbraid Union men, making all sorts of insinuations and applying all kinds of epithets to them, such as "Union-shriekers," "submissionists to old Abe Lincoln," "Black Republicans," "Abolitionists," "Traitors to Virginia and the South." All this and a thousand other things were said and done to *crush* and *damn* the influence of the Union men, and to scare and force them into submission to the *infernal* demon secession,—into the accursed rebellion.

CHAPTER XV.

In the number of the "Christian Banner" of January 10, 1861, we wrote the following:—

"THE CRISIS.

"The crisis is on us! Yes, reader, we are in the midst of a grand revolution. The Rubicon is passed, and henceforth our country shall roll on to glory or to ruin,—which, God only knows.

"Washington City is quite too small a place to hold all the towering minds of this great nation. The geographical boundaries of this vast country are too circumscribed to contain in peace and harmony so many millions of intellectual beings. The people want more elbow-room. They do not die fast enough to make room for one another and for posterity. Nature is too slow in the execution of her duty. Artificial means, the sword and bayonet, must be used to expedite her work of death and destruction. It takes space and territory for mind and matter. The people want more territory for their physical organizations, and more space in which their towering minds can revel. They want more latitude, more liberty, more freedom. Mind is progressing and improving. The institutions of God and our fathers are not sufficiently latitudinous for the people of this generation. There is a great up-heaving of mind, and the laws of God and man must be overthrown and the fragments scattered to the winds. Old things are passing away, and a new order of all things is being introduced.

"Politically, the people profess to be governed by a *republican* form of government; and yet they are gulled, duped, and led on to ruin by a class of unprincipled, aspiring demagogues,—a set of frothy, sophistical, school-boy orators, who rant and foam and talk about the sacred rights of the *dear people*, the hard-working yeomanry, the backbone and sinew of the country. This is beautiful! eloquent! sublime! logical! *ad captandum!*

"The *dear people* are thrown into raptures of political ecstasy by their party leaders, and swear they'll follow them if they land in perdition. Party zeal, political blindness, gross ignorance, religious fanaticism, bigotry, and intolerance have all conspired to produce the present revolution, and to involve our whole country in civil war and one common ruin. The fountain of the great political deep is broken up, and the desolating torrents are bound to flow on, and on, and on, until the question which has so long agitated this whole nation shall be permanently and finally settled. Yes, this question must and will be settled, before peace, happiness, prosperity, tranquillity, safety, and order can ever be restored to our country. It is bound to be done! There is no help for it. Must the sword decide the contest? Must civil war, with all its concomitant train of horrors, be forced upon us? Yes, civil war is already at our very door. Men say by their actions that it *shall* come, that they *will* have war, that the sword must and shall settle the question. Well, let the sword decide the contest, let civil war once begin, and by the time the victory is won, and war ends, thousands who make so much bluster and fuss about fighting will have it to their entire satisfaction. The work of death once begun, the warfare will be one general *mêlée*, from the terrific character of which the mind turns away in disgust, while the heart sickens and sinks into sadness.

"A kingdom divided against itself cannot stand. Where is the civilization, where is the Christianity, of the nation? Brothers going to war with brothers, fathers with sons, and sons with fathers! This is civilization, this is Christianity, this is the spirit of the gospel, is it? Where are the preachers who preach the gospel of peace and bring glad tidings of good things to our ears?

"We regard any class of preachers and pretended Christians who will calmly and deliberately, in their religious deliberative bodies, vote for the breaking up of one of the best Governments the world has ever known, as being no better than whitewashed infidels, traitors to God and their country, and abominable hypocrites, justly meriting the severest censures and warmest execrations of the wise and patriotic everywhere. God save our country from the damning influence of all such sects and parties."

In the same number of the "Christian Banner" we published the following prayer, with a brief remark:—

"MILITARY PRAYER.—The Secession Convention at Charleston, S.C., was opened on last Monday week by the Rev. T. R. English, who prayed to God, saying, 'If, in thine inscrutable providence, we should be called upon to encounter the perils of war, may our arms, in the day of battle, be under thy shield and protection. May our wives, our daughters and sisters, freely give up their husbands, brothers, and sons, and in the day of battle may they encourage them to stand firmly in their places in the assertion and vindication of their rights.'

"The conflicting parties, if it were possible, would place the All-Wise Ruler of the Universe in as awkward a predicament as they have got the President of the United States. If he answer the prayers of the secessionists, he must disregard and offend the people or the North; and if he regard the prayers of the Northern people, he will offend the secessionists. So, what is he to do? He will certainly make no compromise with sin nor sinners, but will do right. Therefore, he cannot consistently answer the prayers of both parties. Nor do we intend any irreverence in this remark."

It will be recollected that about this time the Representatives in the Congress of the United States from the Gulf States manifested the most morbid indifference as to what was being done in Congress, some of them declaring that they felt no interest there, as their States were in convention and would soon pass ordinances of secession, and they were only waiting the action of their States. A correspondent from Washington, writing under date of January 6, 1861, says,—

"The Alabama and Mississippi delegations held a caucus last night, and afterwards telegraphed to the conventions of their respective States, advising them to secede immediately, saying that there is no prospect of any satisfactory adjustment of difficulties. They resolved to remain here, however, and await the action of their States."

These Representatives were sent by the citizens of their respective States to transact the business of the Federal Government, and to guard the interests of the whole country, as well as the special interests of the people of the States which they represented. They were sworn to observe the Constitution of the United States, and were receiving pay from the Government for every hour they held their seats in Congress. In palpable violation of their solemn oaths, in violation of the high and responsible obligations they were under to their constituents and to the whole country, instead of discharging their duties as statesmen and patriots, they were constantly engaged in holding caucus-meetings and plotting treason against the Republic, while the troops at home were taking the arsenals and forts that belonged to the Federal Government. A correspondent writing from Mobile, under date of January 4, 1861, says,—

"The United States arsenal and forts at this place were taken on yesterday at daylight by the Alabama troops. They contained 78,000 stand of arms, 1500 boxes of powder, 30,000 rounds of musket-cartridges, and other munitions of war. Fort Morgan, situated eight miles below Mobile, was taken this (Friday) morning by the Mobile troops, and garrisoned by two hundred men."

What constitutional right had the State authorities of Alabama, or any other State, to seize and take violent possession of the "United States arsenals and forts," or any other property belonging to the United States? Was this not a most wicked usurpation of power, and that, too, while these very States were represented in the Congress of the United States? The resolution declaring the right and duty of Florida to secede passed the Convention on the 7th of January, 1861, by a vote of sixty-two ayes to four nays. A committee of thirteen was appointed on secession, and their ordinance for secession was adopted; and at this very time the Representatives from Florida occupied their seats in the Congress of the United States. Determined, as they were, prior to the meeting of Congress, to secede, why did they take their seats at all? Only the better to enable them to carry out their diabolical plot of breaking up the Federal Government. They had determined to accept of no compromise, however satisfactory to the border States that compromise might be.

CHAPTER XVI.

In the number of the "Christian Banner" of January 24, 1861, we wrote and published the following:—

"Look to your interest.—An appeal to the people, etc. etc.—At a time like the present, no man who has a head, a heart, and soul, can look on with morbid indifference upon the probable destiny of his country. Our God first, and our country next. Without God we could have no country; and without a country we could have no existence,—*here, at least.* When liberty of thought, conscience, speech, and press are taken from us, we don't wish to remain a citizen of this lower world any longer. And if we are proscribed, it matters little whether it is by popular opinion or the sword: the results are the same.

"At a time like the present, every citizen should think calmly, rationally, and act deliberately and decidedly. This is no time for child's play. Every thing that freemen hold near and dear this side of heaven is at stake. The question is, shall we remain passive in the hands of corrupt, ignorant politicians, or shall we, as freemen, take our own rights into our own hands, and defend and protect our rights in our own way and upon our own responsibility?

"Five States have declared to the world that they are out of the Union. These five States are *now* all in a universal warlike commotion. War, war, war! fight, fight, fight! is the perfect order of the times. Have the people counted the cost? Are they prepared to shoulder the enormous expense, the awful taxation, which war must inevitably produce? The seceding States may be prepared for all this. But is Virginia prepared for it? What products has she by which to raise millions of surplus money at this time to carry on a civil war? Already in debt as she is, and all her citizens involved head-and-heels, more or less, in debt, how are thousands and millions of money to be raised to begin and carry on an unending or an exterminating war?

"Is it necessary that war shall come? No: there is no necessity for it at all. Our national difficulties can be settled, and they ought to be settled, without war. Why is this great hurry to precipitate all the slave States out of the Union before Lincoln is inaugurated? Can he free the negroes? No. Can he move the forts and arsenals out of the South? No. Can he force Southern men to act and fight against their own interests? No. Well, then, what can he do? If five States can secede in opposition to the wishes of President Buchanan, why cannot ten secede in opposition to the will and wishes of Mr. Lincoln? He cannot prevent them from seceding after he comes into power. And if he and his party were to make war on them for seceding after he gets into power, he and his party would be more apt to make war on them for seceding before he came into power. So that there is nothing possible to be gained by madly rushing out of the Union, and every thing to be lost. Let us, therefore, not be too hasty in this matter.

"The South will be forced to come to some understanding with the North in relation to the national property, commerce, &c. &c. This the slave States can do better while under the Federal Government and in the Union than after they take themselves out of the Union and from under the protection of the Federal Government.

"Let the border States stand firm, and *demand* their rights; and, if they fail to obtain them, then let them all act in harmony, and go together. It will be time for them to act when they have used and exhausted all means for redress and failed to obtain it.

"The election of members to the Virginia State Convention comes off the 4th of February, and we would again caution our readers to be careful for whom they cast their votes; and, when they shall have the action of the Convention referred back to them for their final decision, let them thoroughly understand the subject, and then act with as much deliberation as if their eternal salvation depended on the result of their action. If the border States do not secede, we think there is yet hope that all our national difficulties will be settled without war; but, if they secede, we firmly believe that the result will be a general war between the whole of the *free* and of the *slave* States,—which will result either in the subjugation of the South by the North, or of the North by the South.

"We are firm and decided in the stand which we first took,—namely: we are for saving the Union, if possible; but, if this *cannot* be done in justice to the South, then we are for the South. But, because others should wish to rush hastily into ruin, this is no reason why we shall. Let conservative men deliberate and act with firmness, and the Republic may yet be saved."

"Five States have declared to the world that they are out of the Union." It will be recollected that South Carolina seceded in December, 1860. In a Congressional correspondence, dated Washington, January 21, 1861, the reporter says,—

"Mr. Hunter, upon request, was excused from serving any longer as chairman of the Committee of Finance,—stating, as the reason of his request, that his State was about to change her political position.

[How did Mr. Hunter know, three months in advance, that his State was going to secede?]

"Mr. Polk presented a memorial, with signatures covering fifteen quires of paper, all wrapped in the 'American flag,' praying the adoption of the Crittenden resolutions as amendments to the Constitution.

"Mr. Slidell moved to take up his resolution, in effect censuring the President for not earlier sending in the nomination of Mr. Holt as Secretary of War.

"Mr. Yulee announced the receipt of official intelligence that his State [Florida] had seceded, and said that he and his colleagues were no longer Senators of the United States. He read a valedictory, in which he gave the reasons which induced Florida to secede. Mallory — Yulee's colleague — also delivered a valedictory.

"Mr. Clay, of Alabama, in behalf of himself and Mr. Fitzpatrick, also withdrew from the Senate, in consequence of official intelligence of the secession of Alabama.

"Mr. Davis announced the secession of Mississippi, and made a speech, after which the seceding Senators all rose and left the hall,—first taking leave of their old associates."

A telegraphic despatch, dated Milledgeville, January 19, 1861, says, "The Convention, at 2 10 P.M. to-day, passed the ordinance of secession by a vote of 206 to 89."

Another despatch, dated Augusta, January 19, 1861, says, "Our city is illuminated with fireworks, and cannons are firing, in honor of the secession of the

State. Bells are ringing, amid great enthusiasm and rejoicing. Georgia is free."

While matters were thus progressing at the South, the conservative men at the North were holding meetings, and passing series of resolutions, in reference to the course which should be pursued towards the seceding States of the South. As a specimen of some of these resolutions, we give the following, adopted at a large and enthusiastic meeting held in the city of New York by the working-men of that city:—

"*Resolved,* That we regard the present movement of several of the Southern States, in resuming the powers they delegated to the General Government, as an effort to preserve our Constitution from being overthrown by Abraham Lincoln, as his party-platform requires and demands him to do.

"*Resolved,* That we are for the Union,—the Union of our fathers; for the Constitution,—the glorious charter of our liberties,—as expounded by the recognized authority, upon the basis of equal justice, liberty, and immunities to all the citizens of all the States."

"*Resolved,* That, believing that the people of the Southern States are, and have ever been, content to remain in this Union under the Constitution as originally designed, we deeply sympathize with them in their unwilling resistance to an incoming Administration, which, by a perverted and unauthorized construction of the Constitution, tends to destroy their peace, welfare, and happiness.

"*Resolved,* That we are firmly and unalterably opposed to any and every attempt on the part of the Government or the people of the North to coerce the

Southern States, or any one of them, into submission to the will of the majority of the people of the North, when that will has been authoritatively declared by the Supreme Court to be in opposition to the true construction of the Constitution of the United States.

"*Resolved,* That we will, by all proper and legitimate means, oppose, discountenance, and prevent the Republican party from making any aggressive attempt, under the plea of 'enforcing the laws' and 'preserving the Union,' upon the rights of the Southern States, believing, as we do, that any such attempt can only result in a protracted and destructive civil war, to attain an end which that party can really and peaceably accomplish by abandoning their hostility to the South, and declaring their willingness to abide by the Constitution as interpreted by the Supreme Court and accepted by all conservative men of the country.

"*Resolved,* That we regard the Republican party, which, to use the language of Jefferson, 'has wriggled itself into power under auspices of morality,' as embodying the policy that Great Britain has pursued for a quarter of a century in endeavoring to equalize the races on this continent,—to reduce white men to a forbidden level with negroes, and thus overthrow not only the Union, but destroy the glorious free institutions which, seventy-six years ago, our fathers extorted from an unwilling despot; and, if any additional evidence be needed to show the alliance of the so-called Republican party with the monarchists of Great Britain to dissolve this Union, regardless of its fearful consequences, it can be found in the fact that its recognized leaders in Congress have deliberately rejected Senator Crittenden's Compromise, although it is well known that it does not grant the South her full, just, and equal rights under the Constitution.

"*Resolved*, That we demand that our representatives and servants, (and not our rulers, as some ignorantly style them,) both in our national and State Legislatures, shall at once initiate movements for a peaceable solution of our difficulties, so that civil war may be avoided, and the wheels of business may again begin to move, and remunerating labor return to thousands now out of employment and suffering from the stubborn refusal of the Republican party to grant the South her just rights under the Constitution.

"*Resolved*, That the State Legislature be respectfully requested to convene the people of this State in convention, for the purpose of securing an expression of public sentiment upon the new and startling issues which a few weeks have so rapidly evolved; and the Chair is directed to appoint a committee of five gentlemen to present these resolutions and this request to the Legislature."

We give the above resolutions in full, that the reader may understand that the secessionists of the South had assurances which were satisfactory to them that, under any and all circumstances, they would receive an overwhelming abundance of assistance from the North in the event that the "incoming Administration" should attempt to "enforce the laws" under the pretence of preserving the Constitution and saving the Union. The conservative men at the North were as ignorant of the real spirit and determination of the secessionists of the South as were the Black Republicans of the real and true condition of the slaves of the South; while the secessionists of the South were equally ignorant of the spirit and determination of the conservative men of the North. We presume that the conservative men at the North had never anticipated an attack on the flag of the Union by secessionists.

The secessionists had determined to accept of *no compromise* which might be offered. This they declared in the outset. Hence, with the leaders of the secession party, any and all compromise was a *foregone* conclusion. The conservative men at the North thought, or affected to think, that these leaders actually wanted a compromise, the Constitution respected, and the Union saved; whereas they had *determined* on *immediate, complete,* and *eternal* separation from the "old Union." Presuming, in part, at least, on the aid and assistance of the conservative men of the North, and the aid and assistance of "fifty thousand Knights of the Golden Circle," said to have been organized in the free States, they struck the fatal blow. Terrible was the disappointment,—but just what every sensible man, under the circumstances, might have expected.

We believe that the conservative men at the North were honest and sincere in their assertions of friendship for and sympathy with the South. And, had the Southern States remained in the Union, and observed on their part the Constitution inviolate, and Mr. Lincoln had waged an aggressive war upon the South, for the ostensible purpose of liberating the slaves of the South, we honestly believe that hundreds of thousands of men in the *free States* would have risen up as one man and united with the South and annihilated the Black Republican party. But when the Southern States seceded, and first struck a blow at the *sacred* flag of our country, this was more than the conservative element of the North had expected; and, seeing that the secessionists were the aggressors, the inaugurators of civil war, they, by force of circumstances, if not from principle and patriotism, became united, and resolved to protect and defend the time-honored flag of their country, preserve the Constitution, and, if possible, save the Union.

The intelligent reader cannot fail to observe, likewise, that the expressed and published opinions of the conservative men of the North in relation to the fixed purpose of the Black Republican party in waging war upon the South in order to free the negroes were well calculated to rouse the suspicions and indignation of the Southern people.

That the leaders of the Black Republican party, *proper*, wanted the Union dissolved, to the end that they might more speedily and effectually accomplish their unholy purpose in abolishing slavery in the South, they did not pretend to conceal. Knowing the terrible results that would necessarily follow in the event of breaking up the Government, we opposed it until we rendered ourself odious with the secession party, and wellnigh lost all our patronage before we discontinued the publication of the "Banner."

The following chapter will show how fully and clearly we portrayed the horrors that would certainly befall Virginia in the event of her seceding. For all which faithful warning we are a refugee among strangers. Thank God, we have a clear conscience. We intended good to our country, even if we did wrong.

CHAPTER XVII.

In the number of the "Christian Banner" of the 31st of January, 1861, under the head of "Random Thoughts Shot at a Venture," we wrote and published the following six short chapters, which have since the war began been denominated the "*Predictions of the 'Christian Banner,'*" how justly we leave the reader *to decide:*—

"Chap. I.—*Read, Think, Determine, and Act!*—Our soul is disgusted, our heart sickened, at the school-boy bombast and *politician* eloquence of the day. This is no time for tropes, figures, and rhetorically turned periods. Political stump-speaking has infused deadly poison into the heart of the whole body politic. War, pestilence, destruction, and death are at our very door, staring us full in the face, and yet *upstart politicians*, would-be statesmen, and leaders of the people *dare* to discuss and harangue the people on abstractions which the speakers themselves never can comprehend, and stop to read long sentences and paragraphs about the opinions of men who are dead and gone and have no part nor lot in the awful tragedies which are now being acted out all over our country.

"Were the present political aspirants and seekers-to-be-leaders of the people influenced by the wisdom and patriotism of the immortal statesmen and patriots whose opinions they *affect* so ardently to admire, but which they are incapable of appreciating, then our country would not be lacerated, rent, and torn into fragments, as she now is. 'Tis all a sham, a hypocritical show, an empty bubble, a false pretension of patriotism, honor, virtue, truth, and justice.

"Political tricksters and ecclesiastical knaves, urged and driven on by cupidity for wealth, position, and power, have reduced our country to the shameful state of degradation in which she is now held up to the astonished gaze and inexpressible derision of all the civilized nations of the world. And still *freemen* must acquiesce, must close their mouths, hold their peace, stifle their consciences, pander to the cupidity and yield to the will and implicitly obey the dictations of caucusing, intriguing, wire-working, life-absorbing, blood-sucking, political aspirants, or else be persecuted, proscribed, *ostracized!*

"Never, while we have brains to think, a heart to feel, a tongue to speak, a hand to write, and a soul to save, will we become the dupe of fools, cowards, knaves, and traitors, nor tamely and meanly submit to the gag-law of any political or ecclesiastical associations, confederations, or parties of men this side of eternity. Cowards, traitors, loungers, spongers, and loafers may shift, twist, turn, and change their political positions and religious relations with every popular tide that drifts the scurf and scum of all political degeneracy and ecclesiastical depravity to the surface, and for the sake of their bread and butter, grog and cigars, petty offices, and a little mushroom notoriety, succumb to the biddings and behests of their impudently-presumptuous, tyrannical leaders, while honest men, freemen, brave men, and patriots, look on with pity supreme, and turn away with loathing and disgust inexpressible!

"'Liberty or death!' should be the watchword of every American citizen. Liberty of conscience, liberty of speech, liberty of action, and liberty of the press, should be the uncompromising demand of all freemen, and they should submit to nothing less."

"CHAP. II.—It is argued that secession is constitutionally right. Grant it. But is it expedient? That is the question. Many things may be lawful which are by no means expedient. Secession or revolution, under certain circumstances, would not only be constitutionally right, but absolutely necessary. Is this the case now? Has the time actually come, and do the circumstances absolutely demand the secession of any one or of all the slave States? If it be unconditionally necessary for one to secede, does the same necessity demand that all shall secede? Has the work of secession and revolution commenced and progressed in a way to prove it expedient and to commend itself to the world?

"The ostensible causes of secession are: first, to save the South from further Abolition aggressions; and, secondly, to free the country from the continual agitation of the slave question. The objects sought to be gained by secession are: first, to *permanently* establish the institution of African slavery; secondly, to extend slave territory; and, thirdly, to reduce the price of slave labor. Will secession accomplish all this? Some seem to think so. They are woefully mistaken.

"Never will the vexed question of African slavery cease to be agitated so long as there are Abolitionists in the North and slaves in the South. The fixed determination and settled principles of Abolitionists are, *never, never* to give up the conflict until African slavery is exterminated. This is their object, their design, their work. They do not pretend to disguise the fact. So that nothing can ever be gained by secession on this score.

"Will secession save the South from further Abolition aggressions? If so, how? Secessionists say, 'We will form treaties and enter into leagues with the Abolitionists after we secede, and, for the sake of our trade, they will spare our slaves.' Have they said so? Have they promised to do this? No: *they have not, and they never will.* Are they not bound by leagues and treaties now under the Constitution? and do they observe them? If they violate treaties and break leagues under the Constitution and while they are in the Union, what assurances have we that they will make leagues and treaties and observe them inviolate after they get out of the Union and are free from all constitutional restraints and obligations? If they perpetrate depredations in the Union and under the influence of the Constitution, they will do it much more abundantly after the Federal Government is broken up. They will never enter into any treaties nor form any leagues with the South, on which the continuance and perpetuity of African slavery are contemplated. This is a fixed fact.

"Dissolve the Union, break up the Federal Government, and will not the same proximity still exist between the *slave* and *free* States that exists now?

"Divide the Union, and the same morbid moral sentiment will remain in the hearts of Abolitionists that drives them on to daring deeds of madness now.

"Divide the Union, and a thousand new causes of hate and eternal animosity will spring up among all parties.

"Divide the Union, break up the Federal Government in advance of terms and treaties of separation between the North and South, and the door for any subsequent equitable separation is forever closed, and the key lost in the depths of eternity.

"Divide the Union, and the floodgate is hoisted through which a concentration of curses will flow that baffles all human thought to conceive.

"Divide the Union, break up the Federal Government, and civil war begins, which will only end in the domination of the South over the North, or of the North over the South.

"Dissolve the Union, and military and ecclesiastical despotism, or absolute monarchies, will supplant the tree of liberty and all the blessings of freedom.

"Dissolve the Union, break up the Federal Government, and the liberty of conscience, the liberty of speech, the liberty of action, the liberty of the press, and the liberty of a once free, independent, prosperous, and happy people, are gone, and gone forever.

"Dissolve the Federal Government, and the reign of terror begins.

"Dissolve the Union, and an *era* more to be dreaded than the dark ages commences.

"Dissolve the Union, and the *guillotine* will take the place of the 'Star-Spangled Banner;' and whoever dares to speak a word against despots and tyrants, off will go his head.

"Dissolve the Union, and the *many*, the *dear* people, the hard-working *yeomanry*, will all become the vassals of the *few*.

"Dissolve the Union, and all the poor will become the veriest menials of the *lords* and *rulers* of the people.

"Are Virginians prepared for all these things? If so, dissolve the Union, break up the Federal Government, and the work of death and desolation is done!

"If the slave States conquer the free States, then the institution of African slavery *may* continue for the next half-century; then will slave labor be reduced to an insignificant price; then *may* slave territory be extended. But, before all this is gained, our country will be drenched in blood: most of those now living will never live to see slave territory expanded; they will never realize the glories of cheap slave-labor; they will never need it! Even should the South succeed, will the spoils be worth the fight, the crown, the sacrifice? Answer us, mothers, you who have sons and love them! Answer us, wives, you who have husbands and look up *to* and rely *on* them for protection! Against a foreign enemy every citizen should lift his hand, and risk his life, and sacrifice all things for his country and his country's glory! It is not so in the present case. They are bone of our bone, flesh of our flesh, our brethren, our fellow-citizens. How, then, dare we, being brethren, as we are, go to war with one another?

"But suppose the *free* States should conquer the slave States? Then African slavery is exterminated! Never would the victorious North enter into any treaty with the subdued South in which the continuance of African slavery were contemplated. The idea is supremely preposterous. If, therefore, the Federal Government be broken up, and civil war follow,—which it *certainly* will,—and the free States subjugate the slave States, then African slavery, slave territory, and slave labor are all at an end. Extreme Abolitionists want the Federal Government broken up, because this, they say, will hasten the abolition of slavery. The present process is too slow for them. They want to accomplish the work at once.

"CHAP. III.—*What can Virginia gain by secession?*—Suppose it were possible for a peaceable separation of the Union to be consummated, and that a Southern Confederacy of all the slave States were formed: what would Virginia gain by the operation? How can she be benefited in the least conceivable degree by uniting her destiny with a cotton or Southern Confederacy? The cotton States say they don't want to sell negroes,—they want to buy them at the lowest possible prices. Their income is from cotton and sugar produced by slave labor: therefore they want negroes to raise cotton and sugar. Hence it is to their interest to get negroes as cheap as possible. We say 'their interest,' because they are going in for their *own interest* in *dollars* and *cents*. This no one will deny who understands the subject. Hence the process by which the cotton and sugar States are to be built up and *enriched*, should they succeed, is the very process by which Virginia is to be pulled down, impoverished, and degraded.

"For example, a Virginia farmer owes a cotton-planter ten thousand dollars, and has no means by which to raise the money, except from the sale of either his land or his negroes. He dislikes to give up his home, and if he were to propose to sell it to the planter, 'No,' says the planter, 'I don't want your land: it is of no use to me: I cannot transport it to South Carolina, Georgia,

Florida, &c. &c.; but I will take negroes at fair valuation to the amount of my claim, otherwise you must pay me the cash.'

"'What is a fair valuation?' asks the Virginia debtor.

"'I can buy first-rate cotton-field hands,' says the cotton-planter, 'for $250 per head; but as you owe me, and are in a 'tight place,' in order to favor you I will allow you $300 per head for good field-hands, but not a *cent more.*'

"So the rich cotton-planter, to satisfy the insignificant claim of ten thousand dollars, drives off *thirty-three* negroes, *good* field-hands, who to him are as valuable as if he had paid one thousand dollars per head for them.

"Can Virginia afford to raise negroes at $300 per head? No; she cannot. Hence it will be observed that precisely in the same ratio as negroes depreciate in value, Virginia is impoverished, and the cotton and sugar States are built up and enriched. We have never yet heard the first good reason given by any one why Virginia should secede; nor can any one point out a single blessing that will be received by her in the event of her seceding, unless the abolition of slavery from her territory be a blessing.

"Look at the present state of things in Virginia and in the South. Large slave-holders in Virginia, who, twelve months ago, were supposed to be worth one hundred thousand dollars, are now not worth more than two-thirds of that amount; and *the day that Virginia passes the ordinance of secession, negro property in Virginia will become comparatively valueless.* The cotton and sugar States are not at all affected by the depreciation in the value of negroes in Virginia, because, if there should be a decline in cotton and sugar, the price in labor is so much cheaper that they can need only raise more produce to make up for the loss in prices.

"*Virginia's action of secession is virtually Virginia's action for the abolition of all her slave property. Secession is virtually abolitionism. Secession is submission. We are no abolitionist; we are no submissionist; and, therefore, we are no secessionist.* If this be *treason*, our head is ready for the guillotine! But who is the *executioner?*"

"CHAP. IV. *What will Virginia lose by secession?*— If Virginia secede from the Federal Government, she will certainly lose all her negro property.

"She will lose thousands of her noblest sons and fairest daughters.

"She will lose her money and credit, and wind up in bankruptcy and ruin.

"She will lose her horses, corn, meat, silver-ware, and valuable household-furniture by midnight assassins, plunderers, and highway-robbers; banditti will prowl and swarm through the country worse than Egyptian locusts.

"She will lose many of her fine residences, beautiful villages, and thriving towns.

"She will lose all her peace, quiet, and happiness during the whole period of a long-protracted civil war.

"She will lose many of her sanctuaries, and the regular, undisturbed public worship of Almighty God.

"She will lose the kind feeling, friendship, affection, and love which now exist among friends, neighbors, citizens, and relatives.

"She will lose her schools, academies, and colleges, and all facilities of educating her youth.

"She will lose all she has gained in agricultural improvements, all her prosperity and thrift.

"Her territory will become a common battle-field, and her soil be saturated with the blood of the wounded, dead, and dying.

"In a word, she will lose all that she now holds near, dear, and sacred, and her history, honor, and glory will end in seas of blood, when the din and strife of the battle-field and the thunders of civil war shall have passed away.

"Is Virginia prepared for all these things? If she be, then let her secede, and the sooner the better."

"CHAP. V. *Has every possible effort been made to save the Union?*—Has every possible effort been made to save the Union that statesmen and patriots ought to have made? Why did not Southern Senators and Congressmen take their stand in the Senate-Chamber and Congress halls, with the Constitution in one hand, and, if necessity demanded it, a bayonet in the other, and swear by the God of their fathers that the Federal Government should be honored and maintained, and that the South should have her rights in the Union, or that their own lives should be sacrificed on the altar of liberty, on the altar of their country? Then all patriots' hearts would have beaten in unison, and Abolitionists would have quailed before the influence of the united band of American patriots, and peace and prosperity would have continued.

"Did not most of the Representatives from the cotton and sugar-growing States manifest a spirit of morbid indifference to the interests of the Federal Government, from the beginning of the present session of Congress up to the time they resigned their seats? Why was this? Because, prior to the session of Congress, they had determined to secede from the Union, and, therefore, felt no interest in the welfare of the Union, and did nothing to save it, but every thing they could do to break it up. Have not their leading men said that neither the enactment of the 'Personal Liberty Bills,' 'nor the election of Abraham Lincoln' to the Presidency of these United States, was the cause of their secession, for that they had desired for 'upwards of thirty years' to separate themselves from the Union?

"And, finally, when Virginia officially sends her messenger, Judge Robertson, to advise and consult with them in this extreme hour of peril, South Carolina officially spurns him, and resolves to enter into no consultation with him for the sake of the public good. And now we are told that if the seceding States will return to the Union, Virginia will not secede; but, unless they do, Virginia *must secede*,—she must go with her Southern sister States. Gentlemen tell us that it is a disgrace, a degradation, to submit to and live under the Administration of Mr. Lincoln. Then the idea is simply this: if the cotton States will submit to the *infamy* of serving under the incoming Administration, Virginia will! This is cool impudence, is it not? If it be no disgrace to serve under the incoming Administration *with* the cotton States, it is no disgrace to serve under it *without* the cotton States. And, on the other hand, if it be a dishonor to serve under the incoming Administration without the cotton States, it is a dishonor to serve under it with the cotton States. Why, then, do gentlemen tell us that unless the cotton States return into the Union, Virginia ought to go and must go out of the Union? Are they serious when they talk to us in this way? Do they wish the cotton States to come back into the Union and thus disgrace themselves and cause Virginia to be dishonored? Why, then, place the secession of Virginia on any such ridiculous condition? The fact is, gentlemen who argue in this style want no compromise, and they are determined to accept no compromise, however acceptable and satisfactory it might be to the people.

"Why did not the cotton States and the whole South secede in the winter of 1859 and 1860, immediately after the 'John Brown raid'? Were not these obnoxious laws about which so much complaint is now made on the statute-books of the Northern States then? Why was not the Federal Government broken up then? Have any new developments come to light since? Why, then, this upheaving of heaven and earth to precipitate all the Southern States out of the Union before the commencement of the incoming Administration? Are Virginians to be scared and driven headlong and blindly into ruin? Will freemen be forced into measures? No, never, never, while God reigns, and truth, justice, patriotism, and liberty remain among mortals! We repel a threat, whether it comes from men or *demons*, from earth or perdition!

"We claim rights, and are determined to have our rights; and if Virginia and all the border States will stand firm, shoulder to shoulder, we confidently believe that we can yet obtain all our rights in the Union and under the Federal Government. It will be attended with much less expense and hazard for the States which have already seceded to return to the Federal Government, than for all the border States to follow in the wake of the seceding States. And if they shall never wish to return, let them remain in peace. Let no blood be spilt."

"CHAP. VI.—The cotton States have made their election, and are rejoicing at it. They all claim to be sovereign, independent republics. They boast of their ability to protect themselves, but, should they need help, they are looking to England and France. Strange alliance this! But England and France want 'King Cotton,' and the cotton States want cheap labor,—that is, negroes for about $150 per head.

"The cotton States, in making their election, consulted neither the wishes nor the interest of Virginia, nor those of any of the border States. They have acted with reference to their own secular interests and individual safety, and that only. Is Virginia, therefore, under any obligation whatever to follow these States out of the Union? No; and if she should, she will act with more imbecility than we had supposed her capable of. Virginia and the border States have now to look to their own safety and interest, and in doing that they may, if they will, save the whole country from desolation and ruin. Let them remain in the Union and avail themselves of the provisions of the Federal Government, and demand their constitutional rights, and if they fail to obtain them, and after all are forced to fight, let them fight with the 'Stars and Stripes' floating over the battle-ground. But if Virginia and the other border States remain firm, we confidently believe that the whole difficulty will at last be settled amicably, and that no blood will be spilt. The States that have already gone out of the Union, or any others that may hereafter go, let them go and remain in peace. The idea of instituting civil war to force them to come back into the Union is ludicrous!

"Take time, and let the *people*, North and South, fully understand the subject and weigh all the consequences, and, upon reflection, we believe that the concentrated good sense, patriotism, and influence of the conservative element within the Federal Government, North and South, will save the country from war and bloodshed!"

ANNOTATIONS ON THE ABOVE CHAPTERS.

CHAP. I. "*School-boy bombast.*"—It will be remembered that, at the time the above chapters were written, *little* politicians and *small* lawyers were making flowery speeches on the positive beauties and anticipated glories of secession, which were well calculated to tickle the ear and please the fancy of superficial thinkers, or rather of those who were not capable of thinking and of reasoning logically on any subject. These bombastic stump-speakers, by trying to make a show of learning, eloquence, and deep research into the mystical and abstruse subjects which were agitating the whole nation, played upon the passions and presumed upon the ignorance and credulity of their hearers, and, we are sorry to say, with too serious effect.

"*Upstart politicians.*"—During the *reign* of the "Order of the Sons of Temperance" in Virginia, hundreds of *orators* were manufactured out of all sorts of material, which but for that *order* would never have had even a mushroom notoriety, but would have remained quietly in their even and unbroken line of obscurity until the general resurrection. In like manner, secession became all of a sudden the great manufacturing machine for orators, and fathers became astounded at the latent powers of eloquence and the deep unfathomable fountain of political wisdom, patriotism, and chivalry which burst forth from the *precocious* boys. These *new* orators and *wee politicians* never failed to have a crowd of brainless hearers, who were always *surcharged* with gas, cocked and primed, ready to huzza! huzza! huzza! whenever the *orators* spoke of the "blue-necked, white-livered Yankees," the "old black-hearted Abolitionist, Abe Lincoln." And when they would speak, as they always did, of the "Union-shriekers," the "followers and admirers of old Abe Lincoln," the "traitors of the South," "men unworthy to be called the sons of Virginia, and who ought to leave the South, because they left the *slime* behind them as they walked the streets of Fredericksburg," the *huzzas* were absolutely deafening. These were some of the ignoble, unmanly, unfair, lying, and rascally means resorted to by secessionists to "fire up the Southern heart" and to force Virginia out of the Union.

"*Proscribed,—ostracized.*"—It is needless to inform the reader that the "Banner" had become odious with all secessionists, not only in the cotton and sugar States, but even in Virginia; and while we were writing and publishing our articles in favor of the Union, and opposing the secession of Virginia, we were receiving from five to twenty discontinuances to our paper almost every day. We saw that the unalterable determination of secessionists was either to coerce every man of influence into secession, or crush him into annihilation, *damn him, his business and his influence.*

"*Change their political positions.*" It was truly astonishing to witness the rapidity with which men wheeled into the secession ranks,—and men, too, who had been as violently opposed to the *locofoco* party—which was the Breckinridge secession party—as they were to Lincoln and the Black Republican party. Some men had told us during the Presidential canvass that they had rather see Lincoln elected than Breckinridge; and, strange to say, these were among the first men to change their political *status* as soon as secession was openly advocated and began to be popular; because it was boldly proclaimed by orators and editors of the secession fraternity that Union men who longer opposed the South—that is, secession—would not be countenanced nor trusted with any post of honor or office of profit, either in the civil or military departments of the Southern Confederacy. And it is a well-known fact in Virginia that the secession papers in Richmond opposed the promotion of any and all men who were not original secessionists. Why did the "Richmond Examiner," for example, so virulently oppose the Hon. Alexander Hamilton Stephens's being a candidate for the Vice-Presidency of the Southern Confederacy, in the spring of 1862? Simply because of his "antecedents,"—his strong Union proclivities. Mr. Stephens was originally an uncompromising Union man, and this with the "*Examiner*" was a crime sufficient to damn him, politically, in all coming time. As the secession road grew wider and wider, or as secession became more and more popular, thousands upon thousands pressed together and walked therein to their own destruction and the hurt and ruin of all others. "There is a way," says Holy Writ, "that seemeth good unto a man, but the end thereof is death." If secession be not the direct and unmistakable road to political and national *death*, that seemed good unto secessionists, then there is no reliance to be placed in facts.

CHAP. II. "*Is this the case now?*"—We had never supposed that Virginia had been oppressed to such a degree by the Federal Government as to justify her in revolting against that Government. Having been a citizen of the State of Virginia for more than twenty-five years, during a considerable portion of which time we have been both a free-holder and the owner of slaves, we claim to have some knowledge of the condition of affairs in that State; and our honest conviction is that Virginia was never in a more prosperous condition than she was in at the time of Mr. Lincoln's election. Nor do we believe that there was any just reason why the tide of prosperity that was flowing over her whole territory should have been retarded or interrupted by the election of Mr. Lincoln. We presume that, by the present time, thousands of Virginians think as we do.

"*The ostensible causes of secession.*"—One grand and never-failing argument, employed and urged with great vehemence by the advocates of secession to force Virginia out of the Union, was that it would save the South from further Abolition aggressions, and free the State and country from the continual agitation of the slave question. Has secession accomplished this? Let facts speak for themselves. We told Virginians that they would bring Canada to their very doors if they voted the State out of the Union. They laughed at our folly, mocked at our kind admonitions and warnings, and branded us as "a traitor to the South," "an enemy to Virginia," "a submissionist to old Abe Lincoln," and an "Abolitionist." We bore it all with patience, and were willing to endure a thousand times more, if we could have saved our happy, beloved country. But *judicial blindness had seized the people; they were demented.*

"The objects sought to be gained."—The Virginia advocates of secession argued that secession would permanently establish the institution of slavery, and extend slave territory over millions of acres of land, thus opening a great and effectual door to make slavery more valuable in Virginia than it had ever been; whereas, unless Virginia did secede, an Abolition *cordon* was being established, by which negroes in the State would soon become valueless either for sale or hire,—and then what would become of men, and whole families, who were dependent on the sale and hire of their negroes for support? This would be a terrible calamity on Virginia,—that is to say, a terrible calamity upon the proud, broken-down, mushroom aristocrats and *first families of* Virginia! God knows, there are more would-be aristocrats and would-be aristocratic families in Virginia than can be found anywhere on the same *area* of territory this side of either *heaven* or *hell.* To this class of citizens, the idea of negroes becoming valueless was terrible,—yea, more terrible by far than civil war with all its concomitant horrors!

While secessionists in Virginia were anxious to force the State out of the Union for the purpose of permanently establishing the institution of slavery and advancing the value of slave property and slave labor, the Gulf States wished to secede for one prominent reason, among others, that they might reopen, with impunity, the African slave-trade, for the purpose of securing cheap slave labor. Such were some of the unhallowed motives by which the ambitious and ungodly leaders in this *infernal* rebellion were influenced to break up the Government of the United States, and introduce and establish an order of things more in accordance with their own proud, ungodly, and ambitious aspirations. Have their sanguine hopes been realized? Let facts answer the question.

"*They will never enter into any treaties.*"—We believe that African slavery, especially in Virginia, will virtually wind up with this war. When the war ends, there will be but few negroes in the State, and they will be of but little value. Secession was the death-blow to African slavery, not only in Virginia, but in the whole South, as is now constantly being demonstrated. Nor do we believe that any treaties will ever be made by the Federal Government and the South which will give any guarantee to the latter for the safety and perpetuity of the institution of African slavery.

"*Vassals of the few.*"—If the Gulf States could have succeeded, and the African slave-trade been reopened, the fate of poor white men in the South would have been forever sealed. And if the Southern Confederacy had her independence now, and a negro-oligarchy were established, what would be the condition of "poor white people" in that Confederacy? Every sensible man of observation in the South and in the slave States can readily answer this question.

"*Divide the Union.*"—Does not the same proximity exist between the slave and free States, with the additional fact that Virginia is wellnigh abolitionized? Does not the same morbid moral sentiment still remain in the hearts of Abolitionists, with the additional fact that it becomes more and more intense? Have not a thousand new causes of hate and animosity sprung up among all parties? Is not the door for any subsequent equitable separation forever closed, and the key lost in the depths of eternity? Has not the flood-gate been hoisted through which a concentration of curses flows that baffles all human thought to conceive? Has not civil war begun, which will only end in the domination of the South over the North, or of the North over the South? Has not a military despotism supplanted the tree of liberty and all the blessings of freedom? Are not the liberty of conscience, of speech, of action, of the press, and the liberty of a once free, independent, prosperous, and happy people, gone forever? Has not the reign of terror commenced, and is it not progressing? Has not an *era* more to be dreaded than the dark ages commenced? Is not every one who *dares* to speak a word against despots and tyrants proscribed,—*ostracized?* Have not the *many*, the *dear people*, the hard-working yeomanry, become the vassals of the *few?* If they have not, why are they forced from their homes and driven off like sheep, at the point of the bayonet, to gratify the *hellish* ambition and to try to carry out the plans of a *few* leaders? Answer us, will you? If such be the state of things in this early period of the rebellion, what will it be before it ends?—and, should a permanent dissolution be effected, what would the poor whites do in slave States?

CHAP. IV. "*What will Virginia lose by secession?*"

—Has she not already lost nearly one-half of her negro population? Has she not lost thousands of her noblest sons and fairest daughters, her money and credit? Is she not already bankrupt and ruined? Has she not lost her horses and stock, corn and meat, silver-ware and valuable household-furniture?—many of her fine residences, beautiful villages, and thriving towns?—her peace, quiet, and happiness?—her sanctuaries, and the regular, undisturbed worship of Almighty God?—the kind feeling, friendship, affection, and love which existed among friends, neighbors, citizens, and relatives?—her schools, academies, colleges, and all facilities of educating her youth?—all she has gained in agricultural improvements, her prosperity and thrift? Her territory has become a common battle-field, and her soil is saturated with the blood of the wounded, dead, and dying. She is losing all that she holds near, dear, and sacred, and her history, honor, and glory are being ended in seas of blood, and will thus end, when the *din* and *strife* of the battle-field and the thunders of civil war shall have passed away. All these things has Virginia already lost; and the half can never be told, and the end is not yet.

Chap. V. "*Virginia officially sends her commissioner.*"—In proof of the correctness of our remarks relative to the course pursued towards Judge Robertson, who was officially sent from Virginia to consult with the authorities of South Carolina, we here give a series of resolutions which were unanimously adopted by the Legislature of South Carolina, in reference to Judge Robertson and the character of his mission:—

"CHARLESTON, *Jan.* 28.—The Legislature has adopted the following resolutions:—

"*Resolved,* unanimously, That the General Assembly of South Carolina tenders to the Legislature of Virginia their acknowledgment of the friendly motives which inspired the mission intrusted to Judge Robertson, her commissioner.

"*Resolved,* unanimously, That candor which is due to the long-continued sympathy and respect which has long subsisted between Virginia and South Carolina induces the Assembly to declare, with frankness, that they do not deem it advisable to initiate negotiations when they have no desire or intention to promote the ultimate object in view. That object is declared in the resolution of the Virginia Legislature to be the procurement of amendments to, or new guarantees in, the Constitution of the United States.

"*Resolved,* unanimously, That the separation of South Carolina from the Federal Union is final, and she has no further interest in the Constitution of the United States, and that the only appropriate negotiations between her and the Federal Government are as to their mutual relations as foreign States.

"*Resolved,* unanimously, That this Assembly further owes it to her friendly relations to the State of Virginia to declare that they have no confidence in the Federal Government of the United States; that the most solemn pledges of that Government have been disregarded; that, under pretence of preserving property, hostile troops have been attempted to be introduced into one of the fortresses of this State, concealed in the hold of a vessel of commerce, with a view to subjugate the people of South Carolina; and that even since the authorities at Washington have been informed of the present mediation of Virginia, a vessel of war has been sent to the South, and troops and munitions of war concentrated on the soil of Virginia.

"*Resolved*, unanimously, That, under these circumstances, this Assembly, in the renewed assurances of cordial respect and esteem for the people of Virginia, and high consideration for her commissioner, decline entering into the negotiations proposed."

The Legislature, or General Assembly, declared "that the separation of South Carolina from the Federal Union is final," and the secession orators of Virginia declared that they would never "*submit* to the Administration of Abe Lincoln;" that before they would do this they would leave Virginia and locate somewhere within the bounds of the anticipated Southern Confederacy; that they wanted no compromise,—all they wanted was a final and eternal separation from the "old Union," which had now become to them odious; that it was a degradation, a dishonor, to Virginia, the *Old Dominion*, the "Mother of States and of Statesmen," to submit to Black Republican rule; and then they would argue that unless some compromise was adopted, that would bring back the seceded States into the Union, Virginia must secede. Hence we asked, "Are gentlemen honest, are they sincere, when they talk to us thus?"

The fact is, the original leaders in this *accursed* rebellion never intended to accept of *any* compromise that might be offered; and all their temporizing about conventions and this, that, and the other measure was only to gain time and opportunity to prepare the *passions* of the people for secession, and to swindle them out of their rights and drive them into the same abyss of treason with themselves.

"*Immediately after the John Brown raid.*"—Why did not Virginia and the whole South secede immediately after the John Brown raid? Because the Southern heart had not been sufficiently fired up. The leaders had not made all the necessary preparations. Floyd had not sent all the munitions of war belonging to the Federal Government down South. The *loco-foco* party had not been defeated; they were living and faring sumptuously on the spoils of the "hateful old Union;" they were afraid then to talk openly before the *dear* people about breaking up the Federal Government,—the old Union. And during the Presidential canvass even the Breckinridge party denied the charge of being disunionists, and of intending to secede: Newton and Yancey were isolated exceptions. They kept the people in the dark as to the true and real policy they intended to pursue. The party was defeated, and so soon as defeat came, and they could no longer rule the Government, they determined to ruin the country; and they have proved but too successful. But, thank God, in ruining the innocent and in trying to upset and overthrow the Government, they themselves, or at least some of them, will get upset, overthrown, and ruined forever. This is one of the games in which the actors, as well as those acted upon, may receive a hurt, a deadly wound. And we predict that, by the time this war is fully ended, but few of the leaders in the rebellion will be found living in the United States to enjoy the spoils.

"*Let no blood be spilt.*"—We had prayed and hoped that some compromise might be made by which to keep the border States in the Union, in which event we trusted that the few States which had already seceded might be brought, in process of time, to see their error and come back again into the Union. And we still believe that if the border States had all taken a firm, decided stand *in* the Union and *for* the Union, the whole difficulties could, and ultimately would, have been settled without the shedding of so much blood. The preceding chapters, it will be remembered, were written during the time that conventions were being held all over the country for the purpose of compromising the national difficulties. Men, from force of circumstances, were constantly changing,—hopeful to-day, but doubting again to-morrow. After having written the leading editorials of the 31st of January, 1861, we find the following paragraph immediately following in the last column containing our editorials. Intelligence received from Charleston, South Carolina, induced us to write it.

"We fear, from all that we can learn, that, before the Commissioners at Washington shall be able to meet and effect any thing for the permanent adjustment of our national difficulties, the *seceding States* will plunge the country into civil war. There is but little doubt that an attack will be made on Fort Sumter in a very short time. South Carolina seems bent and determined at every hazard to break up the Federal Government. Her reckless course is destined to bring down upon her the unqualified condemnation of all sensible men and true patriots."

The great mystery to secessionists has always seemed

to be how we can so bitterly oppose secession and still be a friend to the South. We think that the scenes now being acted out before the eyes of all are a sufficient solution of the problem. There never was a man born on Southern soil who was, or is, or can be more devoted to the South than we are, and, as we have often said, our uncompromising devotion to the South causes us to utterly detest secession, because secession has ruined the South. We love the South and *the people* of the South, but the leaders of secession we abhor. And all true friends of liberty and republican government will abhor and detest them in all coming time. It is because of our devotion to the South that we are a refugee *to-night.* We love the South, but we love the Union more.

CHAPTER XVIII.

THERE'S HOPE FOR THE UNION—UNION CANDIDATES ELECTED TO THE STATE CONVENTION BY A LARGE MAJORITY—GENERAL REMARKS, ETC. ETC.

In the "Christian Banner" under date of February 7, 1861, we wrote and published the following editorial, under the head of "Random Thoughts Shot at a Venture:"—

"In the far-off distance light appears, the clouds begin to dissipate, hope revives, and quiet, peace, and happiness may yet be restored to the bosom of our lacerated country.

"Virginia, like a towering colossus, stands sublimely grand in all her dignity, looking down with sympathy and compassion at the waywardness, recklessness, and stubbornness of her less influential sisters.

"Neither the terrible thunders of the North, nor the lashing, furious billows of the South, though rolling mountain-high, can move her from her firm, dignified, independent position. Well may her sons feel proud of their birthplace, and her fair daughters boast that they were born on her sacred soil.

"We confidently trust that the action of Virginia is the harbinger of our political salvation and that of our whole country. The destiny of more than thirty millions of souls—may we not rather say a nation's destiny?—depends upon Virginia's action. She will submit to no wrong; she will compromise her honor with no people; she will demand nothing but what is just and fair,—her equal rights. *And these she will have.*

"If, after Congress has failed, and every compromise hitherto presented to restore peace to our country has proved futile, Virginia should now, in the very last hour of peril, work out the salvation of the nation, even Washington in heaven may have cause for deeper joy and increased happiness, and boast among angels that his was the honor of being born on Virginia soil,—that his was the honor of saving that soil from the curse of British tyranny,—and that Virginia has, or can have, the imperishable honor of driving back to their lurking-holes the hateful Black Republicanism and fanaticism of the North, and of quelling, harmonizing, and calming down the wild and wicked insurgents of the South.

"From the election-returns of candidates to the Virginia Convention, we discover that the State is conservativo, by an overwhelming majority, and, also, that a large majority-vote is given to refer the action of the convention to the people, either for their rejection or approval and ratification. This is as it should be. The sovereign power is lodged in the people. If they wish to go out of the Union, let them vote *themselves out*, and then they will have no one to blame. This will give the people time to think on the subject, and will enable them to vote more intelligently and safely.

"Let the kindest fraternal feelings exist among us all, remembering that we are all brethren. We are far from believing that the Union or conservative members of the convention will in the least degree compromise the rights and honor of Virginia. Should they fail, however, to obtain sufficient guarantees for her safety and the protection of her rights under the Federal Government, then they will act as one man in defending her safety and securing her rights in every honorable way, with firmness and promptness. This is all we ask; it is all we can expect; it is all we wish.

"Whatever securities Virginia may be willing to accept will, we think, be satisfactory to all the border States, and should be so to *all* the slave States. Conservative men will yield no sooner to the aggressions of the North than will secessionists. It is the wish of conservative men to exhaust all possible means and make every honorable effort to restore peace and harmony; but, if they fail at last, then they will all strike together,—strike a blow that will be terrible in its results. Let Black Republicans remember this. Secessionists, as we understand them, think that all efforts have been made, and, having given up in despair of ever reconciling difficulties, are in favor of immediate, unconditional secession, at the dread hazard of civil war and all the terrible consequences resulting therefrom. We oppose rash and hasty action, when all we have and all we are is at stake."

"*Overwhelming majority.*"—The majority of votes cast for Union candidates to the Virginia Convention was upwards of sixty thousand. With this majority in favor of the Union, we could hardly suppose it possible that Virginia could be *dragged* out of the Union. But we were deceived in our calculation so far as the action of the convention was concerned; but, so far as regards the voluntary action of the people of the State of Virginia we were not mistaken. Virginia was *lied*, *swindled*, and *forced* out of the Union, as the sequel of this work will prove. Never was there a system of greater, *damnable* political villany and downright rascality imposed on any people since God made the world, than that which was imposed on the people of Virginia by the leading secessionists of the State and by the members of the State Convention, as we shall show in a subsequent chapter. At the close of the above editorial of February 7, 1861, we wrote the two short paragraphs following:—

"☞ A thousand guns for the 'Old Dominion' on the result of the late election for candidates to the Virginia Convention! Now, if she saves the Federal Government and causes the 'Stars and Stripes' to continue floating over our homes, she shall be entitled to ten thousand guns from every prominent town and city in the State, and glory, honor, and salvation to her sacred soil forever."

"☞ When we hear fellows boasting of their bravery, and expressing such great anxiety to fight! fight! fight! we think to ourself, 'Poor boys! when the poetry and glory of fighting shall have passed away, and stern realities come, many of you will wish yourselves at home holding on to your mammas' apron-strings.'"

"*Hope revives.*"—Virginia had given a sweeping Union majority vote. The Border States Convention was in session at Washington City, and a telegraphic despatch from Washington stated that "Ex-President Tyler, on taking the chair to-day, [the 5th of February, 1861,] delivered an address which was eulogized by those present as highly patriotic and conciliatory." General Scott had thrown troops into Washington City for its defence, and considered the city a safe place of residence on the 4th of the approaching March. Maryland had not seceded, and seemed to stand firm for the Union,—as she still continues to do. Things seemed to be brightening up; and Union men in Virginia began to feel hopeful that the border States would all remain in the Union, and thus save the country from one common ruin. True, there were many disheartening circumstances when we took an impartial view of things on the other side. Secessionists in Virginia were moving every power and straining every nerve to carry Virginia out of the Union. The seceding States were seizing Government property everywhere within their territory, thus provoking a collision, if possible, with the Federal Government.

Most of the foreign ministers at Washington City had sent off despatches to their respective Governments, stating that the Government of the United States was practically dissolved. Lieutenant James Jewett, United States Navy, had been arrested at Pensacola by the State authorities of Florida, who would not permit him to depart unless upon his parole of honor that he would never take up arms against the State of Florida. Senator Crittenden, of Kentucky, upon hearing of this outrage being perpetrated upon a gallant son of his own State, became indignant, and advised Lieutenant Jewett to proceed at once to the Secretary of the Navy and report the facts, which he did. Warlike preparations continued to progress at Charleston, South Carolina, and an attack on Fort Sumter was daily expected. The times were indeed trying to the hearts and feelings of all true patriots.

CHAPTER XIX.

In the number of the "Christian Banner" of February 14, 1861, under the head of "Random Thoughts Shot at a Venture," we wrote and published the following leading editorial, and several shorter paragraphs :—

"SUNDRIES.

"We have always scorned to dabble in the muddy waters of political strife. Having fixed principles as a citizen, we have ever tried to observe them. For the last twelve months, however, we have written more or less almost every week on the fearful calamities which threaten our glorious country.

"We saw the perilous condition of the Republic, and in our zeal, we have written to try to help save it. We knew that, if our country were broken up and civil war should begin, there would be an end of all our liberties and blessings, political, social, and religious. We have written our views freely, fearlessly, and independently. If any have taken exceptions, we can't help it. We think, however, that the time will come when our course will be commended by all sober-thinking, patriotic citizens.

"So soon as the political storm which is now agitating and convulsing our country shall have passed away, we intend to pursue a different course from that which has occupied our attention for the last year. We begin to hope that the storm will pass over without civil war,—that the Federal Government will continue,—that confidence will be restored,—that peace and tranquillity will once more dwell in our midst,—that business will become active, and that all things will go on prosperously.

"If Maryland, Virginia, North Carolina, Kentucky, Tennessee, &c. &c., remain firm and steadfast, and a compromise of our Federal relations shall be adopted which will prove satisfactory to these States, we confidently believe that some if not all of the seceded States will ultimately return to the Union. If they should not, however, let them have their own *Confederacy*, and enjoy in peace and tranquillity all the blessings and privileges of which they are capable.

"If any of the New England States, or any of the

ultra-abolition States, wish to *slab* off, let them go and do the best for themselves that they can. It will not be many years, in our humble opinion, until all the seceded States will be anxious to return to the old Union of their fathers. So that, after all, the present national excitement may result in infinite good to the whole country. If, however, the seceded States, and those, if any, which may hereafter secede, shall never return to the Union, all sections can go on and govern their own affairs without detriment to each other, and the whole country may continue in peace and prosperity.

"If the 'Peace Conference' now in session in Washington City shall adjust a plan satisfactory to the border States, this is all we can expect or hope for at the present critical crisis. And we again repeat, and would impress it upon the minds of our readers, that if the States which have already seceded *will not* come back *into* the Union, this is no reason why the border States shall go *out of the Union.* There is a principle or law in natural philosophy that supposes the smaller bodies to be attracted by the larger. But in the present case the smaller bodies, or seceded States, seek to *force* the larger bodies, or non-seceding States, and bring them under their influence.

"We would again say to our readers, be as hopeful as to the future, under all the trying circumstances, as possible; and, as cold winter is passing away, and spring-time, with all its glories, is approaching, be cheerful, and go to work in good earnest, and make large preparations for abundant crops. The Lord reigneth: let the earth rejoice, and the children of men be glad! Surely our country cannot be broken up, laid waste, and ruined as easily and as quickly as some people suppose."

"Who could have supposed, twelve months ago, that the question of Union or no Union would have been brought out squarely before the people, claiming their votes so soon? As strange things as this will happen in less than ten years. Remember what we say."

"If the hearts of many of the odious politicians of the day were half as soft as their heads, then would our country be free from danger."

"How are ministers of the gospel *now* to obey the great commission of their divine Lawgiver, 'Go ye into all the world and preach the gospel to every creature'? Northern Abolition fanatics can't go South and preach with impunity, nor can Southern fire-eaters go North and preach with any good effect. A pretty state of things, truly!"

From the following brief article the reader can form some idea of the persecution to which Union men had to submit in the town of Fredericksburg as early as the 14th of February, 1861, the date of its publication:—

"Why is it that secessionists talk of compromise with derision? Why is it that they wish to precipitate Virginia out of the Union? Why is it that they call conservative or Union men '*Submissionists,*' '*Black Republicans,*' '*Abolitionists,*' '*Traitors and enemies to the South,*' &c. &c.? Are secessionists more intellectual than Union men? In what have they displayed it? Are they more patriotic? What proofs have they given of the fact? Are they more brave? Why then did they vacate their seats in the Senate and Congress halls of the United States, thus virtually surrendering all their rights into the hands of their enemies? Why, in the hour of their country's peril, did they retreat into the Gulf States, having as a safeguard the Atlantic Ocean on the one side, and the border States between them and danger on the other side? There is no *submission* in all this, is there? Very brave, is it? In what have Union men compromised their honor or dignity? It is not honorable, not dignified, for a man to stand his ground and fight for his rights on his own soil, and sacredly maintain the trust the people have confided in him! But it is very honorable, quite dignified, for a man to throw down his legal weapons of defence and run away, and *belt* on the sword, and swear if the enemy comes to him he'll thrash him out! This is very brave, is it?

"What rights have secessionists to protect that Union men have not? Have Union men no civil, religious, and domestic rights to protect? We think it bad policy for secessionists who would break up the peace and harmony of the Government, and plunge the whole country into civil war, to be accusing their fellow-citizens, who are trying to pour oil upon the troubled waters and are making all possible efforts to bring about peace and harmony, of being '*Submissionists*,' '*Black Republicans*,' '*Abolitionists*,' and '*Traitors*' and '*Enemies to the South*.'"

The above are specimens of some of the milder opprobrious epithets which secessionists applied to Union men by way of *convicting* them of true patriotism, and converting them to treason and all the *damnable* horrors and curses resulting from it. The efforts used to *browbeat, cow,* and *force* men into the ranks of secession beggar all description. And while Senators Hunter and Mason and others at Washington City were doing any thing else than "pouring oil on the troubled waters," secesh understrappers, politicians, and fifteen-shilling lawyers were haranguing the people through the country and stirring up all the baser and vindictive passions of the ignorant and credulous classes of the people. They sneered at the idea of *any* compromise. None but "Traitors to the South," "Submissionists," "Black Republicans," "Abolitionists," "Old Lincolnites," "Union-shriekers," and "Cowards" wanted to compromise with *blue-necked, white-livered* Yankees! To listen to the stentorian and verbose orations of many of these hopeful politicians and statesmen, one would be induced to suppose that their lungs were made of brass, and that they had ransacked the vocabularies of earth and hell to gather epithets sufficiently strong and damnable to apply to *Union men, to the old Union, to the old Federal Government, to old Abe Lincoln, to the old Flag of the Union, to black-hearted submissionists, to Union-shriekers, to Abolitionists, to traitors to Virginia and the South, to Southern Yankees, &c. &c.* Our heart, even now, saddens at the painful recollection, and we turn away from the subject in disgust. Poor fellows! If they have not already done so, they will see, and feel too, the full effects of their folly before this war shall have closed. May God in mercy save them!

CHAPTER XX.

HOPE FOR THE UNION WANES—JEFF DAVIS'S SPEECH IN MONTGOMERY—GENERAL REMARKS, ETC. ETC.

In the number of the "Christian Banner" of February 21, 1861, under the head of "Random Thoughts," we wrote and published the following:—

"'Tis folly to try to hope longer for an amicable adjustment of our Federal or national difficulties. The star of hope has gone down beneath the hill of despair. To talk longer of compromise is sublime nonsense,—superlatively ludicrous. No compromise would at the present time bring back the seceded States. Mr. Davis, in his Inaugural Address, says,—

"'I enter upon the duties of the office for which I have been chosen with the hope that the beginning of our career as a confederacy may not be obstructed by hostile opposition to the enjoyment of the separate and independent existence which we have asserted, and which, with the blessing of Providence, we intend to maintain. We have entered upon our career of independence, and it must be inflexibly pursued. If a just perception of mutual interest shall permit us peaceably to pursue our separate political career, my most earnest desire will have been fulfilled. But, if this be denied us, and the integrity and jurisdiction of our territory be assailed, it will but remain for us, with a firm resolve, to appeal to arms, and invoke the blessings of Providence upon a just cause.'

"In his address at the depot, on arriving in Montgomery, Mr. Davis said,—

"'We are now determined to maintain our position, and make all who oppose us smell Southern powder and feel Southern steel, if coercion be persisted in. We will maintain our rights and our government at all hazards. We ask nothing, want nothing, and will have no complication. If other States join our confederation, they can freely come on our terms. Our separation from the old Union is complete. No compromise, no thought of reconstruction, will now be entertained.'

"If President Davis be a correct exponent of the views of the people of the six seceded States, then the *Rubicon* is forever passed. Why, then, talk about compromise any longer? The border States must be *forced* to join the Southern Confederacy on just such terms as she may be pleased to receive them. 'They can freely come on our terms.' Hence they have no voice in the matter at all. Are *freemen* to be *menaced* and talked to in this way? So the border States at last have to yield to the dictates of the seceded States!

"A provisional Government! Remember that the laws of this provisional Government are only to continue for the term of one year, until permanent laws are enacted and a permanent constitution adopted. Will the laws of this anticipated firm confederacy be favorable to the interests of Virginia and the other border States? Who can tell? Who can believe that they will? What guarantees have Virginia and the border States that this new confederacy will not reopen the African slave-trade? None whatever! If the African slave-trade is not reopened, then the seceded States will be forced to purchase slaves from Virginia. One thing is certain: they are going to get their negroes just where they can purchase them cheapest. This is a *fixed fact.* We have not a doubt that thousands and tens of thousands of African negroes will be smuggled into the cotton States and sold into bondage, in defiance of all laws to the contrary. We are afraid of the *wooden horse!* There are deep groans within!

"It now behooves Virginia to demand such guarantees as will secure her own property and safety, without having any reference to the seceded States. And if Virginia is satisfied that her property will be protected, she ought to be contented and remain in the Union, and then business will become active, confidence will be restored, and prosperity will follow."

"ANOMALY.

"The history of the world cannot furnish another instance of such an anomaly as is now presented to the mind of the student in these United States, or, rather, in these disrupted States. Within ninety days the greatest republic the world has ever known has been broken up; two separate and distinct confederacies exist; two antagonistic Congresses are in session; two Presidents are ruling; universal preparations for war are being made by both confederacies; confidence is everywhere destroyed; all kinds of business are stagnated; all descriptions of property are depreciating in value to insignificance; people are everywhere crushed beneath the heavy liabilities resting upon them; bankruptcy is threatening the whole country; millions of dollars are being levied to purchase munitions of war; Legislatures, conferences, and conventions are being constantly held; money must be raised to pay all these expenses; the people must be taxed to starvation to pay all this wicked expenditure of money; and, think, not as yet has a single battle been fought, a single gun fired,—except at the 'Star of the West,'—nor a single life lost.

"Positively, the scenes now being acted out beggar all belief. And yet the people tamely submit! Yes, submit to be gulled, duped, and led about by ambitious, designing politicians, just as if they were cattle, to be muzzled, yoked, and driven wherever the owners wish. *Do freemen submit? Will freemen* submit to the galling yoke of despotism being placed upon their necks by petty tyrants, who are only scrambling for public spoils, position, and power? Will they suffer their pockets to be drained of the last farthing, starve their suffering wives and destitute families, to support, uphold, and continue in office, power, and position, a set of worthless public mendicants? Are freemen afraid to speak out their sentiments? Are they afraid to act the part of free-born citizens? Are they afraid to say that they have souls and are determined to save them? It would seem so!

"Fellow-citizens, think! Out of your hard earnings the members composing the present *extra* session of the Virginia Legislature have to be paid! What are they doing there for the good of the country? What have they done? They have called a convention. Yes, and your hard earnings must foot every bill of every member of that convention! They have sent commissioners to confer with the seceded States. For what? Did they not know before the commissioners were sent that the seceded States would accept of *no* compromise? Why, then, send them? If they have business to do as a legislative body, why do they not accomplish it at once, and save the country from the expense of paying them to remain in Richmond, drinking, feasting, and frolicking at the expense of the Commonwealth? Rome burns, and Nero sits on his tower, singing on his lyre the destruction of Troy!

"We are tired and disgusted with hearing about plans and compromises, seeing that secessionists are determined to accept of no compromise whatever. And we now urge the people, independently of politicians, to adopt some compromise which shall be satisfactory to the people, and let the whole North and South vote upon it; and, if the people are safe and satisfied, let politicians 'go by the board.'

"The children of Israel, for a number of years, were governed by a *theocracy;* but they were not satisfied. God could not govern them to their liking. They wanted a king, and God permitted them to have a king; and the result is well known to all Bible readers. The American people were once free and happy; but we fear they will never rest until they are reduced to kingly tyranny and despotic oppression.

"Objections are made to Mr. Lincoln as the chief magistrate of these United States, because he is a sectional President! Who elected President Davis? Was he elected by the popular vote of the six seceded States? Was the popular vote of these States taken at all? Did any State or States in the Union, except the seceded States, have any voice in his election? Look at it, will you? And now we are urged and must be forced to fly for refuge to this newly *self-created* Confederacy of six States, without having any voice or representation either in Congress or as to the Presidency! Thank God! all freemen are not sold yet, and there still live men who know their rights and are not afraid to defend them. Nor do we believe that the eloquence of Mr. Preston nor that of all the commissioners from the seceded States will be able to move Virginia from her dignified, patriotic position. Should the hearts of the members of the convention, however, become *fired up*, and they, in an unguarded moment, pass an ordinance of secession, we ardently trust that the *people* of Virginia have the good sense still remaining to veto the act, until we know that sufficient guarantees will not be given to secure the safety and protection of the border States.

"Two confederacies! Two Presidents and Vice-Presidents! Two separate and independent Governments in the 'United States of America'! Great God! who can realize the fact! Truly we have fallen on evil times. How can a collision be avoided? Well, let us wait and see. The knowing ones may call us a fool and traitor *now*, and say that we have no sense; but, if the future does not reveal the folly of *the fools*, then *we* shall be perfectly willing to be set down as a *fool* by the learned and knowing ones of the day. May the Lord pity the *folly* of *fools*, and save our country from ruin!"

"Blessings of Providence."—Jeff Davis, in the very beginning of his career, tried to impress upon the

minds of the people that God Almighty was *particeps criminis* in his *damnable* plot of treason against the Government of the United States of America. He preached up to the people a God of battles, blood, and thunder, powder, and steel. "We are now determined," he says, "to maintain our position, and make all who oppose us *smell Southern powder and feel Southern steel,* if coercion is persisted in." To what extent Jupiter and Neptune, or the God of battles, of Southern powder and Southern steel, have aided the cause of this *usurper* of authority, is well known to the reader and to the American people. But, if Mr. Davis thus ardently repudiated coercion when applied to himself and his wicked rebellion, why did he himself afterwards persist in trying to coerce individuals, communities, and States into his Confederacy? But more of this in a future chapter; and a dark chapter it is,—one which will astonish the reader.

"*Virginia Legislature.*"—The members of this extra session of the Virginia Legislature were all members who had been elected to the Assembly of Virginia before the question of secession was ever sprung upon the people. This was a Breckinridge-Democratic Legislature, composed of men who were determined, if possible, to dissolve the Union, or to aid in its dissolution to the utmost extent of their influence. They had no State constitutional authority to order a convention without first taking the vote of the people of the State as to whether there should be a convention or not. They knew, or believed, that if the question of a convention or no convention for the purpose of taking into consideration the expediency or inexpediency of dissolving the Union were squarely and fairly brought before the people, there would be no convention. But with that Legislature the secession of Virginia was a *foregone* conclusion; and they *usurped* the *authority* of calling a convention, and then remained in session during the session of the convention to act as an outside pressure upon that convention to force Virginia out of the Union. *This*, facts abundantly prove, and we shall say more on the subject hereafter.

"*Why, then, send them?*"—Why were commissioners being sent *to* and *from* Virginia, *to* and *from* the Southern Confederacy, for the purpose of compromising difficulties, when Mr. Davis openly said, "We ask nothing, want nothing, and will have no complication. Our separation from the old Union is complete. No compromise, no thought of reconstruction, will now be entertained"? Strange as it may now appear to the intelligent reader, the leaders of disunion, the orators of the secession party, still urged upon the people that unless some compromise was devised and adopted, which would bring back the seceded States into the Union, Virginia must secede. It was all a *deep, damnable plot of treason*,—a trap set to catch Virginia and force her out of the Union,—a political swindle, a trick and cheat, imposed upon her, for which she will hold the guilty culprits responsible after this war shall have ended,—if they are then living; and, if not, her wrath and fiery indignation will be hurled upon their guilty souls throughout the undying ages of eternity. The souls of the thousands slain on Virginia's soil will rise up in the day of judgment, and condemn the guilty leaders in this wicked rebellion, because by it they were unexpectedly forced into battle, and consequently hurried unprepared into eternity and before the bar of the Righteous Judge of all the earth. Woe! woe! woe! be unto the leaders of this rebellion, both in time and in eternity! And when this war shall have closed, there will be a fearful reckoning with the people.

A special despatch to the "Petersburg Express," dated Richmond, February 27, 10½ P.M., announced the following intelligence:—

"A member of the Virginia Legislature has just received the following despatch from Washington:—

"'The Peace Congress have agreed upon a plan of adjustment, which, it is hoped, will prove satisfactory to all parties. The object was consummated to-day.

"'The Peace Convention have adjourned and reported to Congress.

"'We fire a salute of one hundred guns in the morning, in honor of the great event, by order of the Government.'

"It is said that Ex-Governor Wise remarked, when he heard the above read, that one hundred were quite enough.

"The secessionists here do not at all relish the news from Washington. Several prominent members of the State Convention left here to-night for Washington."

Why did not the secessionists at Richmond "at all relish the news from Washington"? And why did "several prominent members of the State Convention" leave Richmond "post-haste" for Washington as soon as they learned the result of the Peace Conference? Does not the reader fully comprehend the whole design? Secessionists relished nothing that had the slightest and most remote semblance to "a plan of adjustment" which might "prove satisfactory to all parties."

A Washington correspondent of the "Richmond Dispatch," in a letter to that paper after the inauguration of Mr. Lincoln, explains the whole matter. The correspondent says,—

"Lincoln threatens war because he knows his hands are tied. War is not the thing we ought to fear. Peace is our destruction; war our salvation."

The "Alexandria Gazette," in commenting on the above, said,—

"Is not this significant? Is it not 'rule or ruin'? Will not the people of Virginia mark this? Will they yield themselves to those who hold and express such sentiments,—sentiments destructive to their best and dearest interests and utterly subversive of their highest hopes? We are to desire war, civil war, bloodshed, every thing calculated to ruin us, so that secession may be carried out here and protected elsewhere! Never!"

While secessionists at the South were working the wires of intrigue to consummate their "infernal plot" of *treason* against the Government, evolving every approachable and available element by which to overturn the Republic and dissolve the Union, the conservative element of the North was doing every thing possible to save the Union and keep the Republic from wreck and ruin.

The Working-Men's National Convention, which assembled in Philadelphia in March, 1861, passed the following resolutions:—

"*Resolved*, That we, the working-men of the United States, without distinction of party, believe that, as a consequence of the sectional controversy now agitating our country, we are now approaching the verge of national, social, and financial ruin; that our material prosperity, our hopes of happiness, and future security depend upon the preservation of the Union.

"2. That in the mere abstract questions which have been used to distract and divide the honest masses the working-men have no real interest. As we can hardly hope for a safe solution of pending difficulties through the politicians of the country, we therefore exhort our brethren to lay aside all their feelings, surrender forever the ties that have bound them to favorite leaders, and unite in one solid column for a single purpose, the preservation of the Federal Union.

"3. That the Territorial question ought to be settled on a constitutional basis; [and the resolutions then go on to endorse the Crittenden compromise.]

"4. That the Union must and shall be preserved, and the co-operation of our brethren is invoked to 'hurl with speedy hands the accursed traitors who have with impunity desecrated the inmost sanctuary' of freedom.

"5. [This resolution denounces all attempts made by partisans or public papers to promote disunion, and that the ship of state has been too long confided to men who are unworthy of the trust, and who have permitted her to run upon the quicksands of sectional strife; we will, therefore, vote against aspiring demagogues, and vote for firm and patriotic men.]

"6. [This resolution denies the right of any State to secede, but deprecates the use of coercive power by the General Government, as the Government rests upon the will of the people, the source of all political power.]

"7. [This resolution deprecates the election of any man to any public trust who has by any means endeavored to prevent a just settlement of the present difficulties.]

"8. [The Legislatures of the different States are requested to repeal all personal liberty bills that may violate any constitutional principles of the people of the United States.]

"9. [The working-men of the thirty-four States are recommended to form associations pledging themselves to lay upon the altar of their country all party predilections, and to maintain the Union of all these States, 'one and inseparable, now and forever.']"

If the secessionists of Virginia and the other border States had wished or desired a compromise which might have proved satisfactory to all parties, why did they not co-operate with the Union men of the border States and with the conservative men at the North? No: they asked for no compromise; they wanted no compromise; and they determined to accept of no compromise; and, therefore, the sin of all the evils which have befallen Virginia and the whole South rests upon the guilty souls of these leading arch-traitors, who, by lying, intrigue, and rascality *generally*, forced Virginia out of the Union.

While secessionists in Virginia were effecting the secession of the State, the Southern Confederacy was enlisting troops to be hurried into Virginia as soon as the ordinance of secession was passed by the convention; so that, on the day of election, when the action of the convention was to be voted on by the people of Virginia, they would have to vote for secession at the point of the bayonet. This is no false coloring to the subject, as subsequent events proved, and as we shall be able to show before we are done with this accursed plot of treason against our blessed country.

CHAPTER XXI.

SECESH CAUCUS CLIQUES—GREAT SECESH MEETING AND UNION MEETING IN FREDERICKSBURG—IMPOSITION OF SECESH ORATORS—SECESH REMARKS, ETC. ETC.

On the first Monday in March, 1861, at Spottsylvania Court-House, that being county-court day, a *clique* of secessionists met *then* and *there*, and passed a set of resolutions, among which was one instructing the representative from the county of Spottsylvania and the town of Fredericksburg to the Virginia Convention, which was then being held in the city of Richmond, to urge the immediate passage of an ordinance of secession, the representative from this county having been elected a member of the convention as a Union man by an overwhelming majority. These resolutions were hurried off to Richmond to influence the representative in his future course of action, and published in the public newspapers as being the wish of the voters of the county. Thus was the representative imposed upon, as were also the voters and people of the county. Be it remembered that *fifteen-shilling* lawyers and *sub-editors*, or some *worthless office-hunters*, were generally at the head of all these treasonable *cliques*.

On the following Friday night this same party called a town-meeting for the purpose of *imposing* and *forcing* the same set of resolutions upon the voters and citizens of Fredericksburg. This meeting was largely attended and ably represented by those who had respectively advocated the interests of Bell, Breckinridge, and Douglas during the Presidential campaign of 1860. Eight consecutive *disunion* speeches were delivered by eight lawyers. The speakers who had advocated the cause of Bell and Douglas during the Presidential canvass declared themselves wholly converted, head and heels, soul and body, to the inexpressible beauties, undying excellencies, and transcendently sublime glories of secession, and most unmercifully and vindictively denounced all as *Abolitionists, traitors, submissionists,* and *Lincolnites,* who would any longer stand up for the *old Union,* or the flag of the old United States. On this occasion the *stentorian* style was admirably imitated by all the speakers. They seemed to try to what an astonishing height they could raise their voices, and to what an extent they could be heard; they were verbose, vehement, denunciatory, dogmatic, impudent, insolent, disgusting, and highly insulting; but as for common sense, good logic, sound argument, and mathematical demonstration, there was none of it,—except that they demonstrated their own folly and final ruin by their own treasonable course of conduct. That this would prove to be the result of their action was clearly demonstrated to our own mind at least.

If Virginia did not secede immediately, one was going away out west of the Mississippi River, the Father of

Waters, and leave his "beautiful farm which you" (the audience) "see every day; and if Virginia did not secede, and if *he*, the speaker, did not leave Virginia, his "wife is going any way, as she has determined not to live under old Abe's Administration." Another was going to *root up roots* out of the ground and make his wife and children do the same for a living, before he and they should become the subjects of old Lincoln's tyranny and despotic rule. Another was going to face the cannon—yes, walk right square up to the cannon's mouth and wade in blood up to his neck—before he would ever submit to the despotism of a Black Republican Abolition Administration. It was a great time with secessionists. The rapping and clapping and loud huzzas were frequent, long, and deafening. Oh, they were a merry, jubilant set of fellows that night! If it had been an old-fashioned Methodist camp-meeting, and a thousand sinners had become converted to God, the enthusiasm and extravagance could not have been surpassed.

Strange as it may appear to the reader, not one of the pugnacious orators who were going to turn the world upside down and play the *devil* generally on that ever-memorable night has ever yet faced the mouth of a roaring cannon, or waded in blood up to his neck, or even been in a battle, so far as we know. One of the most popular and prominent of all who spoke on that occasion subsequently offered for the Congress of the Southern Confederacy, but, getting shamefully defeated, he afterwards became attached to the staff of one of the Confederate generals, with the title of major annexed. This man was a prominent Breckinridge Democrat, a great admirer of Jeff Davis, a thorough secessionist, a despiser of the old Union, and a scorner of the "Stars and Stripes." He was rich, and with his party, before the war began, influential; but since the war commenced his negroes have left, his "beautiful" residence and splendid farm have become the head-quarters of the generals of the Federal army, and his farm a common camping-field. He is now comparatively poor, and, except with original secessionists, his influence is gone, and gone forever.

Another one of the *eloquent* orators on that occasion was a Breckinridge Democrat; but during the reign of Know-Nothingism he was a great *Know-Nothingist*, and, if we are not mistaken, he is emphatically a *Know-Nothingist* yet, having learned nothing since,—a *nine-shilling* lawyer, a worshipper of Jeff Davis, a despiser of the old Union, a scorner of the "detestable flag of the Federal Government," but a devoted friend, a sincere lover, of the one thing which most traitors admire, *whiskey*. This man was for a short time a lieutenant in a company when the rebellion first broke out, but, when the "tug of war" actually came, fearing, as was supposed, that he might get into a fight and by some unforeseen accident *might* "get hurt," resigned his office; and when the conscript law took effect, and scouting-parties were hunting out and picking up fighting-men in, around, and about Fredericksburg, we understand that this poor fellow, this would-be hero in time of peace, when there was no danger of "getting hurt," was slipping and sliding, dodging, running, and hiding, from place to place, to keep from being caught and forced into the conscript army to fight against "*submissionists* and the *disciples* of old Abe Lincoln"! He had declined all idea of fighting "old Abe Lincoln" and "the *blue-necked, white-livered Yankees.*" He found it was much easier to make treasonable secesh speeches, and be *huzzaed* by brainless knaves and foolish boys, than to fight the "vandals of the North," and consequently, like "Jerry Sneak, he turned edge-ways and became invisible," or, like the return on a constable's warrant, *non est inventus.*

But to return to the meeting. All the orators of the night and of the occasion having delivered themselves of the eloquence which was pent up within them, and the thunders of the loud huzzas having died away, the resolutions were read and the vote taken, and pronounced by the chair to be unanimous, with but one solitary exception. One poor, thoughtless fellow in the vast assembly said *no* to the resolutions,—when a simultaneous shout like deafening thunder arose, "*Put him out!* put him out! put him out!" whereupon one of the *tender-hearted* lawyers, (and they all have tender hearts, reader,) who had just delivered himself of a treasonable speech, and seeing unconditional glory, honor, and immortality ahead, said, "*No, no, no:* don't put him out; he is evidently intoxicated." The inference, therefore, to be fairly drawn was that none but a drunken man would dare to vote against the resolutions; while the actual fact in the case was, that this poor fellow's carcass only escaped being *kicked* out of the public courthouse into the streets on the plea of his being drunk.

The meeting having adjourned, we left the courthouse, seriously cogitating upon the lamentable scenes which had just been acted out, and the awfully alarming state of public affairs generally, and, like the old prophet of whom we read in the Bible, from the depth of our soul we exclaimed, "Lord, they have killed thy prophets, digged down thine altars, and I am left alone, and they seek my life." Like the old prophet, however, we were mistaken; for in that very assembly there were many who had never bowed the knee to the image of Baal, and who in their hearts despised the *demon secession*, as subsequent events proved.

Resolutions which were passed by these secesh caucus-meetings, which were everywhere being held through the country, were hurried off to Richmond to the representatives in the State Convention, as we have already said, to force and influence them to vote for the immediate secession of Virginia; otherwise, on their return home they would be held accountable to their constituents for not having obeyed instructions. These resolutions were also published in the public newspapers, and largely commented on by editors, to influence and force the people into secession, and to prepare their minds and hearts for action at the election that was to take place relative to ratifying or rejecting the final action of the Virginia Convention.

Many of the meetings which were held and at which were passed resolutions instructing representatives in the convention to vote for immediate secession were composed of but few individuals, and they, for the most part, original secessionists of the baser sort, while the resolutions professed to be a fair representation of the sentiments of whole cities, counties, and communities. The intelligent reader cannot fail to see that in this way, if the members of the convention, in consequence of their superior advantages, were not imposed on, the people through the State were.

To counteract the false impressions produced by these resolutions so far as the town and citizens of

Fredericksburg were concerned, the Union men of Fredericksburg determined to hold a Union meeting in the court-house on the following Monday night after the secesh had held theirs. On Sunday morning we were waited on by Union gentlemen to know if we would deliver an address on the following night, provided they could "get up" a meeting. For reasons satisfactory to ourself, we told them we would. We had written for our country, were willing to speak for our country, and, if necessary, would die for our country. The notice being short, and for a Union meeting, and there being no chance to announce it in any of the town papers, as there was no daily paper in town, and no paper published on Monday, we calculated on quite a small attendance.

No sooner, however, had it become known that there was to be a Union meeting than the secessionists went to work to devise ways and means by which either to turn the Union meeting into a secesh meeting, or, if they failed in that, to create a "row," and break up the meeting entirely. Facts subsequently developed proved this to have been the determination of the opposition party. At the head of this plot there were men who should have blushed to engage in such meanness. *But to what depths of crime and meanness will not treason stoop?*

On entering the court-house on Monday night, we found it perfectly filled. Ignorant of the plot of the secessionists either to turn the meeting into a secesh meeting or attempt to annihilate it, we were surprised to witness so large an attendance; for never had we seen the court-house more thoroughly crowded than on that ever-memorable night, the 11th of March, 1861.

Immediately after the meeting was organized, and the committee appointed to prepare resolutions for the meeting had retired, the chair, in the name of the meeting, expressed a desire to hear an address. Instantly the secessionists called out for a certain lawyer, who had been a Douglas elector during the Presidential canvass, and one of the men who had spoken on the previous Friday night. At the same time the Union men were calling on us to take the stand. Being seated in the crowd, before we had time to rise and get fairly on the way to the speaker's stand, the secesh lawyer was on the stand and had commenced his speech. We returned to our seat until he had finished He "put it on thick and heavy" to the *Union-shriekers, submissionists, Abolitionists, &c. &c.* We looked at him, and wondered all the time, thinking to ourself, "How changed! how fallen!" We had listened to him on the previous Friday night; we had heard him when advocating the cause of Douglas, the Union, the Constitution, and enforcement of the laws. Then he was manly, dignified, eloquent, logical, and patriotic. As a friend, we loved him; as a citizen, we respected him; as a patriot, we admired him. Now, as a traitor to his country, we pitied him; for his treason, we *scorned him.* Scarcely had he finished his last treasonable sentence when a shout was raised for another secesh speaker to take the stand. They called on this occasion for their ablést and most popular speakers. Again the Union men called on us to take the stand. Feeling under obligation to our friends, but infinitely more to our country, we walked upon the stand, where, to our surprise, we found the last secesh orator who had been called out was standing and trying to gain the hearing of the audience.

Here followed a scene that beggars all description. For upwards of fifteen minutes the tumult was like the continuous roaring of many waters,—each party calling on their speaker to *go on, go on, go on,* and each swearing that the speaker of the other party should not speak. It was a rich scene for civilized, patriotic, Christian men! But it was a *struggle* between patriotism and treason, a *struggle* for our country and all the blessings of freedom. Finally, however, the house was brought to order, and we addressed the meeting for about an hour and a half, amidst the huzzas and hisses of that vast assembly. During the time we were speaking, some cowardly, unprincipled scoundrel, a sinner against God, and a traitor to his country, threw an egg at us from the extreme part of the house; but, losing its force before it reached us, it struck a young man who was seated directly in front of us, on the back of the head. Why did this *outlaw* bring eggs with him to a public meeting, unless he had anticipated a *mob* on the occasion? Had he no preconceived design in doing this? Had he no accomplices committed to aid in creating a *mob* and breaking up the meeting? Why was he not instantly rebuked, arrested, and committed to jail for so outrageous an act? Because the leaders of the secession party in that house, on that occasion, sanctioned the infernal act, and would have joined in a general mob, but that they found the Union party much stronger than they had expected. Why were the secesh orators, and the very men, too, who had delivered speeches on the previous Friday night to the same people and in the same house, on the same stand,—why, we say, was an attempt made by their party to force them upon the meeting? And why did these speakers so promptly take the stand and try to impose themselves on the meeting? *Ay*, reader, the *damnable* principles of the tyranny, anarchy, and mob-despotism of secession were as fully developed on that occasion on a small scale, as they are in the army of Jeff Davis on a large scale. We, however, told them many things, on that occasion, which will be remembered by some until they die.

At the close of our address, a simultaneous shout was raised for a certain secesh orator to take the stand and make a speech. Instantly he was on the stand, overcoat off, and about to begin, when the Union men objected to his speaking, inasmuch as it was a Union meeting, and already one of the secesh orators had made a long disunion speech, and, to the Union men, a very insulting and abusive one. The secessionists swore he should speak, and many of the Union men swore he should not speak; and, amidst hisses, huzzas, clapping of hands, stamping of feet, beating of seats and stoves with walking-canes, &c. &c., the Union men proceeded to extinguish the lights, as they had a right to do, having paid for them, when an instant, general "skedaddling" took place, for fear "somebody" might "get hurt."

Thus, reader, ended the last Union meeting we ever attended in the town of Fredericksburg, Va. We give this case and the facts connected with it, as a specimen of the trickery, villany, and deep, damnable rascality resorted to by secessionists to force Virginia out of the Union. We had no vindictive feelings towards our fellow-citizens,—none but pity for them, and deep, pungent sorrow for the approaching downfall of our bleeding country. And, remember, all this happened more than one month before the capture of Fort Sumter.

It may not be amiss to state, in closing this article, that two of the prominent speakers on the Friday night of the great secesh meeting of which we have spoken were during the reign of Know-Nothingism the strongest advocates of that cause to be found in all the country. One, of whom we have made mention above, was a sort of editor in Western Virginia at that time; and the other, decidedly the ablest member of the Fredericksburg bar, ably advocated the cause of Know-Nothingism. On one occasion, in the court-house in Fredericksburg, and on the same stand where he delivered his speech of treason against the Federal Government, we listened to him speak for four hours at a single stretch, when all the powers and eloquence of his soul and tongue were employed in vindicating the "Union, the Constitution, and enforcement of the laws." What a leap from the sublime to the ridiculous, from the highest and noblest aspirations of patriotism to the deepest and darkest depths of treason! How the sworn advocates of the "Constitution, the Union, and enforcement of the laws" could thus easily wheel into the ranks of traitors and espouse the cause of treason, was, and is still, to us a mystery, an inexplicable enigma, a problem to be solved.

The "Virginia (Fredericksburg) Herald," in noticing the meeting of the secessionists on the Friday night of which we have spoken, says,—

"There has been a reaction, just as we have always said there would be; and it has come like a ground-swell in old Fredericksburg."

To this, in the number of the "Christian Banner" of March 14, 1861, we remarked, in the following brief paragraph,—

"How long has the 'Herald' '*always* said there would be a reaction,' and an upheaving, 'like a ground-swell,' throwing off the scurf and scum, 'Union men, or revolutionists, the allies of Black Republicans, Abolitionists, and traitors,' who 'leave their *slime* behind them as they walk the streets of Fredericksburg'? How long will it be before another 'reaction, a ground-swell in old Fredericksburg,' takes place, throwing off secessionists and those who would precipitate our happy country into a civil war?"

Strange as it may appear to the intelligent reader, the "Virginia Herald" had always been, from the time of our acquaintance with it, (and that was for more than fifteen years,) an uncompromising Whig journal, the organ of that party in Fredericksburg, and the gentleman who was the editor at the time of which we are writing had been an uncompromising Whig, and one of the strongest supporters of Bell and Everett to be found in all Virginia,—a man in whose nostrils the *loco-foco* or *Democratic* party *stunk.* He denounced the Breckinridge party as disunionists during the whole Presidential campaign of 1860, and placed at the head of his paper, as a motto, "The Union, the Constitution, and enforcement of the laws." And early in the month of March, 1861, a little over three months from the election of Mr. Lincoln, he unfurls the contemptible secession flag, and declares to the world openly and publicly in his paper that "there has been a reaction, just as we have always said there would be; and it has come like a ground-swell in old Fredericksburg." *Always*, with the Herald, is about sixty days, and, at the furthest, not more than ninety days!

In the notice the "Virginia Herald" gave of the Union meeting on Monday night, it says,—

"The vote was taken, and, from the sound, we suppose from twenty-five to fifty were in favor of them," (the resolutions.) "The noes predominated largely."

To which we replied, in the number of the "Christian Banner" of March 14, 1861, as follows:—

"Is it possible that our neighbor of the 'Herald' can 'suppose,' 'from the sound' of the vote taken on Monday night, that there were only 'from twenty-five to fifty' Union votes given? He makes a long *jump*, from twenty-five to fifty. Why did he not say from twenty-five to one hundred and fifty? How could he leap to the positive conclusion that 'the noes predominated largely'? We are informed, by a gentleman who was in the crowd, that one man 'yelled' out *no, nine* times. Our honest conviction is that a majority of the voters, and especially of the property-holders, in the town of Fredericksburg are opposed to immediate secession. Time, however, will prove all things."

The "Virginia Herald" said,—

"Mr. Rowe took the stand, and advocated immediate secession."

Why did not the "Herald" state the ridiculous and unfair circumstances under which Mr. Rowe took the stand? And why did he not give a public rebuke to the *wretch* who threw the egg at us while we were speaking? He knew that all these things would not add any thing to the character and influence of the secession party abroad.

The "Fredericksburg News," in a short notice of the meeting on Monday night,—another Whig journal, a strong advocate of Bell and Everett,—said,—

"G. H. C. Rowe and James W. Hunnicutt addressed the meeting in favor of 'revolution and fighting, not secession and retreat.' Anarchy seems to be upon us."

To this we replied, in the same number of the "Banner," namely, the 14th of March, 1861,—

"The reader will perceive that the 'Herald' and 'News' differ widely as to the position of Mr. Rowe. The 'Herald' states Mr. Rowe's position correctly. 'Mr. Rowe advocated immediate secession.' Our position is 'revolution and fighting' if necessary, and 'not secession and retreat.' Let us demand our rights, fight for our rights, and maintain our rights to the death, and, if we fall in the fight, let us fight bravely and die honorably. Never fly from our rights and ignobly yield them up into the hands of our enemies.

"Judging from the proceedings of last Monday night, it would seem that the reign of anarchy and terror is inaugurated. But free men and brave men will never yield to the dictations of tyrants and demagogues."

We have given the above extracts to show to the reader that the secession party resorted to every conceivable means to crush out and annihilate the Union men of Virginia. Their orators *lied*, and slandered the Union party. Their public newspapers *lied*, and slandered the Union men of Virginia. And just as soon as the leaders of the Bell and Douglas parties became converted to secession and were baptized into the cauldron containing the hellish liquid of *Southern treason,* they were as vituperative and vindictive in their denunciations of Union men as the original secessionists. The reader who was not a witness to the scenes which were acted out in Virginia during the year 1861 can form no adequate conception of the state of excitement which prevailed among all classes, sexes, ages, and conditions. Hell was spread out miscellaneously among the people, and all the discordant passions of the whole mass were stirred up, and the devil let loose generally.

We had already become convinced that the real issue between secessionists and Union men was the simple question whether *mind* and *liberty* should govern *institutions* and *tyranny,* or whether *institutions* and *despotism* should govern *mind* and *freedom.* In other words, whether three hundred and fifty thousand slave-holders should rule and govern thirty millions of American citizens, or whether thirty millions of American citizens should rule three hundred and fifty thousand slave-holders. Are thirty millions of men capable of self-government? Three hundred and fifty thousand negro-aristocrats respond, "*No,* they are *not;* and we will engage to rule and govern them." The proceedings of the two meetings of which we have written in this chapter more fully than ever convinced us of the correctness of our former conclusion. The reign of terror and despotism had begun. Reason and liberty were scorned and sought to be trampled into the dust.

CHAPTER XXII.

IN the number of the "Christian Banner" of March 21, 1861, we wrote and published the following:—

"PROVIDENCE—CAUSE AND EFFECT—COMMON SENSE, ETC. ETC.

"It is often said that 'Providence will overrule all things for the best.' We have great faith in Providence; but Providence does not destroy cause and effect, unless when the laws of nature are reversed and miracles are performed.

"To every law of nature there is a penalty annexed, and every infraction of law calls for the enforcement of the penalty. A man thrusts his hand into the fire: the natural and lawful result is, he gets his hand burnt. Why did he not trust to Providence, and thus prevent his hand from being burnt? A man drinks and eats to excess: why does he not trust to Providence to prevent drunkenness and sickness, the natural effects of intemperance? A man on the top of a lofty steeple says, 'I'll jump down, and trust to Providence to keep my neck from being broken by the leap:' what assurance has he that Providence will save him from danger and death? None whatever.

"Eve, when she violated the law of God, might have said, 'I'll trust to Providence.' But what was the result? *Death.* The children of Israel determined to rid themselves of *theocracy*, and demanded a king, and God permitted them to have a king; and the subsequent results are known to all Biblical students.

"Providence permitted our ancestors to emigrate to this delightful country; and when the yoke of British tyranny was laid upon their necks, Providence permitted them to throw it off and to establish a republican form of government. Providence has permitted fanatics to spring up by thousands, and traitors by hundreds, who are now constantly and earnestly endeavoring to overturn this glorious republic. And while they are engaged in this work of national ruin, the effects of which will be, if accomplished, the annihilation of our political and religious liberties, national and individual bankruptcy, war, pestilence, famine, and death, still there are those who constantly say, 'Well, we must trust to Providence: Providence will overrule all for the best.'

"We say, let the people trust to their own good sense in this crisis, and go to work like men and patriots, relying on the mercy and power of God, discarding ambitious, unprincipled politicians, and all may yet be saved. If, however, the people yield their destinies into the hands of these political harpies, their ruin is inevitable. God may permit the overthrow of our Government, and the whole country to be drenched in blood, and the yoke of *military* despotism to be placed on our necks; but when the work of ruin is accomplished, it will be horrid blasphemy to say, 'Providence overruled all for the best.' This would be an infamous libel on Providence.

"God permitted the Jews to be carried into captivity, the land of Judea to be laid waste, Jerusalem and the holy temple to be demolished, his people, the Jews, to be scattered to the four corners of the earth. He permitted his only-begotten son Jesus to be crucified, his disciples to be persecuted, imprisoned, and put to death, the churches to become corrupt. He permitted the supremacy of the Pope to be acknowledged throughout the Eastern and Western Churches, true Christianity for a time to become almost extinct, and the Roman hierarchy to sweep, like a desolating avalanche, over all Christendom. He permitted Roman Catholics to guillotine Protestants by thousands, and Protestants, in their turn, to decapitate Catholics. God permits men now to work their own ruin, and the ruin of those who become their dupes. 'If the blind lead the blind, both shall fall into the ditch' together. It is folly for men to say they trust in God and rely on Providence to overrule all things for the best, when they neglect to do their duty.

"Providence would permit our present Legislature to remain in session until the expenses would bankrupt the whole State of Virginia, unless they should eat and drink themselves to death. Providence permits oratorical demagogues to *fire up* and turn the hearts and heads of the people of one section against the people of another section of our country; to spend millions of money for munitions of war; to go to fighting, and kill one another like wild beasts of the forest. All these things Providence *permits*, but does not *will*.

"And now, if the people would be happy and prosperous, and avoid ruin and death, let them exercise the good common sense which they have, and drop politicians, and shun them as the *carrion-vultures* of society, who are seeking their own promotion and interests at the expense of the good of the people and the salvation of their country.

"If the people *will*, our country can yet be saved. Its destiny is with them. We believe that the *hearts* of the *people*, for the most part, are right and honest, but their heads are turned wrong by corrupt politicians. Some of these country-destroying demagogues have their eye on the Presidential chair, others are looking to the Senate and Congress halls, while others, again, have an eye on foreign missions or home-promotions, to gain which they would move heaven and earth, and sink our country in ruin, and blast the prosperity and happiness of the *common people* forever.

"Every American citizen has an interest at stake in this matter,—the interest of his soul and body,—the interest of his family, his wife and children, and every interest that he holds near and dear on earth. The interest, yea, the salvation, of the whole country, and the interest of every man in it, are now at stake, except politicians, and those who are interested in the downfall and ruin of all others, so they may gain promotion.

"Fellow-citizens, speak the life-preserving word, and save your country! Snatch her from the hands of corrupt politicians as a brand from the everlasting burning, and God will bless you, and posterity will bless you, and your fame shall go down to latest posterity, when the names of corrupt politicians shall have been swallowed up in the deep vortex of eternal oblivion.

"Think, reader! Twelve months ago we would as soon have thought that Christians would say, 'Down with the Bible! down with the Cross of Christ!' as that those professing to be patriots should now say, 'Down with the Constitution! down with the accursed Stars and Stripes! down with the infernal Star-Spangled Banner!' O God, have mercy upon us!"

"FIGHTING IN THE UNION.

"By fighting in the Union we simply mean revolution. If at any time a Government becomes oppressive, and one part of the people, whether a majority or a minority, fail to obtain their constitutional rights, it then becomes their duty to throw off the yoke of oppression by revolution. The Constitution of the United States belongs equally to each and every one of these several States, and guarantees equal rights to all.

"The 'Stars and Stripes' are the guarantee to every citizen for the protection of his person, property, and reputation: if, therefore, any portion of the people of these United States shall attempt to deprive any other portion of the people of these States of their constitutional rights, the oppressed are justifiable in repelling any and all such aggressions at the point of the sword and bayonet, if they cannot otherwise obtain redress.

"If, therefore, as is said, the people of the North have oppressed and made aggressions on the rights of the people of the South, it becomes the duty of the people of the South to state their grievances to the people of the North and *demand* their rights, and, if they fail to obtain them peaceably, then commence revolution, and by force of arms obtain their rights, and repel, put down, and crush out the lawless and oppressors. In this case, the law-abiding and constitution-loving men of the North would unite their influence and efforts with the oppressed and outraged people of the South, and fanaticism would be crushed out, and peace and harmony restored to our country. The Constitution, the 'Stars and Stripes,' the Federal city, and this whole country, belong to all the people of these United States; and we say, let us keep all, or lose all, and our lives into the bargain. *This is fighting in the Union, and for the Union.*"—*Christian Banner*, 21*st March*, 1861.

"What is the Virginia Legislature doing? What has it done? Why do not the people hold primary meetings, and call the *rebels* home? Remember, fellow-citizens, we the *dear people* have to foot all the bills. 'Tis a shame,—an outrage upon the citizens of Virginia.

"The *purpose* of the Legislature *was*, and *is*, to continue in session during the session of the convention, and bring all their outside pressure to bear on the convention, to force that body to pass an ordinance of secession. Time is rolling on, and will drift the present politicians of the day into the shades of peaceful retirement, where they'll live unknown and forgotten and die unlamented. The people should begin to think and to act for themselves. Politicians are looking after their own interests, not caring a farthing for the interests of the people, and, unless the people look to their own interests, politicians will reduce them and the whole country to one common ruin."—*Christian Banner*, 21*st March*, 1861.

"*Call the rebels home.*"—This body of Virginia Legislators voted themselves *the State*, in that they called a State convention, without consulting the wishes of the people of the State, knowing, as they well did, that if the simple question, *convention or no convention*, for the purpose of deciding whether Virginia should secede or not, had been presented, the people of the State would have ignored a convention by at least sixty thousand majority. They *usurped* the power, assumed the heavy and terrible responsibility, and called the convention,—thus placing upon the *necks* of the *dear people* the iron heel of *usurped legislative despotism*, involving the State in debt, and forcing her out of the Union, and thus securing the downfall and utter ruin of Virginia. The unmitigated curses of Virginians and of the whole country will, in all coming time, be heaped upon the *nest* of legislative traitors who, in the winter and spring of 1861, forced Virginia out of the Union, and effected her final and eternal ruin, so far as the happiness and well-being of the then population of the State and of their children are concerned. They were a set of unprincipled, ambitious, aspiring *usurpers* of the rights of the people, violators of the Constitution of the State of Virginia, and perjured scoundrels against the Government of the United States, because, in taking their oath of office, they swore they would observe and protect the Constitution of the State of Virginia, and the Constitution and laws of the United States, when, in fact, they went there with but one object in view, and that was to break up the Government, as their whole course of action and the results of their actions have subsequently proved. They were *rebels*, traitors to God, to the people of Virginia, to Virginia herself, to the Constitution and Government of the United States, and to the whole country. We saw plainly what they were doing, and what they had determined to do, and, therefore, we warned the people of Virginia against them. They ought not only to have been called home, but tried and punished for treason after getting home. All these things, however, may be warnings to others in ages to come, and in this way be productive of good.

The reader will not be surprised when we inform him that our patronage was constantly diminishing, and we saw plainly that we should be forced to discontinue the publication of our paper. We had a large amount of money due us; but this was scattered all over the Southern States, and men, for the most part, had declined paying us, as money-matters had become exceedingly stringent in Virginia, and the stay-law was producing its desired effect, and times were looking squally ahead. We received many very discouraging letters, containing *threats* and making insinuations which, sustaining the relation we did to our churches,—all of which were in the slave States,—tended to disturb what little of peace and happiness we might otherwise have enjoyed. The "Banner" had already become offensive to some even who were members of our churches, in consequence of the decided stand we had taken for the Union and against secession.

All the personal ties and interests we had on earth were in the slave States, and most of them south of the Potomac River. In looking into the terribly awful future, we saw nothing but sorrow, tribulation, privation, and distress before us. The distress of mind and deep anguish of heart which we suffered, none but God could know.

CHAPTER XXIII.

SAINT PAUL AND THE GOSPEL, AND THE REV. DR. GEORGE W. CARTER AND SECESSION—A CONTRAST.

In the number of the "Christian Banner" of March 28, 1861, we wrote and published the following article. We give it entire and complete, just as it appeared in the "Banner."

"THE GOSPEL.

"Gospel signifies *good news, glad tidings*, from the Greek *euaggelizoo, to bring glad tidings, to announce as glad tidings, to declare as matter of joy.*

"At the winding up of the Jewish dispensation, when the *sceptre* was about to depart from the hand of Judah, and the last lawgiver from between his feet, Shiloh comes,—the dawning of the Sun of righteousness appears in the east,—the darkness of the Jewish dispensation is being dissipated,—an angel from heaven is despatched, and comes flying down to earth to announce to the fearful, sorrowing children of men the everlasting and universal good will to all men. 'Behold,' said the angel, 'I bring you good tidings of great joy, which shall be to all people; for unto you is born this day, in the city of David, a Saviour, which is Christ the Lord.'

"No sooner does the angel proclaim Messiah's birth to the shepherds who watched their flocks by night, than immediately a multitude of the heavenly host join the angel, and, their voices commingling, swell the anthem of praise, 'Glory to God in the highest, and on earth peace, good will towards men.' This was a song befitting the angel of God and the multitude of the heavenly host. It was good news from God to all men,—through all time. This is the gospel.

"Said Christ to his disciples, after his resurrection from the dead, 'Go ye into all the world, and preach the gospel to every creature.' The angel of God announced Messiah's birth. The grand discovery that God is reconciled to man must be proclaimed by men *to* men. Hence says the Apostle Paul, 'For when we were yet without strength, in due time Christ died for the ungodly; for scarcely for a righteous [*a legally just*] man will one die; yet peradventure [*perhaps*] for a good [*benevolent*] man some would even dare to die; but God commendeth his love to us, in that, while we were yet sinners, Christ died for us. For if when we were enemies we were reconciled to God by the death of his Son, much more, being reconciled, we shall be saved by his life.'

"The manifestation of the Father's love is the cause of the sinner's reconciliation to God. Saint Paul says, 'All things are of God, who hath reconciled us to himself by Jesus Christ, and hath given to us the ministry of reconciliation; to wit, that God was in Christ reconciling the world unto himself, not imputing their trespasses unto them, and hath committed unto us the word of reconciliation.'

"From this it will be observed that God is reconciled to man; but the difficulty is in getting sinners to become reconciled to God.

"Hence continues the same apostle, 'Now, then, we are ambassadors for Christ, as though God did beseech *you* by us; we pray *you* in Christ's stead, be ye reconciled to God.'

"Is not this plain? Could Heaven make it more so? God unconditionally loved the world. He developed that love by unconditionally sending his Son into the world to die for all men. Christ developed his own love, in that he died unconditionally for all men. Christ died a voluntary death:—'Therefore doth my Father love me, because I lay down my life, that I might take it again. No man taketh it from me, but I lay it down of myself; I have power to lay it down, and I have power to take it again.'

"Christ died a *vicarious* death. He, the innocent, holy, harmless, undefiled, and separate from sinners, died in the stead of sinners, that they might live. 'For Christ also hath once suffered for sins, the just for [or in the stead] of the unjust, that he might bring us to God, being put to death in the flesh, but quickened by the Spirit.' The two great gospel facts are these:—First, Christ died for our sins, according to the old Jewish Scriptures: secondly, he rose again from the dead, according to the Jewish Scriptures. This is the *pith* of the glad tidings sent down from heaven to earth,—from God to man,—to all men. So says the Apostle Paul in his first letter to the Corinthian church:—

"'Moreover, brethren, I declare unto you the gospel which I preached unto you, which also ye have received, and wherein ye stand; by which [gospel] also ye are saved, if ye keep in memory what I preached unto you, unless ye have believed in vain. For I delivered unto you first of all that which I also received, how that Christ died for our sins, according to the Scriptures; and that he was buried, and that he rose again the third day, according to the Scriptures.'

"This was the apostle's theme at all times, in all places, and under all circumstances:—'For I determined,' says he, 'not to know any thing among you, save Jesus Christ and him crucified.'

"After his conversion, Paul preached in the synagogues of the Jews, and declared that Christ was the Son of God. In the midst of infuriate mobs,—in the councils of the Jews,—at the tribunals of governors and kings,—he boldly preached Christ and the resurrection, basing the truth and certainty of the resurrection of all men from the dead upon the fact that Christ rose from the dead. 'But if there be no resurrection of the dead, then is Christ not risen; and if Christ be not risen, then *is* our preaching vain, and your faith is also vain. Yea, and we are found false witnesses of God; because we have testified of God that he raised up Christ, whom he raised not up, if the dead rise not.'

"Now, let us place in juxtaposition the ribaldry of these *learned doctors of divinity*, who are itinerating through the country trying to destroy the purest Government on earth, and bringing our country to bankruptcy and ruin, with the preaching and teaching of the holy apostles of Jesus Christ. Take, as a specimen, extracts from the great speech of the Rev. Dr. George W. Carter, delivered at Phœnix Hall, as reported by the Petersburg (Va.) 'Express.' Read the following:—

"REV. DR. GEORGE W. CARTER'S GREAT SPEECH AT PHŒNIX HALL.

"Dr. Carter proceeded to state and vindicate the views and policy of those who held that the true remedy for their troubles was in secession. He argued that secession was *expedient*,—rendered so by the unfriendly purposes of the Northern people, their seizure of power over us, their deep, radical difference in moral sentiment, which rendered concord hopeless and made them the abiding foes of our forms of social organization. [Applause]. Secession, so far from being a destructive process, was eminently conservative in its effects. He used the term conservative in its political—not in its party—sense. In Texas, his country, when a man had neither the wit to perceive nor the courage to maintain his rights, he generally fell back on that last refuge of imbecility, and called himself '*a conservative*.' Secession was conservative in the true sense. It preserved our rights and institutions by rejecting the control that sought to destroy them. [Great applause].

"'Our Government,' continued the speaker, 'had left local interests to local management, and intrusted only the common interests to common management. This was its grand idea, its inspiration. This, however, the Northern people do not seem to understand. They seek to regulate *our* local institutions according to *their* ideas,—to put the order of things as established among us "in a course of extinction," and to make our four millions of negroes the equals of the white man. The end at which they aim would ruin us. The means by which they would accomplish it revolutionizes the Government. We can submit to neither. Secession is absolutely necessary, both to secure our rights, and to maintain the local authority which is *their* guarantee.' "

"Take the following as a specimen of the reverend doctor's logic, by which he arrives at the culminating-point,—secession.—*Editor Christian Banner.*

"The close of the lengthy and able address of Dr. Carter was fired with frequent bursts of fervid eloquence. He earnestly appealed to Virginians to rally at once to the side of their brethren of the South, and assist them in laying the foundation of an *empire* which held out such unexampled promise of prosperity and happiness. 'The Southern people,' said he, 'are your children,—bone of your bone, and flesh of your flesh,—your descendants. They love you, long for you, wait for you, desire you as their leader. They know you will come and must come; but they are anxious for you to come immediately. For themselves, their course is taken. With you, or without you, they will maintain their position. They are able to do it, and, by the blessing of God, they will do it.' [Tremendous applause.]

"'Some of you,' said the speaker, 'talk of "fighting in the Union."' He scarcely knew which to admire most,—the wisdom or the pluck of such a position. For one, he could fight on no such platform. In the first place, we did not desire to whip the North. If the South conquered them, they would not know what to do with them. Like the buffalo calf, after they were caught they could not be held. [Great laughter.] If he could choose to receive a halter on his neck before he would demand his rights, he would then claim the poor privilege of sealing his lips and bowing without murmur or resistance to the yoke.

"The speaker would say in all kindness to these gentlemen, that, when they thus talked about 'fighting,' they were mistaken. They were not going to fight. They might think they would, but they wouldn't. The anecdote related by the English satirist was peculiarly illustrative of the class of Unionists to which the speaker had just referred. The henpecked husband was ordered under the bed. On one occasion a large number of the neighboring dames had congregated, as usual, to gossip. The poor husband, becoming somewhat excited, *peeped* out. His wife gave him a significant look, and he withdrew his head. The gossip becoming more and more exciting, the poor husband again protruded his head. The wife again shook her finger, but it did not have the desired effect. Becoming enraged, she seized a broomstick and proceeded to force back the objectionable head. The courageous husband succumbed, and again tucked his head under the bed, but protested his courage by declaring that so long as he had the spirit of a man he would peep. [Immoderate laughter.] 'So,' said the speaker, 'with those who will fight in the Union. Mr. Lincoln is reinforcing your forts, filling your post-offices with men of his own selection, and gradually binding you hand and foot. By-and-by he will get you under the Black Republican bed. You may then desire to peep out; but Mr. Lincoln will beat you back with the Federal broomstick.' [Renewed laughter.]

"The speaker had prepared himself for this great work amid much trial and trouble. He had prayed on his bended knees for the Union, but, when he ascertained that it was hopelessly and irretrievably gone, he resolved to do his duty to God and his country."

"Contrast the call of Dr. Carter to itinerate to preach *secessionism*, with the call of Saul to preach the gospel of Jesus Christ. Here's the call, as related by the doctor, and reported by the 'Petersburg Express.'—*Editor of the Christian Banner*.

"An affecting incident was related. One day, while in sad meditation, by his own fireside, upon the condition of the country, and the propriety of addressing his fellow-citizens on these great questions, at their earnest solicitations, his wife observed his sadness, and bade him go forward and never mind what the world said. 'I will pray for you,' she added. His little boy of eight years, who must have obtained his knowledge of public affairs from the papers, said, 'Pa, if all the South will go out, I don't think we'll have a fight; but I think we had better go, fight or no fight.' And then his little daughter, still younger than her brother,—his own dear little Daisy, who was as gentle as the flower from which she derived her name,—said, 'Yes, pa; you and Mr. W. [a member of the family] can help to fight, and God and brother *Jimmy* will take care of me.' 'The man would be worse than *craven*,' said the speaker, 'who, under such circumstances, could fail in his duty to his family and his country.' [Tremendous applause.]"

The following is the comment on the above which we made and published in the "Christian Banner" at the time we published the above speech:—

"This was a powerful call. 'His wife bade him go forward and never mind what the world said.' 'I will pray for you,' she added. He receives his commission from his wife, who promises him her prayers for his success in breaking up the Government and in destroying the country. His little boy of eight years says, 'Pa, if all the South will go out, I don't think we'll have a fight; but I think we had better go, fight or no fight.' An intelligent, 'spunky' little boy, that! And then his little daughter, still younger than her brother, said, 'Yes, pa; you and Mr. W. can help to fight, and God and brother *Jimmy* will take care of me.' Surely 'his own dear little Daisy, who was as gentle as the flower from which she derived her name,' would be safe in the hands of God, with little *Jimmy*, eight years old, to help him take care of her. Intelligent little Daisy! Worthy to be taken care of!

"Who could resist such a call as this to go forth into all the world and preach secession to every creature? He that believes secession and runs shall be saved; but he who stays at home and defends his rights, bravely meeting the foe and driving him back, shall be beaten with the broomstick or be damned. May Heaven preserve us! The whole 'affecting incident' well befitted the speaker, the subject, and the occasion. If secession and Abolition doctors of divinity meet together in the next world, they'll either kick up a row and secede, or else get kicked out themselves. Alas for Christianity! Alas for the Bible! Alas for the pulpit! Alas for our country!

Such were the brief remarks we made on the great

speech of Mr. Carter, at the time we published it in the "Christian Banner."

ANNOTATIONS ON THE ABOVE CHAPTER.

Doctors of Divinity.—Of these *titled divines*, George W. Carter is a doctor of Southern Methodist divinity, as well as of Southern Methodist treason. That he has acted well his part in effecting the eternal and temporal destruction of his fellow-men to the full extent of his influence and abilities, we doubt not. The evidences before us are full and direct to the point.

Does he not profess, according to the discipline of his Church, to be "called and sent of God to preach," and to be "anointed with the unction of the Holy Ghost," to enable him faithfully to perform the work of an evangelical minister of the gospel of the Lord Jesus Christ? To resist his authority and teaching, therefore, is to virtually resist the authority of God and the teachings of the Holy Ghost. If this be not a fair deduction from the premises assumed by the reverend gentleman, that he is "called and sent of God to preach," then he comes before the people with a *lie* in his mouth, saying that he is called of God to preach, when God has *not* called him to any such work, and that he is anointed of the Holy Ghost, when the Holy Ghost has had nothing to do with *him* more than with other hardened reprobates.

For the sake of argument, however, let us suppose that God has "called and sent him to preach." To preach what? To preach the disruption and downfall of the greatest, happiest, and most prosperous nation on the earth, and the overthrow of the purest and best form of human government the world has ever known.

To preach the inauguration of civil war, death to untold thousands, and all the afflictions, sorrows, and woes that earth can inflict upon thirty millions of undying souls. To preach *secession*, the disintegration of the American Republic, the annihilation of liberty and all the blessings of freedom, as absolutely necessary to secure the rights and perpetuity of *our local institutions*,—that is, the perpetual bondage of *our four millions of negroes*, and their future increase forever. To preach persecution, imprisonment, proscription, and death by hanging, and all the terrors of a Southern Methodist orthodox hell, to all *Union men, submissionists*, and *Abolitionists*. To *preach* and send true patriots and loyal citizens to perdition, by tapping them on the head with an old woman's broomstick, because they won't wheel into the line of *divinity traitors* and *be baptized in the pool of Southern treason*. To preach, at all times, in all places, under all circumstances, and at every hazard, the perpetual bondage of African slavery. In a word, God has "called and sent," and the "Holy Ghost has anointed," these reverend divines to preach *negroism* first, *negroism* last, and NEGROISM forever! This is the work and the character of preaching in which these Southern Methodist doctors of divinity have been engaged for the last twenty-five or thirty years at least.

What gave rise to the *severance* of the Methodist Episcopal Church in the city of New York in 1844, which was the entering wedge to the disruption of the Federal Union? *Negroism!* What was the popular topic discussed by the reverend doctors of divinity, Messrs. Wm. A. Smith, Leroy M. Lee, Rev. Mr. Rosser, and a host of other underling divines, when they were *stumping* the State of Virginia in 1849, '50, '51, &c., when all the *divine* eloquence of their souls was thrown into the subject, and they were delivering speeches *nine* hours long,—as in the case of Mr. Rosser,—to fire up the Southern heart, and stir up vindictive feelings against the people of the North? *Negroism!* The Southern Methodist pulpit has been prostituted for the last twenty or thirty years by the preaching of *negroism* to the people, instead of preaching the gospel of the Lord Jesus Christ,—peace on earth, and good will toward all men! These doctors of divinity, and their little, inflated understrappers, have performed their full share of treasonable work in breaking up the Government of these United States. "The Methodist Episcopal Church, South," was based upon *negroism;* and it was this circumstance, more than all others combined, that gained it popularity in the South. The Southern clergy *pandered* to the cupidity, pride, and vanity of slave-holders, because they wanted their salaries, parsonages, sectarian schools, academies, colleges, fine meeting-houses, &c., for all of which they were dependent, to a very great extent, on large slave-holders, cotton and tobacco, rice and sugar planters, &c. Eternity alone can develop the incalculable amount of mischief the Southern pulpit has effected towards introducing the cruel war which is now raging among the American people. The withering and blighting influence of their teachings and preaching was felt in all States, counties, cities, towns, villages, neighborhoods, communities, and families in the whole South. The clergy were *everywhere,* and among all classes, scattering the seeds of discord and strife all over the country. Take, for example, the case of the "Rev. Dr. George W. Carter."

"*In Texas, his country.*"—Why did not the reverend gentleman remain in Texas, his own country? Because "his wife bade him go forward" into Old Virginia and preach secession to every creature. Virginia was slow to understand, and hard to believe, all that was promised by secession orators and written by secession editors, and her delay was about to prove ruinous to the cause of the Southern Confederacy, and, to urge her to take the *suicidal* step, the learned Dr. Carter came on a holy mission from Texas, his own country, to say to Virginia, "The Southern people are your children,—'bone of your bone and flesh of your flesh,'—your descendants. They love you, long for you, wait for you, desire you as their leader. They know you will come, and must come, but they are anxious for you to come immediately." He visited Petersburg, Richmond, Alexandria, Lynchburg, &c.; and everywhere the great burden of his important mission was, Virginia will come, must come, but we "are anxious" for her "to come immediately." He came to strike the *death-knell* of Old Virginia and all her greatness, glory, honor, prosperity, and happiness. He came to urge "Virginians to rally at once to the side of their brethren of the South, to assist them in laying the foundations of an *empire* which held out such unexampled promise of prosperity and happiness." He came, however, in fact, to robe "Virginians" in their winding-sheets, and leave them on the battle-fields to slumber until God shall bid them rise. Can the doctor, with all his "fervid eloquence," undo the awful work of ruin and death, which he aided to the extent of his abilities in accomplishing? Can he restore, by his "fervid eloquence," to their parents, wives, and children, the thousands of sleeping dead who lie on the battle-fields at Yorktown, Williamsburg, Richmond, Manassas, Cedar Mountain?—in a word, the unknown thousands who have fallen in battle and now lie sleeping in death on Virginia's sacred soil? Can he soothe and bind up the aching hearts of aged fathers and mothers, of sorrowing widows and suffering children? What word of consolation could he whisper in their ears? Would he tell them he came from "Texas, his country," to argue that secession was *expedient*,—that secession was conservative,—that "secession was absolutely necessary to secure our rights" and to enable us to hold on to *our four millions of negroes?* Great God! reader, look at the picture. Think of the man,—this learned doctor of divinity,—who was evidently either a *fool* or a *knave*,—and then think that there were thousands on thousands all over the South, of the same *clerical* and *doctor*-of-*divinity* order, who were engaged in the same *hellish* work of dissolving the Union and precipitating the country into revolution and civil war. To say that God Almighty ever called and sent such fools or knaves—for either the one or the other they must be—to preach the gospel of his Son Jesus Christ, is a libel on the wisdom, goodness, justice, and character of Jehovah; and none but *fools* can believe it.

And here we must be allowed to say—and we say it because we know it to be true—that the clergy of the Methodist Episcopal Church, South, and the clergy of the South generally, are worldly-minded, money-loving, money-making, and money-saving men, hard masters, severe *negro*-drivers, and absolute petty tyrants. They are proud, vain, pompous, self-important, self-conceited, dictatorial, intolerant, and proscriptive. And such are the "called and sent of God to preach the gospel of Jesus Christ." Good Lord, deliver us from such a set of theological hucksters, who deal out adulterated truth by the small, for a pecuniary consideration, to God's children, who are hungering and thirsting after righteousness!

"Our four millions of negroes."—The reader cannot fail to observe that to fasten the chains of perpetual bondage on "our four millions of negroes" and their future increase was paramount to any and all other considerations with Dr. Carter and with the whole fraternal band of leading conspirators of the South. Let our sons be butchered upon the battle-field; let ten thousand hospitals be filled with the wounded, the sick, the dying, and the dead; but let us hold on to "our four millions of negroes"! Let thousands of women be made widows, millions of children be made orphans; let one long, loud, universal cry of sorrow, lamentation, and woe go up to heaven; but let us hold on to "our four millions of negroes"! Robe a nation of thirty millions of souls in the winding-sheet, and let angels weep, and all the hosts of heaven stand appalled, and devils damned be jubilant, at the wickedness of mortals, and at the downfall of the greatest, most civilized, and most thoroughly Christianized nation in all the world, but let us hold on to "our four millions of negroes"!

"Their leader."—This was a favorite argument with *secesh* orators. Virginia was to be the *leader* in the Southern Confederacy. On this they poured out torrents of "fervid eloquence." Virginia was to be the great leader in this vast "*empire* which held out such

unexampled promise of prosperity and happiness." Oh, the trickery, the villany, the deep, black, *damnable rascality*, that was employed to coax, swindle, and force Virginia out of the Union, and to consequent ruin, by these *clerical demons* and wicked, aspiring politicians! Let them come and take a wide survey of Virginia's greatness, prosperity, and happiness now, and say if her leadership is enviable! Ay, reader, "beneath the folds of the white robes of the Church lie hid the keys of *empire* and an iron sceptre."

"*Tucked his head under the bed.*"—This, reader, is a specimen of the ridiculous stories and anecdotes that were constantly narrated in the public speeches of these *clerical* and *political secesh* orators, to stir up and excite the baser passions of their audiences to vindictiveness against the whole people of the North. We speak what we do know, and testify what we have seen and heard.

"*Affecting incident.*"—Without questioning the truth of the affecting incident as narrated by the learned doctor, was it not a shameful reason to urge upon an intelligent audience, that a "man would be worse than *craven* who, under such circumstances, could fail in his duty to his family and his country"? That is to say, who would fail in his duty to introduce sorrow, affliction, hunger, nakedness, famine, and death into his family, by disrupting his country and precipitating revolution and civil war, with all their accompanying train of evils and horrors. But "his little boy of eight years said, 'Pa, if all the South will go out, I don't think we'll have a fight; but I think we had better go, fight or no fight.' And then his little daughter, still younger than her brother,—his own dear little Daisy,—said, 'Yes, pa; you and Mr. W. can help to fight, and God and brother *Jimmy* will take care of me!" Precocious *infants* these! There's the story, reader: you can think of it as you please. But why was the story told by the doctor? To stir up the sympathies of his hearers, and to enlist the feelings of men, women and children, old men and old women, little boys and girls, to influence them to raise the clamor and force Virginia out of the Union. Surely the doctor must have thought that he was at a Southern Methodist revival, as such stories are generally employed on those occasions to force people to the "mourners' bench, to *get* religion!" Such, intelligent reader, were the means to which these Southern oratorical traitors resorted to stir up the vile passions and tender sympathies of all classes to influence them to force Virginia out of the Union.

We have extended our remarks and entered thus largely into the details of the "Great Speech of the Rev. Dr. George W. Carter" and the circumstances connected with it, not because it is an isolated case, but as a tolerably fair specimen of the trickery used by the Southern secesh clergy generally, and by political secesh orators, to precipitate Virginia into secession and ultimate ruin. How effectually they succeeded in their work of destruction her subsequent history will show.

In connection with this subject, we will just state that one of the strongest reasons why the females of the South were, and still are, so bitter and vindictive in their feelings towards the "old Union," the "Stars and Stripes," and Union men generally, and the Union men of the South particularly, is owing to the great influence the clergy exercise over their minds. Hence it was argued that secession must be right, "because the women and children believed and said it was right." They believed and said it was right because their preachers told them that *they* believed it was right. And it would never do to call in question the opinions and *dicta* of men "called and sent of God" to preach treason, though black as hell.

CHAPTER XXIV.

IN the number of the "Christian Banner" of March 28, 1861, we wrote and published the following:—

"SIGNS OF THE GREAT UPHEAVING IN THE SECEDED STATES.

"When a boy, we witnessed the great *Nullification* excitement, as it was called, in the State of South Carolina. Then there were *Nullifiers* and *Unionists*, and the contention was as hot between those two parties as has ever been the contention between the North and South. And we now believe that, if the question had then been left to the vote of the *people*, a large majority would have been for the *Union*. Knowing this to have been the case, we have all the time had our doubts as to whether the *people generally* in the seceded States went understandingly and heartily into the act of secession.

"Had it *even* been left to the vote of the people, how could they, in little over five weeks, have informed their minds on so grave a subject so as to be able to cast their votes understandingly? What! enlighten the people of a whole State in the short period of some five or six weeks on subjects which many reading men do not profess to understand? This seems to have been taken for granted by the leaders: hence they *ignored* the *intelligence, will, action, voice,* and *power* of the *people.* And just look at it.

"The *people* of the Southern Confederacy, thus being ignored by their leaders, are now to be regarded as traitors and submissionists, and to be trodden down and crushed out, if they enter a disclaimer against the usurpation of power exercised by their leaders.

"A reaction is bound to take place as soon as the people fully understand the political trap in which they have been caught. A free and independent people do not like to be led as sheep to the slaughter; and, when they once understand the trick which has been imposed upon them, and begin to feel the burden unconditionally placed on their shoulders, there will be a *ground-swell* that will astonish the leaders in this fearful drama, and a revolution which we fear will be terrible in its character. We think it vitally important, therefore, that our readers should understand this subject, and understand it well, as our very being depends upon its final results. Read, in proof of the truth and correctness of the foregoing remarks, the following extracts from Southern newspapers. They speak for themselves. The Tuscumbia 'North Alabamian,' in its issue of the 22d instant, remarking upon the course of Congress at Montgomery, says,—

"However our people in this section of the State may have differed with a majority of the convention touching the policy of that majority on the subject of immediate secession, there should be no division among us in support of the declaration that 'we will sustain the honor and dignity of Alabama, whether assaulted by fanatics North or South.' There has been, however, a manifest distrust or disregard of the popular sentiment by the leading politicians of Alabama, in withholding the secession ordinance from a vote of the people; and the tendency still is, if we are not mistaken in the movements of the political chess-board of those leaders, to remove still further all power from the immediate action of the people. What voice had they in electing members to the Congress now in session at Montgomery? And what voice, kind reader, do you think you will have in ratifying the constitution which that Congress has adopted? By what authority have a President and Vice-President been elected to the Confederate States of America? When you elected your members to a State Convention, did you authorize a bare majority of that body to elect members to a Congress, to form a new Government, and to authorize still further the members of that convention to elect a President, a Vice-President, and other officials? These are questions for your serious consideration."

The New Orleans "Picayune" complains, in the following strain, of "the exercise by the State Convention of a power which has resulted in the assemblage of a Congress at Montgomery composed of citizens in whose election the people had no direct voice, whose action is devoid of any direct responsibility to the people, and whose assumed power was unlimited when assembled; the imposition by the Congress upon the people of the Confederacy of a President and Vice-President in whose election the people had no direct share; and the putting into operation of a constitution without it being subjected to the customary ordeal of ratification or rejection at the ballot-box."

The Tuscaloosa (Alabama) "Monitor" thus sums up its objections to the proceedings of the Alabama State Convention and the Southern Congress at Montgomery:—

"We hold, first, that the ordinance of secession should have been submitted to the people for their ratification or rejection. Secondly, that the ordinance passed by the convention should have awaited the issue of this decision. Thirdly, that the people had the right, and it should have been given them, to have chosen the delegates to a Congress which was to have framed for them a Government for weal or woe. And we now demand that, the Government formed, its President, Vice-President, and officers should be submitted to the people for their approval or disapproval. If it is not, we shall, come weal or woe, attempt to fire the people's heart, to educate the people's mind, to know their rights and to dare maintain them. We are no submissionist; but right is right, and wrong is wrong, and we will not betray our trust. We assert that the people had a right to be heard, and, being heard, to be obeyed. And we intend to keep them posted in what we consider to be an infringement of their rights and of their privileges, let the worst come to the worst. If it be treason against the new Confederacy, make the most of it. We know we are right, and, untrammelled and unawed, we will defend the right."

The Lagrange (Georgia) "Reporter" alludes in the following terms to a spirit of intolerance betrayed by certain representatives of the disunion press of the South. The "Reporter" says,—

"We regret to see a spirit of intolerance manifested by a portion of the disunion papers of this State. They seem to have arrogated to themselves the office of *censor*. Every thing political that does not conform to their ideas of right they denounce as treasonable, and seem to insinuate that any thing but their own views will not be tolerated in the Southern Confederacy. Has the reign of terror begun? Are we in the hands of red republicans? If it has come to this, then we are certainly undone. We are as ready as any man to offer up our life, if need be, in defence of the rights of the South; and we hold that we are no less true to those rights than these Hotspurs when we express our love for the old Union of our fathers. If it is treason for a citizen of the Southern Confederacy to express his dissatisfaction with the present Union, was it not equally as great a crime to denounce the old Union? *Treason has the same definition in the new as it had in the old Constitution.* We hold ourselves to be loyal to the Southern Confederacy, and we greatly deprecate the disposition to inaugurate terrorism in our midst by professed friends."

The Selma (Alabama) "Weekly Issue," a leading secession paper, reasons as follows upon the policy of receiving the border slave-holding States into the Southern Confederacy. The "Issue" says,—

"We do not want such elements in our new Confederacy. We desire no association with unwilling States, who, forgetful of every obligation of political consanguinity, and governed only by a cancerous selfishness, come to us for shelter when they can go nowhere else,—who seek association with their erring sisters only when exiled from the companionship of what they are pleased to regard as their more reputable Northern relatives. No. We have two potent reasons for esteeming the accession of the border States to our ranks a serious misfortune under existing circumstances. First, they would be continually hankering 'after the flesh-pots of Egypt,' and impeding our advance by propositions to return. 'Reconstruction,' in a thousand insidious forms, would creep into our councils and entwine itself around every effort at permanent organization,—would paralyze every struggle for progress, and make the history of our Confederacy an endless alternation of imbecile dynasties. At every session of Congress this subject would be renewed. Our people would be divided, and the collision of parties upon this issue become as fierce and rancorous as it ever was upon slavery between the South and North."

GENERAL REMARKS ON THE FOREGOING CHAPTER.

We have already stated that we witnessed the great Nullification excitement which raged in the State of South Carolina in the years 1830–31 and 1832. Then there were two great antagonistic parties, the Nullifiers and the Unionists, and the contention between them was as violent as had ever been the contention between the North and the South.

John C. Calhoun was the champion and idol of the Nullification party, his followers regarding him as being the embodiment of all political orthodoxy; but, notwithstanding his great moral virtues, his immense wealth, his high order of intellect, and his superior accomplishments, he was unable to convert the whole State to his cherished principles of nullification and disunion.

As we have just stated, there were two vehement parties desperately arrayed the one against the other. Men quarrelled and fought, women quarrelled and fought, boys quarrelled and fought, and mothers with infant children who for want of physical strength and a knowledge of language were unable to quarrel and fight, stuck *blue-ribbon cockades* on their little caps and hats, to let the Unionists know how and what they would do if they were only able. Ministers of all denominations took sides, and nullification and politics supplanted the gospel of Jesus Christ in the pulpits; and the same unholy, infuriate, vindictive spirit and passions were developed then as were manifested between the secessionists and Union parties at the outburst of the present ungodly rebellion; and to what a deplorable extent matters might then have been carried, had it not been for the strong nerve, the moral courage, the iron will and *whole-souled patriotic spirit* of General Jackson, God only knows.

The same spirit of nullification and rebellion which was then at work in the hearts of the children of disobedience, and which has been growing, increasing, and strengthening ever since, reached the culminating-point in December, 1860, in the passage of an ordinance of secession at Charleston, South Carolina, and subsequently by an attack being made on the glorious "flag" of our country, and the inauguration of civil war.

When, in the month of December, 1860, at Pleasant Grove Meeting-House, in Green county, North Carolina, we saw, for the first time since the days of South Carolina nullification, a contemptible *blue cockade*, the sure and unerring emblem of *damnable* treason, sticking on the hat of a shallow-headed Breckinridge Democrat, in a moment our mind was carried back to the days of *blue-ribbon* cockades and South Carolina nullification; and, looking into the dark mysterious future, we trembled as we meditated on the sure and certain consequences. *Then* it was a dark and sad picture to contemplate; *now* we are suffering the stern realities.

Why were the leaders in this rebellion afraid to submit the question to the people whether these conventions should be held at all or not? And why were they afraid to submit their ordinances of secession to a vote of the people of the several States in which they were passed? Simply because they feared that the *vote* of the *people* would thwart their nefarious design to overthrow the Government. This is the only legitimate reason that can be given why the *will, action,* and *power* of the *people* were ignored by these *political Jesuits.* When these Democratic leaders were before the people begging for popular suffrage, they boasted that all power was lodged *in the* people; but as soon as the convenient period, the appointed hour, the set time, arrived to overthrow the Government which the people themselves had created, the stream rose above the fountain, and the *creature* became superior to the *creator*, and all power and authority were wrested from the people, and usurped by a set of tyrants for the purpose of establishing a despotism over the *dear people,* and an *accursed negro-oligarchy* on the *ruins* of *liberty* and the *rights* of *freemen.* These are historical facts, which, black, infamous, and *damning* as they are, the ever-rolling stream of time will carry down to the latest posterity. And this is Democracy,—boasted

Democracy,—Breckinridge Democracy, which was to save the country! Oh, the beauties, the excellencies, the glories, the loveliness of Breckinridge Democracy! Reader, it is nothing more nor less than *demonocracy,*— the power and government of *devils!* Look at the work it has done.

Ditches and pits have been filled with slaughtered men, hills and valleys have been bleached with the bones of our dear sons, fathers, brothers, neighbors, friends, and fellow-citizens, thousands of hospitals filled with the wounded, sick, and dying, loathsome prisons and dungeons filled with harmless, worthy, patriotic citizens, deprived of all the blessings and comforts of home and friends, and made to lie and pine away and die, without a friend to administer to their extreme wants while living or to drop a tear of love and sympathy over them when dying and dead, and all because they loved their country and were suspicioned by traitors. It has made *maniacs* of thousands of men and women. Look, also, at the maimed, the lame, the halt, and the blind: thousands of poor soldiers have their arms or legs shot off; others, again, have their mouths, noses, ears, or eyes shot off or cut up with scimeters, swords, or bayonets, and are otherwise disabled and made infirm for life. Look at the desolated farms, the empty corn and meat houses, the dreary mansions and lonely cottages, all over the country, filled only with destitute women, weeping widows, and poor little orphan children in rags and tatters, starving and crying for meat and bread, the very necessaries of actual existence, and no hand to extend to them relief. Look at the finest country God ever gave to man, laid waste and made desolate by men and beasts employed in the awful work of fratricidal slaughter. Look at a whole nation robed in mourning. Listen to the groans and wails of the sick, the wounded, and the dying. Listen to the melting strains, the weeping, wailing, deep, and loud lamentations of fathers, mothers, wives, sisters, children, brothers, friends, and neighbors. Think of the millions of sorrowful, throbbing, aching hearts,—the floods of tears which have flowed. Think of the unknown thousands of refugees, driven from their once quiet and peaceful homes, thrown among strangers, destitute of the means of support, many of them separated from their wives and children, deprived of all the blessings and comforts of *home, sweet home!* In a word, think of a whole nation immersed in sorrow and woe, and then tell us, reader, that this is not the work of *devils!*

The leaders, fearing to let the people know their infernal design to overthrow the Government, lest they might be defeated by the popular vote at the ballot-box, usurped the whole power, and have completed the work of ruin, and the whole responsibility now rests on them; and to God, the Judge of all the earth, and to the people, they are held responsible for all the horrors, bloodshed, and national and individual evils which have been and are now being produced by this wicked and cruel war. Oh, what a weighty, what a terrible retribution awaits the leaders in this awful drama!

CHAPTER XXV.

In the number of the "Christian Banner" of March 28, 1861, we wrote and published the following editorials:—

"WHEN SHALL THE MILLENNIUM COME?

"When shall the wilderness and the solitary place be glad for them? When shall the desert rejoice and blossom as the rose? When shall the weak hands be strengthened, and the feeble knees confirmed? When shall the fearful in heart feel strong, and fear not? When shall the eyes of the blind be opened, and the ears of the deaf be unstopped? When shall the lame man leap as a hart, and the tongue of the dumb sing for joy? When shall waters break out in the wilderness, and streams in the desert? When shall all these things come to pass?

"When soft-headed, aspiring politicians shall be put to silence by the good sense of the people. When *political tricksters* and *clerical knaves* shall combine in infamous caucuses and secret councils to overthrow the Government and the country, and none but fools shall regard them. When sensible men and true patriots shall combine at every hazard to save the country, and knaves, traitors, fanatics, and treason shall be driven back to their native hell. When sensation speeches, false telegrams, mock compromises, extra legislative sessions, treasonable conventions, shall cease, and fools shall be disregarded by wise, common-sense men, and all shall be forced to attend to their own business, and every one compelled to get his bread by the sweat of his brow. When men shall learn to think and act for themselves, and cease to become the dupes of knavish priests and wicked politicans. When all shall become so thoroughly educated and enlightened as to refuse to let priests and demagogues lead them by the nose whithersoever they will. When the public mind shall have taken the second sober thought, and shall find by actual experience that secession, taxation, war, blood, death, and ruin are not the things they were represented to be, and shall determine to stand by the Constitution of our fathers and cause the 'Stars and Stripes' to wave over all our happy land forever.

"Then shall the waters of prosperity break out in the wilderness, and streams in all our deserts. Then they shall beat their swords into ploughshares, and their spears into pruning-hooks. Nation shall not lift up sword against nation, neither shall they learn war any more. The wolf and the lamb shall feed together, and the lion shall eat straw like the bullock.

"'No more shall nation against nation rise,
Nor ardent warriors meet with hateful eyes,
Nor fields with gleaming steel be cover'd o'er,
The brazen trumpets kindle rage no more
But useless lances into scythes shall blend,
And the broad falchion in a ploughshare end;
The lambs with wolves shall graze the verdant mead,
And boys in flowery bands the tiger lead;
The steer and lion at one crib shall meet,
And harmless serpents lick the pilgrim's feet.'

POPE."

"We have no confidence in the final results of the many sensation meetings which are now being gotten up through the State of Virginia, and the immediate-secession resolutions which are being passed, and the instructions which are being sent to the members of the convention now in session to force them to vote for immediate secession. There are more things in heaven and earth than are dreamed of in the philosophy of wire-working, office-seeking politicians."—*Christian Banner, March* 28, 1861.

At the time of writing the foregoing editorials, the whole country was kept in a continual state of feverish excitement. Sensation meetings were held all over the State, and especially all through the eastern part of Virginia. The speakers always had some secesh "cock-and-bull story," to create a tremendous sensation. Sometimes the news would come direct that England and France had already acknowledged the independence of the Southern Confederacy,—were sending thousands on thousands of munitions of war to the South,—were going to send over their whole navies to crush out the Federal Government at once. Again, thousands from the North were on their way to join the South; the States of New York, Pennsylvania, Rhode Island, Delaware, and Maryland were all on the eve of joining the Southern Confederacy. Such were the means to which secessionists resorted to force Virginia out of the Union.

CHAPTER XXVI.

In the number of the Christian Banner of April 4, 1861, we wrote and published the following editorials:—

"*Position defined.—A new political move.—The Christian's Bible, and the American Constitution.—Startling developments.—But there is no Union now.—Immediate, absolute, and eternal secession.—How is it?—Important consideration.*

"'Tis somewhat provoking, when one is conscious of the honesty and integrity of his own heart and purpose of life, to be misrepresented and slandered as being a traitor and an enemy to his country, and that, too, by his own familiar friends. Nothing is more common *now* than to hear those men who have been true to their country, and have maintained consistency throughout the whole political struggle through which our country has thus far passed, called, by those who please to dissent from them, by the opprobrious epithets of '*Abolitionists, submissionists to old Abe Lincoln, submissionists to Black Republican rule, the vassals of the tail end of the Northern Confederacy,*' &c. &c.

"Let us impartially examine the facts in the case. During the last Presidential canvass there were four candidates in the field. The Bell-and-Everett electors took for their platform 'The Union, the Constitution, and enforcement of the laws.' To this platform the Douglas electors did not object. It was by both parties thought to be sufficiently sound and strong for them to stand on; and hence there seemed to be but little or no material difference, and certainly no important issue, between these two parties, and during the whole canvass, for the most part, they stood shoulder to shoulder. Each one of these parties accused the Breckinridge party of a premeditated design of breaking up the Government in the event of a defeat. This the Breckinridge party denied; and when the ultraism of Newton and Yancey was introduced as evidence, the Breckinridge electors maintained that these men were not the proper exponents of the party, and that they did not reflect the true and correct sentiments of their party. All were opposed to the breaking up of the Union. The Bell and Douglas parties contended that Lincoln's election, would not be sufficient cause for a dissolution of the Union. The idea of disunion and secession was denounced in the most unqualified terms by the Bell and Douglas parties.

"The election came off, and Lincoln was elected. All at once the country is thrown into a state of consternation; business becomes paralyzed, confidence is destroyed, general bankruptcy and universal anarchy threaten the whole country. What had happened? 'Lincoln was elected President!' Well, what of it? Why all this national terror, disorder, and confusion because of the election of a single man to office? What could Lincoln do? Nothing,—positively nothing! The conservative men had the power in both houses of Congress, and could have defeated any measure which might have been detrimental to the interests of the country or of any portion or section of the country.

"Congress meets; and what is the result? Why, the Representatives from the Gulf States said that they felt no interest in the Federal Government,—that their States were going to secede, and that they were only waiting the action of their States. Well, their States seceded, and they vacated their seats in Congress, and left the border States and the whole Federal Government in the hands and at the mercy of their enemies. The Representatives of the slave States are now in the minority, and the 'Black Republicans' can run over us and rule us at will and pleasure. What shall be done? This was the question which stared the border States full in the face.

"All at once the doctrine of secession is advocated in our midst, and disunion is sprung upon the people, and becomes popular and a *petted* thing. South Carolina is gone, and of necessity all the other slave States *must* go with her. 'This is our only remedy.' Yes, secession and disunion, which twelve months ago were execrated everywhere, and openly advocated by *none*—no, not *one*—in our whole community, now become absolutely necessary, as the only remedy by which we can maintain *our honor and get our rights;* and unless we 'back out' and ignobly submit all our rights, yield up the whole *reins* of the Federal Government into the hands of Black Republicans, we must be branded with the odious epithets of '*Abolitionists, submissionists to old Abe Lincoln,*' &c. &c. To tamely yield our rights into the hands of our enemies for fear we shall not be able to retain them if we were to maintain our ground and contend for them, is, in our opinion, submission,—yes, mean, cowardly submission,—a dastardly submission, to which we will never willingly yield or assent!

"That the remedy for the evils which threaten the South is to be found in secession and disunion is what we do not believe, and what yet remains to be proved. Great inducements are held out to us if we will join the 'Southern Confederacy.' The glories arising from the joining of this 'new Southern Confederacy' are all in the distant future; we know nothing of them, and, like Mohammed's heaven of wine and women, they exist only in the sickly imaginations of ambitious, disappointed politicians. We doubt whether one of Mohammed's followers has ever attained to that heaven even unto this day, and we equally doubt whether any one will ever realize the promised glories of this 'new Southern Confederacy,' until after the great general judgment-day of Almighty God.

"All the slave States are interested in the final and equitable adjustment of the slavery question. The border States, however, are much more deeply interested than the Gulf States, because they are and always have been the greater sufferers. It became, therefore, the duty of all these States jointly to demand such securities and guarantees for the protection of their rights as they might wish, or think necessary. This was the duty of all the slave States jointly. Had this been done, and had their *ultimatum* been rejected by the North, then, and in that case, they would have been justifiable in commencing revolution, provided the causes of their grievances were of sufficient magnitude to warrant revolution. Then all the fifteen slave States, with the conservative element belonging to the free States, could have forced their claims, and would have obtained their constitutional rights, despite the fanatical hosts of Black Republicans.

"But this was not done. Seven States seceded, and now, for fear the Black Republicans will overrun the border States, we are urged 'to go with our sister States.' For what? 'To keep from being bound with Lincoln's chain.' 'He is after us, and has his heel of iron, brass, and clay nearly on our necks,' and we must run, or be subdued. 'Run,' eh? 'Run,' reader! This word is not in the chapter, nor this chapter in our book. To run is no part of our programme. We don't run from our enemies. We don't submit and yield up our rights to our enemies without a manly effort to defend them. We are not afraid of President Lincoln; and, if we were, we think it would be bad policy to let him know it,—especially if he meditate harm against us. What! confess we are scared, and run away even before the battle begins? No! never! never! A scared man is half whipped, to say the least of it.

"A desperate effort was made to precipitate civil war, and, consequently, to precipitate the border States out of the Union. The constant cry was, War! war! war! The whole country expected war. War was in the minds, in the hearts, in the feelings, in the mouths, and on the tongues, of all. In parlors, dining-rooms, kitchens, hotels, livery-stables, barber-shops, cars, steamboats, on the highways, by-ways, in the hedges, in pulpits, on rostrums, by day and by night, at home and abroad, at all times, in all places, everywhere, and under all circumstances, the constant theme was war! war! war! Well, war hasn't come yet. Lincoln hasn't caught any one yet! The Black Republican armies haven't come down like 'Hessians' upon us yet, nor do we *now* believe that there is any danger of an attempt being made to do it. Should the attempt be made, however, we are willing to pledge our life that the Union men of Virginia will be among the first and foremost to meet and give them battle and repel and drive them back to their hiding-holes.

"The Union men of Virginia are true to the Constitution as it was left to them by their fathers. They are true to the 'Stars and Stripes;' they are true to their whole country. But, if revolution must come, and civil war cannot be honorably avoided, then they will fight for their rights, and, with the 'Stars and Stripes' proudly waving over their heads, they will fight bravely, and die, covered with glory and honor imperishable, on old Virginia's soil, and, as their names shall be handed down to posterity, their children and children's children shall rise up and call them blessed."

"A NEW POLITICAL MOVE."

"The 'Richmond Whig' publishes the following circular, copies of which, it states, have been sent in large numbers to the country, and asks, 'What does it mean?'

"RICHMOND, VA., 1861.

"Your presence is particularly requested at Richmond, on the —— day of ——, to consult with the friends of Southern Rights as to the course which Virginia should pursue in the present emergency. Please bring with you, or send, a full delegation of true and reliable men from your own county; and, if convenient, aid the same object in the surrounding counties.

"On arriving at Richmond, report yourself and companions immediately to ——, at ——.

["Signed]

"SAMUEL WOODS, of Barbour.
JOHN R. CHAMBLISS, of Greenville.
CHARLES F. COLLIER, of Petersburg.
JOHN A. HARMAN, of Augusta.
H. A. WISE, of Princess Anne.
JOHN T. ANDERSON, of Botetourt.
WM. F. GORDON, of Albemarle.
THOS. JEFFERSON RANDOLPH, of Albemarle.
JAMES W. SHEFFEY, of Smythe.

"Rather suspicious! We fear the Trojan horse! Why not let all the sovereign people know what this great gathering in the city of Richmond means? Why call for 'a full delegation of true and reliable men from your own county'? For what are all these full and reliable delegations wanted? Why *rendezvous* at Richmond, and that, too, during the session of the convention? What kind of aid is to be extended to the surrounding counties? And who are the false and unreliable men at home? 'True and reliable men' are called for,—which necessarily supposes that the *concocters* of this circular think that there are men who are not 'true and reliable.' 'True' as to what? 'Reliable' as to what? Such circulars, at such times as the present, augur no good, we fear to our country. Look at it! Think of it!"

THE CHRISTIAN'S BIBLE AND THE AMERICAN CONSTITUTION.

"Infidels have scorned the Bible, and thousands now treat it with contempt; but what harm has it ever done them? Suppose they should gain the ascendency: would it be safe, would it be wise, for Christians, although in a minority, to declaim against the Bible, and cry, 'Down with it! down with it! down with the accursed book!' simply because infidels are in the majority? What Christian will say so?

"The Bible is understood and interpreted differently, in many parts, by every religious denomination in Christendom. What then? Shall the pedobaptist say, 'Because the Baptists do not understand and interpret the Bible as we do, and seeing that they do not regard us as being their equals as constituted members of the Church of Jesus Christ, not regarding us as being worthy to participate with them in the holy communion of the Lord's Supper, therefore we will dissolve every religious, social, and political *tie* which has hitherto bound us together, and separate ourselves entirely and forever from them, and abandon the old Bible, about the true and correct interpretation of which there has been so much contention, and we will fix up *a Bible* of our own, and go to heaven in our own way, and let the Baptists and the old Bible all go to perdition'? Would such a course of conduct be wise? Would it be safe? Would it be politic? No, it would not; and no *Christian* would say it would be. Because Baptists say that pedobaptists are not their equals, does that make them inferior to the

Baptists in any respect? By no means; and no man of sense believes that it does.

"Every religious denomination of professing Christians interpret the Bible according to their professed understanding of the doctrines and principles which it contains. They all admit, however, that it is a good and great book,—a book of divine origin, the book of God's revealed will to man,—that it will direct all true believers in the Lord Jesus Christ to the kingdom of endless felicity. No sensible man, much less a Christian, will reject the Bible because others do not understand it precisely as he does himself.

"In regard to the Constitution of the United States. What harm has it ever done any American citizen? What true patriot can find fault with it, or *feel* in his heart a wish, a *fixed* desire, to annihilate it? Has it not proved a blessing to us all, and to the whole nation? Who can produce a better? Where can a better be found? 'But there are those who give it misconstructions, and are not willing that all the citizens of these United States shall receive and enjoy the protection which it guarantees.' Grant it. But whose fault is this? The fault is not in the Constitution. The Constitution remains the same pure and holy document as ever. The fault rests with fanatics and traitors, who wish to pervert the Constitution and wrest it from its true meaning, because it thwarts them in their wicked aspirations.

"What shall be done? Shall we abandon the Constitution, cut loose from the salutary restraints of all law and government, and launch out upon the broad ocean of political strife and uncertainty, without chart or compass? How shall we shun the dangers of the sea? And, if we escape total wreck and ruin from the dangers of the voyage, to what harbor shall we be drifted? Shall we abandon a *known, tried, positive good*, and enter upon the wild career of *Utopian* experiments, when our all is at stake? Who but madmen can act so rashly? Shall we join in the cry with those who say, 'Down with the Constitution! down with the Constitution! Down, down with the accursed document!' No, this is not the remedy. The cry should be, 'Down with the violators, down with the desecrators, of the Constitution!' Had this course been pursued with wild fanatics and black-hearted traitors thirty or forty years ago, our country would not now be cursed with the agitation of the slavery question, disunion, revolution, and civil war, as it is and certainly will be. And, having borne with the insults of fanatics and traitors so long and so patiently, shall we now abandon the good old Constitution and the 'Stars and Stripes,' and passively yield up all our rights and institutions into their hands? Never! Never! We now have the Constitution which our ancestors bequeathed unto us: let us cleave unto it until we *positively know* that we have or can obtain a better. We still have a country, in which we have all lived prosperously and happy, and may continue to do so through life, if we will only do our duty. The 'Star-Spangled Banner,' the emblem of untold blessings, social, political, and religious, still waves over our once happy country. As yet, all are permitted to worship God under their own vine and fig-tree, while none dare to molest or make them afraid. Long may those blessings be perpetuated unto us and unto our children. 'Long live the Republic!' "

"STARTLING CONSIDERATION.

"The latent causes which can influence American citizens to rejoice at the trailing in the dust of the 'American Flag' is a mystery we cannot fathom,—a problem we cannot solve. The 'flag' of our country, which was the pride and boast of our fathers, and which in the national horizon was a sign to them, and to us their children, of security and protection not only at home, but abroad, on every sea and in every land,—that men can rejoice at its downfall and exult in its desecration is to us a startling consideration! To us it appears unnatural, ungrateful, unpatriotic, unchristian, unmanly, and wicked in the extreme. To exult over a fallen foe is unmanly and cowardly; but to exult over the dead body of a fallen parent is so unnatural that he who would be guilty of such an act would, by general acclamation, deserve to be branded with the blackest and basest ingratitude.

"What harm has the 'American Flag' ever done to any American citizen? Who has ever been injured by it? Where is the American citizen living, who can lay his hand on his heart, in life, in death, or at the bar of his God, and say that the 'American Flag,' the 'Stars and Stripes,' have ever done him harm? Sooner would we desecrate a mother's grave than we would desecrate the 'Stars and Stripes,' which protected that mother from insult and injury while living, and still watches over her grave, to drive back the approaching enemy and preserve her sacred ashes from the desecrating tread of the wicked and profane! Long may the 'Stars and Stripes' proudly wave over all our happy land!"

"BUT THERE *IS* NO UNION NOW.

"It is said by some that 'there is no Union now.' 'The Federal Government is broken up, and why talk any longer of the Union?' The fact that seven members of a large family, containing thirty-three members, may feel that they have been badly treated by other members of the family, and resolve on quitting the family, and should actually leave, does not by any means prove that the family does not still exist. The family, in fact, still exists, *minus*, however, seven of its original thirty-three members. It, therefore, becomes the duty of the remaining members of the family, who regard the rights of the seven absented members, and who feel *for* and sympathize *with* them, to force the unruly and refractory members still remaining in the family into subjection and obedience to the rules, regulations, and government of the family, or drive them out of the family altogether, and afterwards use their influence to get the absent, injured members to return and all live as one great, harmonious family again. If, however, the members who had previously left the family circle find it to their interest to remain separate and independent to themselves, without serious detriment to the interests of the great original family, let them continue in peace and quietness. Use no arbitrary means to force them back again.

"The American people inhabiting the thirty-three States of this Union constituted one great family. Fifteen States of this great national family feel and complain that they have been badly treated by other members composing this great family, and seven have seceded. Now let the good law-abiding members of the twenty-six States still remaining say to these refractory members of the great national family, You must in all coming time behave yourselves, and submit to the constituted authorities of this great American family, or, otherwise, we will inflict the penalties annexed to the laws of the Federal Government upon you; and, if this will not answer, you shall not live with us; we will *expatriate* you: we are not going to leave the family ourselves, nor will we allow it to be broken up by you; therefore you must give us satisfactory guarantees for your good behavior in all time to come. This being done, then let the twenty-six members of the family affectionately invite the absent or seceded members to return to the embraces of the common brotherhood, and all become members again of the one great American family. If, however, the seceded members think they can live more happily and do better to remain by themselves, and refuse to return, give them the portion of the public inheritance which belongs to them, and let them remain in peace. All this can and ought to be done without war or the shedding of one drop of fraternal blood.

"IMMEDIATE, ABSOLUTE, AND ETERNAL SECESSION.

"If immediate, absolute, and eternal secession be the policy of those gentlemen who are candidates for office under the Federal Government, how, in the event of their election, can they consistently, honestly, and conscientiously take the oath to support the laws of the Federal Government, which will be administered to them on entering into office? It does seem to us that this is a grave question, and one which should be duly considered both by candidates and voters before they act. How can *gentlemen*, on entering into office, swear upon the Holy Bible that they will observe, respect, and protect the laws and Constitution of the Federal Government, when at the same time they are committed and pledged, if possible, to break up the Federal Government? No mental reservation, gentlemen, when you are called up to the Holy Bible! Think of this, gentlemen!"

"HOW IS IT?

"Men from the North come to Virginia, and some of them become so thoroughly *pro*-slavery and *anti*-Union that they become rampant, red-hot, immediate, absolute, unconditional, and eternal secessionists. This being the case, who can say that 'the whole North is hopelessly abandoned to *niggerism*?'

"Many of our Virginia citizens have near and dear relations in the North. Some have fathers, mothers, brothers, sisters, sons, and daughters in the North. Now, let all those rampant, hot-headed secessionists who are emigrants from the North set to work and see if they cannot enlighten their benighted Northern relatives and friends on the subject of African slavery."

"IMPORTANT CONSIDERATION.

"Suppose that what is now called the 'Southern Confederacy' should succeed by a *meagre* majority in getting their 'Permanent Constitution' ratified by the people of the several Confederate States: would there not be a fearful danger of rebellion in this new Confederacy, on the part of the large minority, at any time when they might feel themselves sufficiently strong to throw off the yoke of oppression, and thus produce revolution and civil war among themselves? We think so.

"This is a question of the gravest importance, and one which is worth the serious consideration of all those political leaders who are moving heaven and earth in order to precipitate Virginia out of the Union. Minorities have rights as well as majorities; and those rights should be respected; and if majorities refuse to do so, the minorities, as soon as they feel the weight of oppression, and find, or believe, that they are able to throw off the yoke of tyranny which majorities have forced upon their necks, will rise up in rebellion and assert and defend their rights.

"If, therefore, Virginia shall ultimately secede, the people of the State should have ample time to consider the matter well and thoroughly understand the principles on which they secede, and the reasons why they secede, and all act in harmony; otherwise, terrible results may grow out of a too hasty flight out of the Union. Recent observations convince us how easy it is for a people, led on by ambitious, unprincipled politicians, to repudiate to-day the acts of yesterday, and the acts of to-day they will as readily repudiate to-morrow. To-day they will exalt a *man* to heaven, and to-morrow they will doom him to infamy, without being able to assign a justifiable reason for either act. The work of breaking up and overturning one system of government to establish another, for the express purpose of accommodating and installing politicians in office, is a serious business. The results will be fearful,—the consequences terrible. Remember what we say."

REMARKS ON THE FOREGOING.

"*New political move.*"—We have some important facts to state, and some interesting circumstances to lay before our readers, in connection with the "new political move," and the "circulars" already noticed in the above; which, however, we shall reserve for a subsequent chapter. We hope the reader will, in the mean time, analyze the "circular" and our remarks on the same, that he may be the better prepared for future developments which will be unfolded in the progress of this work.

"*Hessians.*"—It was constantly affirmed by secessionists that old Abe Lincoln, Scott & Co. were coming down upon us with their Black Republican armies, having a huge "chain," to bind us, hand and foot, and, if not to cast us into *outer* darkness, to make slaves of us and of our children forever. On all occasions, the cry was, "The Hessians are coming!" "The Hessians are coming!" "The vandals of the North will soon be upon us!" "The hordes of old Lincoln are coming to ravage the whole South, and especially Virginia!" Thus the country was kept in a state of continual excitement, and terror seized the people, and especially the females, all over the country. We had come to the conclusion, however, that secessionists would commence the war before President Lincoln, and thus save him the trouble, and the Government the mortification, of inaugurating civil war. In this we were not deceived.

"*Candidates for office.*"—In alluding to candidates for office under the Federal Government, we had reference to the candidates in Virginia for the Congress of the

United States, and the State Senate. Virginia had not seceded, and yet these candidates said that if they were elected, they would serve in either Congress; that if Virginia seceded and joined the Southern Confederacy, they would serve in the Southern Congress, but, if Virginia did not secede, they would serve in the Congress of the United States.

Ex-Governor Smith had announced himself a candidate for re-election to Congress, at Spottsylvania Court-House, on the first Monday in April, and was on an electioneering *tour* through the district at the time we wrote the following brief paragraph, which appeared in the number of the "Christian Banner" of April 4, 1861:—

"Ex-Governor Smith is a candidate for re-election to Congress; and as the 'Virginia (Alexandria) Sentinel' and the 'Virginia (Fredericksburg) Herald' have buried the political tomahawk, and now stand shoulder to shoulder on the *rickety* platform of immediate secession, Ex-Governor Smith will, as a matter of course, receive the hearty and cordial support of both these journals; and it may, therefore, be reasonably inferred that his election is sure. Well may it be said that 'Extra Billy is hard to beat.'"

Governor Smith had no opponent more violent in his whole district than the 'Virginia Herald,' up to the time that that journal turned over to *Breckinridge loco-foco treason*,—and no friend more devoted to his political interest than the 'Virginia Sentinel.' No two journals could have been more antagonistic politically than were the 'Herald and Sentinel' before the question of secession and the dissolution of the Union became popular.

We had always been a warm personal and political friend of Governor Smith, and therefore the more deeply regretted the course he pursued in relation to the immediate and unconditional secession of Virginia. It will be remembered that Governor Smith was a Breckinridge Democrat,—a strong supporter of that party,—a strenuous advocate for the immediate secession of Virginia, and a violent opposer of the present Administration. But still, if Virginia did not secede, and if he were re-elected, he would serve in the Congress of the United States. So, likewise, with all the Breckinridge candidates in the State of Virginia. Hence the question arose in our mind, "How can gentlemen, on entering into office, swear, upon the Holy Bible, that they will observe, respect, and protect the laws of the Federal Government, when at the same time they are committed and pledged, if possible, to break up the Government?" To our mind there did appear to be some difficulty in this matter, although to others it might, and we suppose did, seem different.

CHAPTER XXVII.

EVERYBODY IN A FOG—STAMPEDE—RAISING SECESSION FLAGS—PETITION OF R. THOM, ESQ., FOR POST-OFFICE—WHAT THEN?—LET THE NORTH AND SOUTH BE HEARD—SECESSION CONVENTION.

In the number of the "Christian Banner" of April 11, 1861, we wrote and published the following articles:—

"EVERYBODY IN A FOG.

"Yes, everybody is in a fog, and everybody is likely to remain so. All is rumor, conjecture, surmise, predictions. It is said, thought of, talked of, rumored, in certain circles of the knowing ones. It is now sure, almost certain, confidently believed. No doubt war has commenced! will begin, must begin! it can't be helped. Charleston has made, will make, would make, should make, must make, an attack on Fort Sumter. Fort Sumter is, will be, shall be, might be, may be, must be, could be,—positively it is, may, can, might, could, would, should, and shall be evacuated!

"Major Anderson is, has been, or is certainly going to be ordered away from Fort Sumter; now has, or has had, or is going to have, all supplies cut off from Charleston. Fort Pickens has been, will be, must be, shall be reinforced; and then war, blood, and thunder, commingled with cannon-shot and lightning, will deafen, crimson, and illuminate all the beautiful plains of the 'sunny South.'

"Messrs. Lincoln, Scott, Holt & Co. are gathering together millions of Black Republicans, and are making grand military preparations to march down South to take all the 'people's negroes' from them. Already has Lincoln placed 'his big broad iron heel of despotism on Virginia's neck,' and has nearly gotten her chained, clinched, screwed on tight and fast to his horrible Black Republican, Abolition car. Pictures are now being bandied about representing seven States running for life, with lightning-speed, to get out of 'old Abe's clutches,' while Virginia is represented standing with a huge lock-chain thrown around her neck, and 'old Abe's' great big paw hoisted over her head ready to pounce down upon her. 'Run, Virginia! run, Virginia, run!' like a rat from a cat, or 'old Abe' will harness you! Is this manly, brave, heroic? Is this the kind of reason, argument, and logic to frighten freemen into abject submission? Has Virginia become reduced so low in the scale of degradation as to forget and utterly ignore all her former greatness and glory, to become frightened with pictorial representations of rats running from cats, and the ludicrous representation of the rattling of 'old Abe's' despotic Abolition chain? Can a nation of brave men and freemen be awed into submission by ludicrous pictures, scarecrows, raw-heads and bloody-bones? Alas for the fallen greatness and departed glory of a once honored and powerful nation!

"Virginia, to her honor be it said, has not yet taken up the line of march. Let her stand firm, and speak out in unmistakable language to President Lincoln, that, if he wants her slaves, he must 'come and take them'! Then every true heart and strong arm of Virginia's sons would become a Thermopylæ. If Virginia will only stand firm in this trying crisis, imperishable glory will crown her mighty efforts, and posterity will do her homage through all coming time. Virginia can drive away the fog and cause the true light once more to shine. May she never falter, tire, nor become weary in well-doing. As yet all is rumor, conjecture, and guess-work. No one can rightly divine the immediate or ultimate destiny of our once prosperous, peaceful, happy, honored, and glorious country."

"STAMPEDE.

"Reader, do you know what this *big* word 'stampede' means? You can't find it in any of your little dictionaries. It's a *big* word, and is only found in *big* dictionaries, and belongs to *big* folks! In Webster's *big* dictionary it has the following meaning:—'In the Western States, a sudden fright, seizing upon large bodies of cattle or horses in droves or encampments on prairies, and leading them to run for many miles, until they often sink down or die under their terrors.'

"This word has recently been transferred from large bodies of cattle and horses to large bodies of negro-owners, who, it is said, are threatened with a stampede terror, and will actually run away from Virginia and never stop in their flight until they sink down away in the safe, sunny plains of the far distant South, unless Virginia also becomes frightened and secedes and runs away down South too: in which event they promise to stay in Virginia and all go down South together. That will be nice: won't it, now?

"What does all this mean but a threat to those citizens of Virginia who, in the event of danger, are not able to enter upon this stampede? It simply means this: unless those men in Virginia who are now opposed to secession, and who have not the means to gather up their goods and chattels and remove South, turn secessionists and force Virginia out of the Union, they will be left to the mercy of their 'Abolition enemies,' to fight their own battles and defend their own rights as best they can. Does this show that the men who boast and threaten stampedes have any fraternal regard for their poorer brethren who may be forced of necessity to remain and fight and contend for their rights at home on their own native, sacred soil? No. Is not this a daring threat to force men to act contrary to their better judgment, conscientious principles, and patriotic spirit? It is. And does it not argue a cowardly and submissive spirit in those men who forsake the graves of their ancestors, leave their own native soil, and give up their own pleasant homes because of an anticipated enemy? Do brave men act thus? No. Will freemen be awed by such arguments and threats into servile submission to the treasonable will of such men? We hope not.

"But suppose they do go. What then? Will the lovely hills and valleys and beautiful plains of Virginia become desolate, filled with thorns, briers, and thistles, and be abandoned forever? And will the beautiful cottages and splendid mansions of these stampeders become the dwelling-places of wild beasts, bats, and owls? No: there is not a word of truth in the whole of it. It would only hasten the abolition of slavery in Virginia, and free labor would take the place of slave labor, and Virginia lands would advance two hundred per cent. in value. Hence, we argue that men who make such threats are, in fact, the real Abolitionists and submissionists of Virginia, whether they mean it or not. Political demagogues make these threats to 'fire up the Southern heart,' to force Virginia out of the Union. What do you think of that, reader?"

"RAISING SECESSION FLAGS.

"The raising of secession flags, and all the sensation speeches, and telegraph-despatches, and abominable exaggerations and frauds which are being practised upon the people are no signs of permanent and general secession views entertained by the people. Politicians may rave, rant, and try to 'fire up the hearts' of the people, but, as certainly as the sun shines in the heavens, a reaction will take place. It can't be otherwise. And then woe be unto those who have ambitiously and blindly led the people on to ruin."

"PETITION OF REUBEN THOM, ESQ., FOR THE POST-OFFICE.

"We learn that a petition is being circulated through the town of Fredericksburg to obtain signatures to send to the President of these United States, requesting him to retain in office Reuben Thom, Esq., who is now postmaster of the Fredericksburg post-office. We have not had the pleasure of either seeing or signing the petition, though we may yet have the gratification of both seeing and signing it. We sincerely hope that Mr. Thom may be retained in office: first, because he is emphatically a good man; secondly, because he is an old man; thirdly, because he is a responsible and a reliable man; fourthly, because he faithfully discharges the duties connected with his office.

"We are decidedly in favor of his being retained in office, because we are a *Union man,* and desire to see the offices of Government judiciously distributed among citizens of different political sentiments. We desire it, because we wish to see President Lincoln rising superior to these little, petty, political prejudices which influence little minds, and, in the magnanimity of his soul, showing himself superior to party distinctions and influences. We hope he will be retained in office, because we do not think that any one who would seek to get him out of office would be worthy the confidence of the people of Fredericksburg."

Secessionists had sneered at the idea of living under the "Lincoln Government," but no sooner is he installed into office than secessionists get up petitions to be retained in office. "O consistency, thou art a jewel!"

"WHAT THEN?

"Suppose that these gentlemen who are candidates for the United States Congress should be elected, and that subsequently Virginia should secede from the Union: what then will these gentlemen do? Of course they will vacate their seats in Congress. What then? They will seek an asylum in the 'Southern Confederacy.' But will they not have to be re-elected? And is it certain, if Virginia secede, that she will join the 'Southern Confederacy'? This will have to be left to the vote of the *sovereign people!* In any event, we think that these secession candidates, who are trying to break up the Union and to destroy the Government, are in rather an awkward predicament. Remember, then, gentlemen, that if the convention should pass an ordinance of secession, this ordinance will be referred back to the people for their ratification or rejection. Suppose it shall be ratified. The next question is, what course will Virginia pursue? Will she join the 'Southern Confederacy,' or will she 'set up for herself'? In any event, we insist on it, these gentlemen will be in rather a ludicrous fix. In view of all these facts, ought not the Union men of Virginia to be active and energetic in their efforts to elect Union men to fill all the offices both in the State and the Federal Governments? Then we will have men on whom we can confidently rely. Fellow-citizens, think seriously on this question."

"LET THE PEOPLE, NORTH AND SOUTH, BE HEARD.

"Let the people, North and South, be heard. Yes, let them speak their sentiments fearlessly, honestly, and independently of the influence of designing politicians, and they will tell a story that will send terror and consternation to the hearts of those leaders, both North and South, who are trying to overturn and annihilate the best and purest form of government on earth. It is a shame and an awful sin for the people to allow a few aspiring demagogues and rotten-hearted politicians to break up the Government and ruin the whole country."

"SECESSION CONVENTION.

"What does this secession convention, which is to meet in the city of Richmond on the 16th instant, mean? Does that convention intend to depose Governor Letcher and force Virginia out of the Union whether she will or not? This will be a high-handed move, and one which every loyal son of Virginia and the South ought to repel at every hazard. The people of Virginia are not yet prepared to be run over rough-shod by tyrants, without lifting their voice against it."

Such was the character of the editorials of the "Christian Banner" of the 11th of April, 1861.

CHAPTER XXVIII.

THE CONSPIRACY UNVEILED—VIRGINIA SACRIFICED.

In the present chapter we propose to *group* facts and circumstances together, that the reader may more clearly understand some of the influences by which Virginia was forced out of the Union.

On the 11th of April, 1861, at the time we published the editorials contained in the last chapter, Virginia was undulating on the thin surface which covered an iniquitous *sink* of *treason*, deep, dark, and black as perdition itself. In fact, she had been driven to the lofty summit, and stood trembling on the awful precipice of ruin, to overlook which maddened the brain and sickened the heart, while no eye could fathom the terrible chasm below, save the omniscient eye of the great God of the universe.

Already had the Virginia Convention been in session for nearly two months, having organized about the 13th of the preceding February, and up to the 11th of April had failed to pass an ordinance of secession. Every possible outside pressure had been employed to force that body to pass an ordinance of secession, but without effect. The importance of deposing Governor Letcher and of breaking up the convention was boldly advocated by the secessionists. They argued that the convention was too *slow* in its operations. The people (that is, the secessionists) were tired waiting the *tardy* movements of the convention. Hence originated the *plot to usurp the power to depose Governor* Letcher, *to break up the convention, and to put others in their places who would do the work at once.* Hence, also, the call for a new, secret, secession convention, composed of true and reliable Southern-Rights men, to take into consideration "the course which Virginia should pursue in the present emergency."

In a former chapter we alluded to a "new political move," and promised to notice it more particularly in a future chapter. To save the reader the trouble of referring to the previous chapter containing the "Circular," and our remarks on the same at the time we published it, and that he may be the better enabled to comprehend the whole scope and design at a single glance, we will here give them another insertion. Read the "Circular:" it is pregnant with meaning, especially when taken in connection with all the circumstances attending the passage of a secession ordinance by the Virginia Convention, and the overthrow of the Republic.

"A NEW POLITICAL MOVE."

The "Richmond Whig" publishes the following circular, copies of which, it states, have been sent in large numbers to the country, and asks, "What does it mean?"

"CIRCULAR.

"RICHMOND, VA., 1861.

"Your presence is particularly requested at Richmond, on the —— day of ——, to consult with the friends of Southern Rights as to the course which Virginia should pursue in the present emergency. Please bring with you, or send, a full delegation of true and reliable men from your own county; and, if convenient, aid the same object in the surrounding counties.

"On arriving at Richmond, report yourself and companions immediately to ——, at ——

"[SIGNED.]

"SAMUEL WOODS, of Barbour.
JOHN R. CHAMBLISS, of Greenville.
CHARLES F. COLLIER, of Petersburg.
JOHN A. HARMAN, of Augusta.
H. A. WISE, of Princess Anne.
JOHN T. ANDERSON, of Botetourt.
WM. F. GORDON, of Albemarle.
THOS. JEFFERSON RANDOLPH, of Albemarle.
JAMES W. SHEFFEY, of Smythe."

There, reader, is the "Circular;" and to show our opinion of it, and our suspicion of the design of the concocters of the circular at the time we published it, we will here insert our remarks on the subject, so that the whole matter may appear in connection:—

"Rather suspicious! We fear the Trojan horse! Why not let all the sovereign people know what this great gathering in the city of Richmond means? For what are all these full and reliable delegations wanted? Why *rendezvous* at Richmond, and that, too, during the session of the convention? What kind of aid is to be extended to the surrounding counties? And who are the false and unreliable men at home? 'True and reliable men' are called for,—which necessarily supposes that the concocters of the circular thought that there are men who are not true and reliable. 'True' as to what? and 'reliable' as to what? Such circulars, at such times as the present, augur no good, we fear, to our country. Look at it! Think of it!"

A volume is here unfolded for the serious contemplation of the reader, which presents a picture of one of the *blackest plots* of *damnable treason* to be found in the records of the world's history! Why were "large numbers" of these infamous circulars sent to the country?

To what class of persons were they sent? Not to "Union-shriekers, submissionists, and traitors," but to "true and reliable men," who were sworn, no doubt, to exert every influence and power within their reach to force Virginia out of the Union, and, consequently, to effect the overthrow of the Federal Government.

Why was the time of holding this treasonable convention left blank? Were the traitors afraid that there would be a *ground-swell* of Union men *then* and *there*, who might upset the whole conspiracy?

Why were the names of the persons to whom these country traitors were to report themselves "and companions immediately on arriving at Richmond" left blank? Were they afraid that the "submissionists to old Abe Lincoln" might stealthily get into the secrets of their infernal machinations, and report them to the loyal authorities at Richmond?

Why did they leave the place at which these "true and reliable men" and their "companions" were to *rendezvous* blank? Were they afraid that some who belonged to the "tail-end of the Northern Confederacy" would linger in disguise about the place at which they were to report themselves and "companions," and learn something of their diabolical plot, and thus break up the conspiracy?

Whom did they mean by "friends of Southern Rights," but *simon-pure secessionists*, "true and reliable men," who had been *baptized, head* and *heels, soul* and *body*, in the *sink*-pool of Breckinridge *locofoco treason?*

Why did they wish "to consult as to the course which Virginia should pursue in the present emergency"? Were not the members of the Virginia Convention, who had been elected by the popular vote of the citizens of the State, at that very time in consultation "as to the course which Virginia should pursue in the present emergency"?

Why this deep and earnest solicitude for full delegations, but to be able to *usurp* the authority, *depose* Governor Letcher, *burst up* and annihilate the Virginia Convention, organize themselves into a *self-created body, vote themselves the State of Virginia*, as the Legislature of Virginia had already set them the example, and *force* an ordinance of secession upon the people of Virginia, in the event that they should fail to *force* the Virginia Convention to do it for them?

"Please bring with you, or send, a full delegation." Under the circumstances, could language be more significant? At the time these treasonable circulars were being sent all through the "country," an overwhelming majority of the members of the Virginia Convention were Union men. Governor Letcher himself was reported as being a Union man. And there were thousands of the citizens of Richmond Union men, and a majority of them would have remained loyal to Virginia and to the Federal Government to this day, no doubt, had it not been for this treasonable secession convention, and the circumstances connected with it, all of which hurried and forced the Virginia Convention to commit the suicidal act. In view of the strong Union feeling which still burned in the bosoms of the members of the convention and the citizens of Richmond, it was important and absolutely necessary that *full* delegations "of true and reliable men" should be sent from all the counties in Virginia. As if they had said, "We expect *hot work* in Richmond on the *blank* day of the blank month; that is, on the 16th day of April, 1861, we shall in all probability meet with and have to contend against powerful influences and forces: therefore, please bring with you, or send, full delegations of true and reliable men from your own county, and, if convenient, aid the same object in the surrounding counties."

We again ask, what kind of aid was to be extended to the accomplices in treason "in the surrounding counties" to further on the same nefarious object of sending traitors to Richmond? Were they to be aided with clothing, transportation, money to pay their expenses, and munitions of war to enable them effectively and effectually to consummate their infernal plot of treason against the commonwealth of Virginia, and, consequently, against the Government of the United States?

Look, also, at the localities, standing, and position of the men whose signatures are affixed to these treasonable circulars, which were sent in great numbers all through the country! Had not the Hon. Henry A. Wise for several months previous been actively engaged in getting up a "legion" of "minute-men," afterwards known as the "Wise legion?" Was it not in contemplation that these "true and reliable men," thoroughly armed as they were, should be on hand at this great secret secession convention? Who can doubt it? Was not Henry A. Wise the very man to head and lead on an army or mob of *locofoco traitors* to accomplish the diabolical work of breaking up the Government, to the end that he in his ungodly ambition might *usurp* the *power* and become the great leading spirit in the Virginia revolution and *the man* in the new Southern Confederacy?

And where, too, were the "one hundred and twenty thousand members of the order of Knights of the Golden Circle"? The Norfolk "Day-Book," early in the month of December, 1860, contained the following significant paragraph:—

"THE K. G. C.'S AND THE SLAVE-HOLDING STATES.—Colonel V. D. Groner, Knight of the Golden Circle, has returned to this city. He has been to Texas, and returned home *via* Mississippi. His mission South and Southwest was in connection with the order of Knights of the Golden Circle. We learn from Colonel Groner that there are one hundred and twenty thousand members of the order of Knights of the Golden Circle, each one of whom is sworn to stand by the South. They are fully organized, and are constantly drilling, and can be brought into action, if necessary, in two weeks' time."

Here is a conspiracy on a grand scale! One hundred and twenty thousand men, "each one of whom is sworn to stand by the South;" these men were "constantly drilling, and could be brought into action in two weeks' time." Is it not presumable that these *sworn*, drilled, and armed men would be on hand at this secret secession convention, which was to be composed of "true and reliable men"? And does not this clearly explain, also, what the framers of that "circular" meant by "true and reliable men"? Men who had been *sworn* to "stand by the South," or who had been *sworn* to break up the Government in the event that Mr. Lincoln was elected and they themselves were defeated; presuming upon the election of Mr. Lincoln as a sufficient reason to justify them in their diabolical plot to break up the Government, and involve the whole country in one common ruin, in the event that they could not succeed. In other words, here are one hundred and twenty thousand men, who are *sworn* to stand by the "Slave States," or the institution of slavery, even if the Republic be annihilated, the country steeped in blood, and thousands of helpless women made widows and millions of children made orphans! Gracious God! What a dark volume is here unfolded for the contemplation of the reader!

But, reader, this is not all. As was subsequently ascertained, this secession convention was to meet in the city of Richmond on the 16th day of April, 1861; and as soon as we learned the time when this treasonable conclave would assemble, we wrote the following paragraph, which was published in the number of the "Christian Banner" of the 11th of April, 1861, and which we republish, that the *reader* may understand the working of this plot, and that it was talked of and publicly understood, and by the people of Virginia believed to be in contemplation, and of the truth of which there can now be no doubt, not even in the mind of the most skeptical. The following is the paragraph:—

"What does this secession convention, which is to meet in the city of Richmond on the 16th instant, mean? Does that convention intend to depose Governor Letcher, and force Virginia out of the Union whether she will or not? This will be a high-handed move, and one which every loyal son of Virginia and the whole South ought to repel, at every hazard. The people of Virginia are not yet prepared to be run over roughshod by tyrants, without lifting their voice against it."

To effect a collision between the authorities of the United States and the "Confederate States of America" had become, about this time, the one great *mania* of the leading secessionists of Virginia and of the whole South. They said that if a single gun was fired, Virginia and all the border States would certainly secede, and that immediately. A correspondent of the "Richmond Dispatch," writing from Petersburg, says,—

"PETERSBURG, *April* 6.—The excitement here is very great, and the 'war' tidings are discussed at every corner. The people say, 'Let it come.' The indignation of the people at the course of the convention is at a high pitch."

Why was the "indignation of the people" (the secessionists of Petersburg) "at the course of the convention at a high pitch"? Simply because that convention had been in session for nearly two months, and had failed to pass an ordinance of secession. For the sake of precipitating Virginia out of the Union, the secessionists of Petersburg said, "Let it (war) come." This shows the uncompromising determination of the secessionists of Virginia to secede, at the time of which we are writing.

A correspondent, writing from Goldsboro', North Carolina, to the Richmond "Dispatch," under date of April 6, says,—

"GOLDSBORO', N.C., *April* 6.—The news of outfitting the fleet and army at the North is very exciting, and the community wish to hear of an attack on Fort Sumter. The military are ready to assist the Southern Confederacy."

Why did the "community" (that is, the secessionists) in the town of Goldsboro' *wish to hear of an attack on Fort Sumter?* They *knew* that a collision between the Federal and Confederate troops would tend very much to the precipitating of Virginia out of the Union, and then North Carolina would certainly follow.

A despatch from Charleston, South Carolina, under date of April 6, says,—

"CHARLESTON, *April* 6.—We are by no means disappointed at the news, and are now ready to receive our enemies, come as they may. Affairs, however, are culminating. All points have been strengthened, and we are now ready for any emergency. The ball will probably soon open. If the authorities do not soon act, the people may take the matter into their own hands."

"Affairs are culminating." They were then ready, waiting, and anxious for the command to be given to strike a blow at the "flag of the Union,"—to commence the cannonading of Fort Sumter. The impression intended to be made by the correspondent, is that such was the impatience of the people to have the ball opened, that, unless the authorities of the Confederate Government should speedily make an attack on Fort Sumter, the people would *usurp* the authority, *assume* the responsibility, and *inaugurate* civil war themselves. The leaders had already *usurped* the *authority* and *power* of the Government, and were determined to inaugurate civil war, to force the border States out of the Union; and then *libelled* the people, saying that they—the people—had done it,—when, in fact, the people had no voice, directly or indirectly, in the whole matter. It was, therefore, a *libel* on the people, from beginning to end. The people never *usurped* the *power;* they never desired to do it; and the leaders would not have allowed them to do it, even if they had wished. The leaders in this accursed rebellion usurped all the power from the people, did all the mischief, and then, as a sort of *panacea* for the national, political, social, and universal ruin which they inflicted on their country, said, to justify themselves, and to make the people still *think* that they held the power, "the sovereign people did it all." Yes, the "sovereigns have done it." Breckinridge *locofocoism* is the child of the devil,—the spawn of hell,—the enemy of all righteousness,—the destroyer of a nation's happiness,—and would, if possible, demolish all Governments, human and divine, and sink the world in a *sea of damnation*, to sit on a throne of human skulls and shout hosannas to "King Cotton" and the ETERNAL *nigger.* Who would not blush to utter a whisper in justification of a monster so hideous, even in the hearing of *devils damned!*

In order to provoke and hasten a collision between

the Federal and Confederate troops, the secessionists at Richmond despatched the Hon. Roger A. Pryor to Charleston, South Carolina, to "fire up the heart" of the authorities there to make an attack on Fort Sumter before the 16th day of April, the time of the meeting of the secession convention,—knowing that, if this were done, it would be a much easier matter to force the Virginia Convention to pass an ordinance of secession. What man in all Virginia was better fitted for such a mission than Roger A. Pryor?

On arriving in Charleston, he publicly addressed the people, and by his frequent "bursts of unsurpassed, fervent eloquence," he soon set the city in one universal blaze of patriotic enthusiasm; and, the citizens enchained, enraptured, and electrified by his eloquent addresses, it became an easy matter to influence them to determine to commence the work which he desired, above all things, they should do. He told a thrilling story,—and he told that story well. Said he, "I have been asked my opinion relative to the ultimate action of the Virginia Convention. I answer,—the final action of the Virginia Convention depends upon a single contingency! Do you ask what that contingency is?" significantly pointing in the direction:—"*Fire on Fort Sumter, and Virginia is with you!*"

The intelligence went with lightning speed to Jeff Davis, at Montgomery, Alabama. "What shall we do?" was the question. "Fire on Fort Sumter!" was the laconic reply. And be it remembered that on Friday evening, the 12th day of April, 1861, civil war was inaugurated at Charleston, South Carolina, by the authorities of the "Confederate States" firing on the "flag" of the United States of America. The cannonading was resumed on Saturday morning, the 13th of April, 1861, and on that ever-memorable day Fort Sumter fell, and was surrendered up to the authorities of the "Confederate States of America." The time-honored "flag,"—the "flag" respected the world over,—the "flag" which represented the greatest, most powerful, prosperous, and happy nation on earth,—was insulted, hauled down, and made to trail in the dust, and a little, contemptible *secesh flag*, the emblem of treason, and the embodiment of all folly, madness, and wickedness, was run up in its stead. And all this was done by the people who had been protected by that flag all their lives, and their fathers before them.

The effect of the downfall of Fort Sumter on the citizens of Charleston and the South generally may be inferred from the following despatches:—

"[Special despatches to the 'Petersburg (Va.) Express.']

"BOMBARDMENT AND CAPTURE OF FORT SUMTER.

"FIRST DESPATCH.

"CHARLESTON, *April* 13.—The flag on Fort Sumter is down, and a white one displayed in its place. A boat with a white flag is now approaching the city. Major Anderson has not fired a gun for four hours.

"SECOND DESPATCH.

"CHARLESTON, *April* 13.—A terrific explosion has just occurred at Fort Sumter. The fire is still raging. Anderson has fired only twice in three hours. The batteries are pouring it into him. The fleet is still lying idle, though plainly in view. They are now mounting guns on the battery in the city. Roger A.

Pryor, in conveying despatches yesterday in an open boat, was fired on twice from Fort Sumter, but escaped injury. He is busy on duty again to-day.

"THIRD DESPATCH.

"CHARLESTON, *April* 13.—Fort Sumter is ours, God and South Carolina be praised! The surrender is unconditional. Engines are now being taken over there to extinguish the fire. The bells in the city are ringing their joyous peals at the capture of the fort. It is said that there is much loss of life at the fort; but I cannot learn the particulars. There has been no loss on our side.

"FOURTH DESPATCH.

"CHARLESTON, *April* 13.—The most reliable reports from Fort Sumter represent only five men to have been wounded, and that slightly. None were killed. It has been, in this respect, an extraordinary battle. Lieutenant R. K. Meade is certainly unhurt. Preparations have been made to resist the landing of troops upon Morris Island, if it should be attempted to-night; but, after the cowardly abandonment of Major Anderson, no fears are entertained of any such movement. The Confederate troops will take possession of Fort Sumter to-night.

"[**To the Associated Press.**]

"FURTHER PARTICULARS.

"CHARLESTON, *April* 14.—Negotiations for the surrender of Fort Sumter were completed last night, and Major Anderson and his command will evacuate it this morning. They will embark in the war-vessel now off the bar. When the fort was in flames, and Anderson could only fire at long intervals, the men in the Confederate batteries cheered at every shot, but looked defiance at the vessels of war which rode outside the bar without attempting to divert the force of a single battery. Two of Anderson's men were slightly wounded.

"SECOND DESPATCH.

"CHARLESTON, *April* 14.—The steamer Isabel will take General Beauregard to Fort Sumter, which Major Anderson turns over to the Confederate States. Anderson and his men, it is reported, will proceed to New York in the steamer Isabel.

"THIRD DESPATCH.

"CHARLESTON, *April* 14.—Fort Sumter has been turned over to General Beauregard, and Major Anderson has been allowed to salute his flag. Fifty guns were fired from the parapet and casemates. He is embarking on board the 'Isabel,' and will proceed to New York.

"FOURTH DESPATCH.

"CHARLESTON, *April* 14.—A boat is just in from Fort Sumter, and brings intelligence that during the firing of the salute four of Major Anderson's men were mortally wounded by the bursting of two of the guns.

"CHARLESTON, *April* 14.—Last night a boat from one of the vessels outside communicated with General Simmons, in command of Morris Island, bringing the request that one of the steamers be allowed to enter the port for the purpose of taking away Major Anderson and his men. An armistice has been agreed upon, to continue until nine o'clock this (Sunday) morning."

MAJOR ANDERSON'S OFFICIAL REPORT.

"STEAMSHIP BALTIC, OFF SANDY HOOK,
April 18, 1861, 10.30. A.M., via N.Y.

"Having defended Fort Sumter for thirty-four hours, until the quarters were entirely burnt, the main gates destroyed by fire, the gorge-walls seriously injured, the magazine surrounded by flames and its door closed from the effects of heat, four barrels and three cartridges of powder only being available, and no provisions remaining but pork, I accepted terms of evacuation offered by General Beauregard,—being the same offered by him on the 11th instant, prior to the commencement of hostilities,—and marched out of the fort on Sunday afternoon, the 14th instant, with colors flying and drums beating, bringing away company and private property, and saluting my flag with fifty guns.

"ROBERT ANDERSON,
Major 1st Artillery, commanding.

"Hon. SIMON CAMERON."

A correspondent writing from Montgomery, Alabama, under date of April 13, 1861, says,—

"MONTGOMERY, *April* 13.—Fort Pickens was reinforced last night. The news of the surrender of Fort Sumter has been received with immense cheering. The streets are crowded, and the Confederate and Palmetto flags are flying, cannons firing, bells ringing, and great rejoicing."

Such were the jubilant manifestations of secessionists all over the Southern States at the downfall of the American Republic. We might extend our quotations *ad infinitum;* but it would be useless. How was the intelligence of the downfall of Fort Sumter received by the secessionists of Virginia? It was hailed with acclamations of joy everywhere. Taking the town of Fredericksburg as a tolerably fair specimen of the extravagances and ridiculous conduct of the secession element of the State generally, the reader may form a faint idea of what transpired there from the following editorials which we published in the number of the "Christian Banner" of the 18th of April, 1861:—

"On last Saturday evening the news of the surrender of Fort Sumter was received by telegraphic despatch in Fredericksburg,—since which time the greatest excitement has prevailed, and it seems to continue unabated.

"On the receipt of the news on Saturday evening, several guns were fired, the soldiers paraded the streets, several speeches were delivered, many cheers were given, and the doleful 'tiger groans' fell upon our ear like the deep mutterings of demons coming up from the regions of despair. At night bonfires were kindled, as if the actors in the drama were eager for light to see the downfall of the Republic and the departure of a nation's glory! Such is the progress of American civilization, such the character of American patriotism, such the character of American Christianity, in this enlightened nineteenth century!

"Thoughtless children in their infancy, childhood, and ignorance may laugh and skip and play while a dying mother lingers on the verge of eternity; but as soon as the spirit takes its flight into the deep abyss unknown, and the cold, lifeless body is laid low and covered up in the deep, dark, silent grave, and the children find themselves scattered abroad, homeless, penniless, and friendless, thrown upon the cold charity of a heartless world, among unfeeling and unsympathizing strangers,—then they wake up to the sad and startling reality that they have lost a mother, a mother's protection, a mother's blessing, and a mother's love: no one to feel for and love them as a mother did.

"In like manner men may make merry now, while our blessed country, the mother of us all, is convulsed and agonizing in the last throes of existence; but as soon as she sleeps the sleep which knows no waking, we, her ungrateful children, will wake up to the sad and thrilling reality that we have no country, the common nursing-mother of us all, no peaceful, quiet home, no legacy, no inheritance to bequeath to our children to be handed down to posterity. The downfall of our country and the inauguration of civil war seem to us like the madness of men walking, alive, wide awake, into eternity. The thought is terrible beyond conception. Angels might weep, and heaven veil herself in sackcloth and ashes, at the downfall of a country so great and powerful and prosperous as ours. Could our own life be substituted as a sacrifice for the salvation of our blessed country, freely and quickly should the sacrifice be made. We ardently trust in God that the knell of our country's *funeral* has not yet been sounded. We will still try to hope that she may yet be saved.

"Men who will break up their country, impelled by no higher and holier motives than cupidity, ambition, lust for honor, office, position, and power, may live in history, song, and oratory, but they will live only as beacons of infamy to all other treasonable, wicked adventurers through all coming time. Catiline lives, and so does Benedict Arnold,—but 'tis only in infamy. Their names are held in derision, scorn, and contempt by all patriots and good men everywhere."

Let us now return to our investigation of the incidental circumstances connected with the passage of the ordinance of secession by the Virginia Convention. The reader will bear in mind that the attack was made on Fort Sumter by the authorities of the Confederate States, at Charleston, South Carolina, on Friday, the 12th day of April, 1861. Simultaneously with the attack on Fort Sumter and the inauguration of civil war by the Confederate authorities at Charleston, the following proclamation was issued by the President of the Confederate States of America at Montgomery, Alabama:—

"PROCLAMATION BY THE PRESIDENT OF THE CONFEDERATE STATES OF AMERICA.

"Whereas, an extraordinary occasion has occurred, rendering it necessary and proper that the Congress of the Confederate States shall convene, to receive and act upon such communications as may be made to it on the part of the Executive:

"Now, therefore, I, Jefferson Davis, President of the Confederate States, do issue this my proclamation convoking the Congress of the Confederate States for the transaction of business at the Capitol, in the city of Montgomery, on the twenty-ninth day of April, at twelve o'clock, noon, of that day, of which all who shall at that time be entitled to act as members of that body are hereby required to take notice.

"Given under my hand and the seal of the Confederate States, at Montgomery, this twelfth day of April, Anno Domini 1861.

[L. S.]

"JEFFERSON DAVIS.

"By the President.

"R. TOOMBS, *Secretary of State.*"

The question naturally forces itself upon the mind of the reader, what 'extraordinary occasion' had 'occurred rendering it necessary and proper' that President Davis should issue his proclamation on the 12th day of April for the convocation of the Congress of the Confederate States on the 29th day of April, 1861? Who can fail to discover and detect at a single glance the whole scheme devised, and the agencies and means to be used, to consummate a conspiracy against the commonwealth of Virginia and the Federal Government, *black and base as hell?*

President Davis *knew*, and he *knew well*, that important communications would be received by him, and that to make them valid, and at all popular with the people, they would have to receive the sanction of the Confederate Congress. He *knew* that an ordinance of secession would be passed, by which Virginia would be forced out of the Union. He *knew* that delegates, or commissioners, would be sent by the authorities at Richmond, whoever these authorities might be, to *tie* Virginia on to the Southern Confederacy before the people of Virginia should have time to vote upon the action of the convention. He *knew* that Virginia would be literally filled with armed troops before the day of election on which the action of the Virginia Convention should be ratified or nullified by the popular vote of the State. He *knew* that the people of the State would be forced to vote for the ratification of the action of the convention at the point of the bayonet. He *knew* that Richmond would be his *head-quarters*, and he was making his preparations to remove there. He *knew* that Virginia would be the great battle-field and the common burial-ground of this wicked, cruel, and infernal war. Yes, President Davis *knew all these things before he issued his proclamation for the convocation* of the Congress of the Confederate States.

The collision between the two governmental authorities was consummated! The Hon. Roger A. Pryor had thoroughly effected the object and design of his infernal mission to Charleston, South Carolina. The blow was struck at Fort Sumter on the 12th day of April, 1861, and on the 13th day of April, 1861, the fort was captured and turned over to General Beauregard by Major Anderson. On Tuesday, the 16th, after the downfall of Fort Sumter on Saturday, the 13th day of April, the secession convention met in Richmond. Remember the words, "Fire on Fort Sumter, and Virginia is with you!" Pryor had told the authorities at Charleston that unless a collision between the troops of the Federal and Confederate Governments could be effected, the Virginia Convention would never pass an ordinance of secession. We wish the reader especially to bear in mind that on Saturday, the 13th day of April, 1861, Fort Sumter fell; that on Tuesday, the 16th day of April, 1861, the secession convention met in the city of Richmond, Virginia; that on Wednesday, the 17th day of April, 1861, the Virginia Convention went into secret session; and that on

Thursday, the 18th day of April, *Anno Domini* 1861, the Virginia Convention, in secret session, passed and *forced* upon the people of the State of Virginia an ordinance of secession, by which the State of Virginia was declared out of the Union. Virginia was *doomed*, —*sacrificed* on the altar of a set of ungodly, ambitious demagogues and traitors!

As further evidence that it was a part of the *programme* of the traitors of Virginia, in order to fully consummate their *damnable* plot of treason against the State, to invite Jeff Davis and his armed troops into the State for the purpose of *awing* the people on the day of election into the ratification of the action of the Virginia Convention, we submit the following correspondence to the Richmond papers.

"MONTGOMERY, *April* 16.—General Pillow has just arrived with an offer to President Davis of a division of Tennessee troops.

"Everybody is delighted with the encouraging news from Virginia.

"The Cabinet here will wait for Lincoln's proclamation before taking further action.

"Should Virginia unite with us, President Davis will vacate his seat at Montgomery, and Stephens will assume its duties. Davis will then make Richmond his head-quarters within ten days. Beauregard will be second in command. Bragg can take care of Pensacola.

"The Cabinet read Lincoln's proclamation amidst bursts of laughter.

"The Secretary of War authorizes the statement that

thirty-two thousand more troops will be called out to-day to meet Lincoln's men."

On the above correspondence we made the following remarks, which were published in the number of the "Christian Banner" of April 18, 1861:—

"Civil war is inaugurated, and Richmond is to be the head-quarters of President Davis. Why is the seat of war transferred from the Gulf States to Virginia? Has not Virginia used every effort to avert a civil war and to save, if possible, the whole country from ruin? Why, then, make Richmond the head-quarters of a long-protracted civil war, and Virginia the common battle-ground? Such would be the state of universal excitement that business of all kinds, in towns and cities, would be brought to a perfect stand-still, and all agricultural and farming operations would, of necessity, become to a very alarming extent neglected. A long-protracted civil war would devastate Virginia and reduce her to a state of complete desolation. It is horrible to think of, much less to realize.

"If the people of Virginia wish to vote themselves into a civil war, into a common ruin,—their territory into a slaughter-pen of blood and death and all the horrors concomitant upon a civil war,—let them go to the ballot-box and do it. Does Virginia wish to precipitate herself into the gulf of irreparable ruin? Is she prepared for a catastrophe so awfully horrible and revolting? Surely not!"

On the very day the above editorial remarks were

published in the "Christian Banner," the ordinance of secession was passed in the Virginia Convention and forced upon the citizens of the State. One undisturbed *halo* of glory had surrounded the secessionists of Fredericksburg from the time they received the news of the taking of Fort Sumter up to the time that the joyful tidings of the passage of the ordinance of secession by the Virginia Convention sounded in their ears; and then they became absolutely intolerable. The reign of terror then commenced in *earnest*. Worthless men, and little *secesh* boys who had hardly doffed their infant rags, felt fully authorized, being tolerated by popular opinion and legally indemnified by the ordinance of the convention, to offer all kinds of insults and indignities to Union men. Immediately it was proclaimed publicly on the streets that there was no need of an election by the people; that Virginia had seceded; that the members of the convention voted unanimously, with the exception of five or six,—and two or three of these were absent, and would certainly have voted for the ordinance had they been present; that no man would dare to vote in opposition to the ratification of the ordinance; that *tar* and *feathers* and sharp fence-rails would be liberally applied to all *Union-shriekers*, *submissionists*, and *old Lincolnites*, who might any longer dare to express an opinion favorable to the "hateful old flag of the Union" or that the Federal Government should be sustained. It is absolutely impossible for any one who was not an eye and ear witness, and who was not a subject of the infernal goadings continually inflicted on Union men by the silent and open insinuations, insults, and indignities of men, women, and children, to form any correct idea of the intolerant and vindictive spirit manifested, and the ridiculous extravagances to which secessionists, in their treasonable madness, were driven. *It was hell all over, inside and outside.*

With secessionists it was a perfect jubilee, a time of great and universal rejoicing, surpassing in extravagant manifestations of joy and gladness those of the children of Israel on their return to Jerusalem after a captivity and bondage of seventy years in Babylon. Exclamations like the following were heard in all directions:—"Thank God, we are free once more!" "We have thrown off the iron yoke of old Abe Lincoln!" "Thank God, we are once more a free and independent people!" "God and South Carolina be praised for the work they have done!" "Thanks be to God, we can breathe free and easy *now*, since we have gotten our rights and liberty once more!" "Who but fools, submissionists, and traitors to the South, would refuse to be freemen, and submit to be *tied* on to the tail-end of a Northern Confederacy of black-hearted Abolitionists, and the *minions* of old Abe Lincoln?" &c. &c.

The *wee* lawyers, demagogues, and politicians made congratulatory speeches: yes, the *little* orators swelled, raved, ranted, tip-toed, threw back their heads, opened their mouths, and at the top of their voices bawled out, "Fellow-citizens! Glorious news from Richmond! The convention has passed an ordinance of secession, and Virginia once more is free! We have *rent* the chains of Black Republican despotism, and dashed them from us forever!" Then the crowds would almost silence the artillery of heaven with their thundering vociferations of, "Huzza! huzza! huzza! for the convention!" "Fellow-citizens, we are now a free and independent people! Virginia has declared her sovereignty, and the *Old Dominion*, the 'Mother of States and of Statesmen,' is redeemed! Not old Abe Lincoln, but Jefferson Davis of Mississippi, is our President! Jefferson Davis henceforth shall be our leader! To his standard we will rally, and under his banner we will march! He will lead the Confederate army in triumph to Washington City! to Baltimore! to Philadelphia! to New York! to Boston! and will plant the Confederate standard and unfurl to the breeze the *Palmetto* flag over the Capitol of every State in *Yankeedom!*" Then the crowds would shout, "Huzza! huzza! huzza for Jeff Davis!"

This, reader, is only an imperfect sketch, a faint representation, of the ridiculous extravagancies and manifestations of despotism over the people perpetrated by secessionists in Eastern Virginia. We were an eye and ear witness to the course pursued by them in the town of Fredericksburg, and were, moreover, the subject of their taunts and ridicule for more than twelve long months. We speak what we do know, and *testify* what we have *seen*, *heard*, and *felt*.

While secessionists in Virginia were manacling the people at home, throwing around them the chains of political and military despotism, preparing to force them to vote for the ratification of the ordinance of secession when the day of election should arrive, what were Jeff Davis and his accomplices in treason doing at Montgomery, Alabama?

Remember the *words* of the correspondent writing from Montgomery under date of the 16th of April, the very day that the secession convention met in Richmond:—"Everybody is delighted with the encouraging news from Virginia." What news was it from Virginia which so much delighted everybody in Montgomery? The jubilant effect produced upon the secessionists of Virginia at the collision which had been brought about between the Confederate and Federal troops, and the downfall of Fort Sumter, and the certainty that the Virginia Convention would be broken up by an armed mob of secessionists unless that convention passed an ordinance of secession, and that a *self-created body of secessionists* would pass an ordinance of secession and force Virginia out of the Union. In a word, the absolute and unconditional certainty that Virginia would be *forced out of the Union* and *tied* on to the Southern Confederacy by a set of political swindlers and traitors caused "everybody" in Montgomery to be delighted with the "encouraging news from Virginia." Remember, likewise, that General Pillow had just arrived with an offer to President Davis of a *division* of Tennessee troops; that, should Virginia unite with the Southern Confederacy, President Davis would vacate his seat at Montgomery,—would then make Richmond his headquarters within ten days; Stephens would assume the duties of the vacated seat of Davis at Montgomery; Beauregard would be second in command; Bragg would take care of Pensacola; the Cabinet at Montgomery had read Lincoln's proclamation amidst bursts of laughter, (quite dignified and patriotic for a cabinet of statesmen at the downfall and overthrow of their country!) thirty-two thousand more troops were to be called out to meet Lincoln's men. Here was the whole *programme* laid out and sent to Richmond two days in advance of the passage of the ordinance of secession by the Virginia Convention! Was ever such villany, trickery, rascality, and damnable treason *read of, heard of, or thought of, since God made the world?* As to the secession of Virginia, there existed not a doubt in the minds of the members of the Cabinet at Montgomery, because they knew that if the Virginia Convention could not be forced to pass an ordinance of secession, the called convention, composed entirely of "true and reliable" secessionists, would *usurp* the authority and pass it themselves and force Virginia out of the Union.

A correspondent from Montgomery to the Richmond papers, under date of April 30, says,—

"MONTGOMERY, ALA., *April* 30.—Sixteen thousand good troops have just started for Virginia. The question, whether the Confederate Government will remain here or move to Richmond, is now under earnest consideration, and still pending. I will not undertake to state the probabilities of the decision."

The reader will bear in mind that the ordinance of secession was passed in the Virginia Convention on the 18th day of April, 1861; and on the 30th day of April, 1861, twelve days after the ordinance was passed by the convention, "sixteen thousand good troops started" from Montgomery, Alabama, "for Virginia;" and that the day of election, on which the citizens of the State of Virginia were to vote on the all-important question of ratification or no ratification of the action of the convention, did not take place until the 23d day of May, 1861, being more than one whole month from the passage of the ordinance of secession by the convention to the time when the vote was to be taken by the citizens of the State; and this time, too, was given, not that the people might coolly and deliberately decide on a question involving the *whole* of their worldly interests, and perhaps, likewise, their eternal destinies, but for the purpose of giving time and opportunity to the authorities of the Confederate States to crowd armed troops into Virginia, to be ready to *awe* the citizens of the State into *submission* on the day of election. We ask if this was fair play. Was it not a usurpation of authority? Was it not wresting the power from the *people* of Virginia, and placing it in the hands of a few petty tyrants, a few infernal traitors?

As early as the 5th of May, 1861, the "Lynchburg Virginian" said,—

"Six additional companies of the 3d Regiment of Alabama Volunteers arrived in this city about five o'clock yesterday morning. The entire regiment is now here, together with all its officers, except Colonel Withers. Lieutenant-Colonel Lomax arrived with the men yesterday."

Regiments of troops from Texas, Arkansas, South Carolina, Georgia, Mississippi, and North Carolina, arrived in Fredericksburg early in the month of May, long before the day of election. Why were thousands on thousands of armed troops from all the *seceded States* hurried into Virginia, and stationed in all the important cities, towns, and villages, before the people of the State had even voted on the question of ratification or no ratification? Why were thousands of armed troops stationed at Richmond, Petersburg, Lynchburg, Fredericksburg, Norfolk, Portsmouth, Hampton, Yorktown, Williamsburg, Alexandria, Harper's Ferry, &c. &c.? Who is so blind and stupid as not to be able to perceive the whole design at a single glance? The design was, to *awe* Virginia at the point of the bayonet into submission, on the day of election, to vote for the ratification of the ordinance of secession. If five thousand votes had not been cast by the citizens of the State, on the day of election, for the ratification of the ordinance, still Virginia would have been forced out of the Union by *foreign votes* and *military forces*. Who knows, to this day, the number of votes polled on the 23d day of May, 1861? The official returns, if ever received at Richmond, the head-quarters of treason, were never published to the world. Virginia was declared out of the Union by a large majority of votes *voluntarily* given by her citizens; which *was*, and *is*, and *will forever* remain a slander and *libel black as hell* upon the citizens of the State of Virginia.

When the candidates were elected to the Virginia Convention, there was a majority of sixty thousand votes cast for the Union, and a large portion of these voters were in favor of the Union on the 23d day of May, 1861. Men were made to vote the secession ticket by force of circumstances, and influences which they could not control. Influential secessionists told their neighbors that, unless they voted for secession, neither they nor their children could ever command any standing or position in the country; that they would be brought under the *ban* of public censure, and would always be regarded as *traitors* and *tories*, and would become odious as were the *tories* and *traitors* of the Revolutionary War; that their property would be confiscated, taken from them and given to the Southern Confederacy; that the *damned* Yankees would come and take their negroes, if they had any, and, if they had none, they would take them, their wives and children, and make slaves of them all; that the Yankees would come and insult their wives, outrage their daughters, rob them of all their property, and play the *devil* generally. If they wished to frighten the Yankees, make the Federal Government "back down," and avoid civil war, "go and vote for secession." If they wished to stand fair in society, and command respectability in the communities in which they might live, "go and vote for secession." If they did not wish to be *damned to infamy* themselves, and consign their children to the scorn and contempt of all mankind, "go and vote for the ordinance of secession." If they wished to keep their *snug* little farms and comfortable homes, and their little property of whatever kind they had collected around them, "go and vote for secession." If they wished to keep themselves and their children from becoming slaves to old Abe Lincoln, "go and vote for secession." If they wished to save their wives and daughters from the insults and injuries of the vandals of the North, "go and vote for secession." If they wished to keep the Yankees from stealing and taking away their negroes, "go and vote for secession." If they wished to permanently establish the glorious institution of African slavery, "go and vote for secession." If they wished to get rich, educate their children, associate with the *first families of Virginia*, roll and shine in splendor in the world, "go and vote for secession." If they wished to throw off the yoke of serfdom to old Abe Lincoln, and be freemen, independent, happy, and prosperous, "go and vote for secession." If they wished to live in the Southern

Confederacy, under the purest, wisest, and best form of government in the world and in the greatest country on earth, "go and vote for secession." If they wished to escape the horrors of civil war, and wanted a peaceable separation, "go and vote for secession." If they were true and pure *Democrats*, and wished *Democratic doctrines* to prevail,—and, unless they did prevail, the country could not be saved,—"go and vote for secession." Unless they had turned traitors to their party, and had forsaken the *good old Democratic* principles of their fathers, "go and vote for secession." If they wished, or expected, either themselves or their children ever to fill any office of wealth or honor, either in the civil or military departments in the Southern Confederacy, "go and vote for secession." If they were friends to good old Virginia and her noble institutions, "go and vote for secession." Unless they intended to turn traitors to their native State, the *Old Dominion*, the mother of States and of statesmen, in this her great and grand struggle for freedom and independence, "go and vote for secession." If they were friends to the South and to Southern rights and institutions, "go and vote for secession." If they were not traitors, Abolitionists, and Union-shriekers, "go and vote for secession." If they were not submissionists, and did not wish to become the vassals of Lincoln's despotism, "go and vote for secession." If they were not *old Lincolnites*, and did not want to be *tied* on to the tail-end of the Northern Confederacy, with an old rail-splitter at its head, "go and vote for secession." And, finally, if they wanted to hold on to all their rights and institutions, political, religious, social, moral, and domestic, real and imaginary, and especially to the institutions of

African slavery and *Breckinridge locofocoism*, which two institutions embodied all blessings, human and divine, past, present, and future, for this world and all worlds to come, for all time and through all eternity, "then go and vote for secession, like men."

Such, reader, were some of the influences which were brought to bear on the action of the people of Virginia prior to the day of election; in addition to which, bear in mind that at least one hundred and fifty thousand armed troops from the seceded States were stationed at all the important points in Virginia, prepared to *awe* the people into submission.

And as to the vote in the Virginia Convention, we were told that it was unanimous,—there being only some five or six members who did not vote for the ordinance of secession; yet when, subsequently, the injunction of secrecy was removed from the acts of that convention, it was ascertained that there were about forty-seven members of the convention who never did vote for the passage of the ordinance at all. And this was another *damnable* swindle,—a downright imposition on the people of Virginia.

No sooner had the convention *forced* the passage of the ordinance of secession than it set to work to *tie* Virginia forcibly on to the Southern Confederacy; to accomplish which, commissioners were appointed by the convention and hastened off to Montgomery, to make sale of Virginia in the quickest time and on the best terms possible. The Richmond "Examiner" of about May 1, 1861, contained the following editorial in relation to the delegates who were appointed to the Congress of the Confederate States :—

"DELEGATES TO CONGRESS.

"The convention, on Monday, appointed the following gentlemen delegates to the Congress of the Confederate States:—

"R. M. T. Hunter, Tide-Water.
"Wm. C. Rives, Piedmont.
"Judge Brockenbrough, Valley.
"Judge Camden, Northwest.
"W. R. Staples, Southwest.

"Two of the State's representatives in the Peace Conference were elected,—Rives and Brockenbrough,—while Mr. Sedden, one of the wisest heads and the most patient hearts that Virginia contains, the third member of the Peace Conference not in the convention, was nominated and rejected. So, it seems, were Mr. Jenkins and Abdiel, always 'faithful found,' in the northwest of the State, and Mr. Bocock on the other side of it. In their places the convention chose a Mr. Staples and a Mr. Camden. What they are, the convention only knows. All we can learn of them is the general report that they were microscopic, but very venomous, submissionists some time ago. If they now are any thing better, we shall be very glad; but at present it would appear that this delectable body that continues to rule over us, and will long rule over us, has chosen for Virginia's embassy to the South three enemies and two friends of the Confederacy; and this will be the fitting finis of a session which should be remembered as one of the most remarkable chapters of parliamentary iniquity ever recorded in history."

In the number of the "Christian Banner" of May 2,

1861, we published the following editorial remarks on the above article of the "Examiner":—

"Is it not an alarming usurpation of authority that the Virginia Convention should have appointed gentlemen to the Congress of the Confederate States at all? Was this the purpose for which the convention was called? We did not so understand it. Is it not an alarming usurpation of power that the convention should unite the destinies of the Old Dominion with the 'Confederate States of America' before the vote of the citizens of the State is taken on the question? Are a million of freemen to be bartered and sold, and handed over to other authorities, without being consulted, and without their knowledge or consent, by a convention of men elected by the people to transact other and different matters? If we understand the subject, the convention was called together to decide on the policy as to the passage of an ordinance of secession or non-secession: after which the action of the convention was to be referred back to the *sovereign people* for their ratification or rejection. The whole matter is pre-arranged and virtually fixed, and then the people are called on to vote for all the questions together! If this be the beginning of our new order of things, what will the end be?"

Already had the Virginia Convention not only passed an ordinance of secession and sent delegates to the Congress of the Confederate States, but had actually

"*Resolved*, That the President of the Confederate States, and the constitutional authorities of the Confederacy, be, and they are hereby, cordially and respectfully invited, whenever in their opinion the public interest or convenience may require it, to make the city of Richmond, or some other place in this State, the seat of the government of the Confederacy."

The Richmond "Examiner" said,—

"The presence of Jefferson Davis in Richmond would be worth an army of fifty thousand men. He is the man for this hour. He would be obeyed. He could inspire confidence, and order, and energy everywhere. With others our troops will fight, and perhaps win the battle; but with him the victory would be sure, and chance certain."

The reader cannot fail to observe the keen thrust the "Examiner" makes at the "very venomous submissionists," and the "three enemies of the Confederacy," as also the thrust it makes at the whole convention when it says, "This will be the fitting finis of a session which should be remembered as one of the most remarkable chapters of parliamentary iniquity ever recorded in history." Why this editorial reflection on the reputation of Rives, Camden, and Staples? Simply because they were "some time ago very venomous submissionists," or, in other words, Union men. This, with the "Examiner," was sufficient evidence to convict them as being enemies of the Confederacy, and which should politically *damn them to infamy.* The "Examiner" opposed any one holding office in the Southern Confederacy whose antecedents on the question of secession were not above suspicion. Hence, also, the "Examiner's" reflections on the convention, an overwhelming majority of the members of which were Union men or "venomous submissionists" up to the time of the attack on Fort Sumter. The "Examiner" had great faith in Jeff Davis, because he was an original secessionist, and if he would only come to Richmond and issue his mandates "he would be obeyed." His "presence in Richmond would be worth an army of fifty thousand men" in subjugating the State of Virginia! Well, Jeff Davis came to Richmond, and brought with him his vast army, and had all his troops scattered over the State on the day of election,—which, however, was nothing more than a mock-election; for, long in advance of the day on which the vote of the State was to be taken, the Democratic press of the South denounced every man who might dare to vote for the Union as being a *traitor* and an *Abolitionist*, who should be hung or else driven out of the South. And if they remained at home on the day of election, thus refusing to vote for secession, it would be evidence sufficient to convict them of having sympathy for the "old detestable Union," and they, too, should be driven out of the South, and all their property should be confiscated. And the Richmond "Examiner" declared that all who "professed recent conversion to secession were hypocrites," and of course ought not to be trusted.

Such, kind reader, were the coercive agencies and influences employed to force Virginia out of the Union and to utter ruin. Nor was this all. Civil war was already inaugurated in Virginia. Gosport Navy-Yard, at Norfolk, Virginia, was already seized by the Confederate authorities, and the munitions of war were secured in great quantities, while thousands of troops were constantly being sent from the South to Norfolk and Portsmouth. Read the following despatches:—

"NORFOLK, *April* 20, 1861.—The navy-yard was fired at one o'clock this morning, and the two ship-houses, sail and rigging lofts, and the marine-barracks destroyed, together with the ships 'Pennsylvania,' 'Columbia,' 'Raritan,' 'Germantown,' 'Dolphin,' and 'New York.'

"Every cannon was spiked, and all the small-arms destroyed. Gosport is now in flames. The Federal troops have escaped in the 'Cumberland' and 'Pawnee.' Three naval officers are under arrest in Norfolk."

"*April* 21, 1861.—The 'Pawnee' left this morning at four o'clock. She is now at Old Point. The 'Cumberland' could not pass the obstructions. Before leaving, the infamous scamps fired the navy-yard, and the 'Pennsylvania' is now in a mass of ruins."

About this time, also, the following despatch was received by Governor Letcher of Virginia, which seemed to favor the general impression among the secessionists of Virginia that there would be a universal *ground-swell* of the secessionists of Maryland, and that she would be *out* of the *Union* and *into* the *Southern Confederacy* in the shortest conceivable time, and that the insurgents of Maryland and Jeff Davis and his army would form a junction in Washington City, depose the Government authorities, and take possession of Washington.

"ALEXANDRIA, *April* 22.—Lieutenant Charles Carroll Simms, late of the U. S. Navy, and attached to the Navy-Yard at Washington until one o'clock to-day, has just arrived here, and reports that reliable information has reached Washington that the 7th Regiment of New York was *literally cut to pieces* this morning, between Annapolis and Marlborough, by the Maryland troops.

"C. E. STEWART,

"*Colonel* 175*th Regiment*."

The night on which the news was received at the Fredericksburg Railroad depot of the destruction of Gosport Navy-Yard, and that the 7th Regiment of New York was *literally cut to pieces*, we were present, and listened to two enthusiastic speeches which were delivered to the crowd at the depot by two rampant, original secession orators, who had just arrived from Richmond with the "glad tidings." At the close of the last speech, after the deafening roar of the loud huzzas had partially died away, a *fiendish* shout was raised in the crowd, with the cry, "Where's Major Williams?" "Where's Major Williams?" "*Yes, God damn him,*" was responded, "where is he?" "Where is he?" "Damn him, let's tar-and-feather him and ride him on a fence-rail!" Not knowing but that our turn would come next, and having left Major Williams in our office when we started to the depot to learn the news, we hastened back to our office, it being on Main Street, only about two squares from the depot, and reported to the major what had occurred at the depot. Being fearful that they might come to our office in search of him, in the event they went to his house and could not find him at home, as he frequently visited us, which was known by many, we proposed to him to spend the night with us, which offer he unhesitatingly accepted, and, conducting him through a back room out of our office and up two flights of stairs, he was soon ensconced in a warm bed in our dwelling, and thus spent the night. Major Williams was a Union man, and was subsequently arrested and confined in prison for at least six months, only having received his discharge in the month of October, 1862, being exchanged for secession prisoners whom the Federal authorities arrested in Fredericksburg and lodged in the Old Capitol at Washington City. The major frequently visited us in Washington City after his release, during the time we remained there a refugee; and the story he relates of the sufferings of Union citizens while in prison is most revolting. We believe his report, because we know him to be a man of truth and perfectly reliable.

We state this circumstance that the reader may be advised of the violent opposition and vindictive feelings which were manifested by secessionists towards Union men in Fredericksburg and throughout Virginia at least one month in advance of the election for the ratification or rejection of the ordinance of secession by the citizens of the State.

In further evidence of the truth of our statements in this work, read the following correspondence from Lynchburg, Va., which we published in the number of the "Christian Banner" of April 25, 1861:—

"ANDY JOHNSON SALUTED IN LYNCHBURG.

"LYNCHBURG, VA.—Andy Johnson, late United States Senator from Tennessee, passed through here to-day on his way from Washington to Tennessee. A large crowd assembled and groaned him and offered every indignity he deserved,—including pulling his nose. Every effort was made to take him off the cars.

"The demonstrations were first suggested by Tennesseeans. Great difficulty was experienced in restraining the populace. Johnson was protected by the conductor and others, who begged that he might be permitted to proceed home and let his own people deal with him. He denied sending a message asserting that Tennessee should furnish her quota of men."

From the above the reader will discover that even United States Senators who were in favor of the Union could not pass through the State of Virginia to their homes and families in other States without being in danger of crowds of armed mobs offering every *indignity* and *insult* to them, including the *pulling* of their *noses*. They groaned him; they offered every indignity he deserved, including the pulling of his nose; every effort was made to take him off the cars. Why did Senator Johnson *merit* all this abuse? Simply because he was a patriot, loyal to his country. Why, or for what purpose, did they wish to take him off the cars, but to do violence to his person? Be it remembered that Tennesseeans were the first to make demonstrations of every sort of insult and to offer all kinds of indignities to United States Senators on Virginia soil. This was one of the great designs the Confederate authorities had in view in sending troops from other States into Virginia,—to make demonstrations of insults and to offer indignities to Union men. Why did not the military and civil authorities protect Senator Johnson? Because this would, perhaps, have thrown a *damper* on other large crowds, who subsequently might wish to offer insults and indignities to Union men. The conductor and others *begged* that he might be *permitted* to go home, and let his own people deal with him. *Begged* that a United States Senator might be *permitted! permitted* to go *home!* Great God! Was ever such insolence known? And that, too, in Old Virginia, "the

24*

Mother of States and of Statesmen," and in the town of Lynchburg! And all this damnable despotism was acted out in Virginia a month in advance of the vote of the people on the action of the convention.

As we have already said, thousands of armed troops were sent from the seceded States to crush Virginia,—to force her out of the Union,—to establish a military despotism over the people,—to *awe* them into servile submission to the infernal conspiracy of Davis and his band of traitors. This was the freedom, the independence, of the people of Virginia and of the whole Southern Confederacy. These were the men who denounced the despotism of the "Lincoln Government" and the "tyranny of the old *infernal* Union." These were the men who shouted against *coercion*,—who boasted of the liberty of the press, the liberty of speech, the liberty of action,—all of which simply meant that everybody had to write, speak, and act precisely in harmony with all that the original secessionists wrote, spoke, and did, and nothing else; and this was *freedom!* Yes, the freedom of slaves, the freedom of serfs,—and the only freedom exercised by the *people* with impunity within the Southern Confederacy since its organization. God knows it, and the people in the Southern Confederacy know it, and they will tell the thrilling story to the world when the time comes. Talk about the "tyranny of the North," the "despotism of the Lincoln Government"! Where is greater despotism to be found this side of *hell*, than that which has been, and now is being, exercised over the poor, swindled, down-trodden *people* in the Southern Confederacy? Every vestige of freedom—every right and privilege—have been wrested from them, and then these God-forsaken, heaven-daring, hell-deserving traitors presume to deliver lectures and write essays *to* and *for* the dear people, setting forth the horrors of the "despotism of the North,"—"the tyranny of the Lincoln Government,"—"the despotic Government of the *Old Union*"*!* Absolutely, men who have never been goaded by the curses of secession cannot sympathize with those who have. Secession is unmistakably the broad road and the wide gate which lead to destruction, and thousands there be who go in thereat. Secession is the shortest and most direct route to hell.

Positively, secession is the most damnably aggravating curse by which mortals can be goaded this side of the infernal regions. Secessionists forced *the people* by the most terrible threats of every evil on earth, and that, too, at the point of the bayonet, to go and vote for the ratification of the acts of the Virginia Convention, to the end that they might "hit them in the teeth with it" in all time to come. The leaders in this rebellion, who forced the people to submit to their will and pleasure, and who forced Virginia out of the Union, are themselves now submitting to the will and pleasure of their own *slaves*, and to many other things, of which they had never dreamed when, two years ago, they were anathematizing Union men and shouting hosannas to Jeff Davis, "King Cotton," and the everlasting "nigger." If they shall prove successful in ruining all others and the whole country, they themselves will be ruined in the end. This is right and just in the sight of all heaven. The leaders are the ones on whom the whole curse of this war should fall, if it were possible.

Again, on the 17th day of April, 1861, one day in advance of the passage of the ordinance of secession by the Virginia Convention, Governor Letcher issued the following proclamation:—

BY THE GOVERNOR OF VIRGINIA—A PROCLAMATION.

"*Whereas*, seven of the States formerly composing a part of the United States have, by authority of their people, solemnly resumed the powers granted by them to the United States, and have framed a Constitution and organized a Government for themselves, to which the people of those States are yielding willing obedience, and have so notified the President of the United States by all the formalities incident to such action, and thereby become to the United States a separate, independent, and foreign power; and whereas the Constitution of the United States has invested Congress with the sole power "to declare war," and, until such declaration is made, the President has no authority to call for an extraordinary force to wage offensive war against any foreign power; and whereas, on the 15th instant, the President of the United States, in plain violation of the Constitution, issued a proclamation calling for a force of seventy-five thousand men to cause the laws of the United States to be duly executed over a people who are no longer a part of this Union, and, in said proclamation, threatens to exert this unusual force to compel obedience to his mandate; and whereas the General Assembly of Virginia, by a majority approaching to entire unanimity, declared, at its last session, that the State of Virginia would consider such an exertion of force as a virtual declaration of war, to be resisted by all the power at the command of Virginia, and, subsequently, the convention now in session, representing the sovereignty of this State, has reaffirmed, in substance, the same policy, with almost equal unanimity; and whereas the State of Virginia deeply sympathizes with the Southern States in the wrongs they have suffered and the position they have assumed, and having made earnest efforts peaceably to compromise the differences which have severed the Union, and having failed in that attempt, through this unwarranted act on the part of the President, and it is believed that the influences which operated to produce this proclamation against the seceded States will be brought to bear upon this commonwealth if she should exercise her undoubted right to resume the powers granted by her people, and it is due to the honor of Virginia that an improper exercise of force against her people should be repelled:

"*Therefore*, I, John Letcher, Governor of the Commonwealth of Virginia, have thought proper to order all volunteer regiments or companies within this State forthwith to hold themselves in readiness for immediate orders, and, upon the reception of this proclamation, to report to the Adjutant-General of the State their organization and numbers, and prepare themselves for efficient service. Such companies as are not armed and equipped will report that fact, that they may be properly supplied.

"In witness whereof, I have hereunto set my hand, and caused the seal of the Commonwealth to be affixed, this 17th day of April, 1861, and in the eighty-fifth year of the Commonwealth.

[L.S.]

JOHN LETCHER."

Did the Constitution of Virginia authorize "the General Assembly" of that State to "declare at its last session, by a majority approaching to entire unanimity, that the State of Virginia would consider such an exertion of force a virtual declaration of war, to be resisted by all the power at the command of Virginia? Was this *declaration* of "the General Assembly" ever brought out squarely and publicly and explained to the people of Virginia? Was the vote of the sovereign people of the State ever taken on this question? And did one-tenth part of the voters in the State ever understand this declaration, or even know that it had ever been made by the Legislature? Why did "the General Assembly" of Virginia make this *declaration* so far in advance of the difficulties which subsequently were so suddenly sprung upon the country, if not to forestall and ignore the intelligence, will, and power of the people? Was not this *declaration* on the part of the General Assembly *virtual secession?* And was it not a direct invitation to the Gulf States to secede, and to make Virginia and the other border States the battle-ground of this ungodly war? They say to the rebellious States, *Secede,* if you wish, and we will stand between you and the authority of the United States Government, and, if that Government attempts to enforce the laws, we will protect you by resisting the enforcement of the laws "by all the power at the command of Virginia:" there shall be no *coercion.* Of what use are the laws of the Government if they are not to be observed and enforced? The trickery, treachery, and treason of that accursed *locofoco* General Assembly of Virginia were *damnable!*

And by what authority did "the convention now in session, representing the sovereignty of this State, reaffirm in substance the same policy with almost equal unanimity"? Was this the object for which the convention was called? No: it was not, nor did the people so understand it. Was not the *reaffirmation* of the *declaration* of the "General Assembly" by the convention virtual secession, and an unqualified invitation to the Gulf States to secede and make Virginia the slaughter-field of this shocking rebellion? The convention, in reaffirming the declaration of the "General Assembly," virtually says to the Gulf States, Secede, and we will stand between you and all danger: our territory shall become the common battle-ground, and we will fight your battles for you. These declarations and reaffirmations in time of peace, even had they been submitted to the people, would have passed unnoticed and uncared-for by the great majority of them, because they did not understand them, nor the design for which they were thrust upon them. The object and design of the leaders, however, were to get the people fully committed on all subjects which would aid them in the overthrow of the Republic.

If there were a majority of the people in Virginia "approaching to entire unanimity" in favor of resisting the enforcement of the laws of the United States Government, why did the electors of the Bell and Douglas parties take for their motto during the Presidential campaign of 1860, "The Union, the Constitution, and enforcement of the laws"? And what did the political editors, the advocates of these two parties, mean when they headed the columns of their journals with the *motto*, "The Union, the Constitution, and enforcement of the laws"? Did they mean nothing?

After all, it is evident that the members of these two dignified bodies were lamentably deficient either in good sense or true patriotism, or both; and to the latter opinion we very strongly incline.

By what authority did Governor Letcher in his proclamation affirm that "seven of the States formerly composing a part of the United States have, *by authority of their people*, solemnly resumed the powers granted by them to the United States"? Did he not *know* that the *authority of the people* of these States had been set aside and totally ignored by the leaders of these States? He did. And he knew also that at that very time the Legislature and Convention of Virginia were trying to wrest all power from the people of Virginia. But why elaborate further on this terribly black chapter in the political history of Virginia? The glory and honor, influence and dignity, power and greatness, of the *Old Dominion*, "the Mother of States and of Statesmen," is swiftly passing away.

The conspiracy is unveiled. Virginia and the whole South are sacrificed. Awful is the responsibility of the leaders in this wholesale work of ruin and death, blood and carnage, and terrible is the retribution which awaits them.

CHAPTER XXIX.

In the "Banner" of April 25, 1861, we published the following editorial:—

"DIABOLICAL WICKEDNESS.

"Having for months past anticipated with almost prophetic precision the inevitable results in the event of 'certain contingencies,' we are in mind prepared to meet the very worst that can befall our country and our fellow-citizens.

"We have for more than twelve months been warning our countrymen of the awful dangers ahead. The subject has borne with terrible weight upon our mind, both by day and by night, at home and abroad, in the sacred and secret retirements of life, and in the great congregation. Hence we are prepared to meet the very worst that can now come; and our constant and religious object in writing and conversing on this subject as we have done, was, and is, if possible, to so influence the actions of our countrymen as to avert civil war, and, consequently, all its train of horrors; and that, if we should ultimately fail to accomplish this object so devoutly wished, we might prepare the minds of our readers to look for the horrible calamities which must certainly befall them.

"Having done all that we could do to secure peace to our country, we now feel in our heart that we have a clear and honest record before Heaven and earth, and, having acted faithfully and honestly, are, therefore, ready and willing to meet the issue, be that issue what it may.

"This is a war in which every one is individually interested to the extent of his earthly existence. If continued, it will result in a war of extermination, as we have always predicted. Can it not yet be arrested? Shall a nation of Christians be butchered, to gratify the unhallowed and unbridled ambition of a few blood-thirsty tyrants and despots? Shall innocent females and children, aged fathers, and the youth, the young men, the flower and hope of our country, fall in one common ruin? What folly! what madness! what *diabolical wickedness!*"

GENERAL REMARKS.

The month of April, 1861, will ever be memorable in American history as recording the most thrilling events which have ever occurred on this great continent. In this month thousands of *secesh flags* were "thrown to the breeze" throughout the rebellious States; the "Stars and Stripes" were hauled down and made to trail in the dust; civil war was inaugurated at Charleston, South Carolina, by the Confederate troops firing on the "flag of the Union;" Fort Sumter was surrendered to the Confederate authorities by Major Anderson; the Virginia Convention passed an ordinance of secession, and sent commissioners to the Confederate Congress to *tie* Virginia on to the Southern Confederacy; Gosport Navy-Yard and the Arsenal at Harper's Ferry, Va., were burned by the United States troops, and afterwards seized by the Confederate troops; Andrew Johnson, a United States Senator, had his nose pulled by a mob in the town of

Lynchburg, Va.; thousands of armed soldiers from the rebellious States were sent into Virginia and stationed at Norfolk and Portsmouth, Hampton and Yorktown, Lynchburg and Fredericksburg, Richmond and Petersburg, Alexandria and Harper's Ferry, Manassas and Acquia Creek, &c. &c., to awe the people of Virginia into servile submission to the arbitrary will of despots and tyrants; the reign of terror commenced, and the fate of Virginia was sealed, in April, 1861. Thus was Virginia environed on the 23d day of May, 1861, when the people of the State were called on, at the points of a hundred thousand bayonets, to vote for the ratification of the ordinance of secession which was passed by the Virginia Convention on the 18th of April, 1861. Thus circumstanced, what were Union men to do, and what could they do, but humbly and patiently submit and *bide* their time?

CHAPTER XXX.

THE LAST EDITORIALS OF THE "CHRISTIAN BANNER" OF 1861—GENERAL AND CLOSING REMARKS.

In the number of the "Christian Banner" of May 9, 1861, we published the following editorials:—

"THE PEOPLE OUGHT TO KNOW.

"Blow ye the trumpet! Warn the people of their danger! Cry aloud, and spare not! Recreant is he who, when he sees danger approaching, cries, 'Peace, peace and safety,' when there is neither peace nor safety, but sudden destruction at the door. If there be no danger, why, in the name of all that is sacred and humane, has our country been kept in a state of such unparalleled excitement for nearly six long months? If there be no danger of war, as some affect to believe, and if there never has been any danger, as others affirm, then we are forced to the conclusion that no age or country has ever been cursed with a class of such consummate knaves and fools as the political leaders in the farcical drama which is now being acted out in our wretchedly distracted country.

"Do the leaders presume upon the ignorance and credulity of thirty millions of freemen to effect their ambitious schemes to *wriggle* themselves into office, and to hold on to the offices they now fill?—now crying out, 'War, war, war!' until they create a sort of universal panic, which they keep up sufficiently long to accomplish their nefarious designs, and then trying to allay the excitement and calm the passions of the infuriated masses of the people by whispering in their ears, 'Peace, peace.' 'There will be no war.' 'There is no danger of war.' 'We never thought there would be any war.' 'All will be settled without the shedding of fraternal blood.' 'This is all unnecessary excitement,' &c. &c.

"Are freemen to be made slaves and brutes, to be gulled, duped, and led about by knaves whithersoever they wish? If there be no danger of war, then the leaders in this national, tragical affair justly merit the execrations of all good men on earth and all the hosts of heaven above. If, however, there be danger, then the people ought to know it, and prepare themselves for the threatened calamities which are about to befall them.

"If an enemy designed to fire our house or to take our life, would we not be thankful to any one to forewarn us of the danger? Then we could prepare to meet it and defend ourself. 'But the people ought not to be alarmed. There is no occasion for it.' No, no: 'the people ought not to be alarmed: 'tis all nonsense to talk about war, and frighten the people for nothing.' Ignorance may be bliss when and where there is no danger; but it may prove fatal when and where there is danger. Then we say to all our readers, there is danger,—imminent and immediate danger,—danger at *any moment* and *everywhere*. The people both in towns and country should be on their watch-towers both by day and by night, and every hour and every moment. 'Tis wicked to act, in such times as the present, like silly boys walking in the night, whistling to keep each other's spirits up, all the time scared half to death for fear of seeing wandering ghosts from the 'spirit-land.'

"Danger has been *forced* upon us, and there is no concealing the fact any longer; and it would be unrighteous in us, as an editor, to cry, 'Peace and safety,' when there is neither peace nor safety. We feel for our friends and fellow-citizens; and, because we do feel for them and love them and wish them well, we warn them to prepare themselves for coming danger. We have for more than twelve long months, and almost every week during that time, warned our readers that, in the event of 'certain contingencies,' ruin, danger, and death await us in the future. These contingencies are wellnigh consummated; and we now say to one and all, prepare for the worst. Be not alarmed to madness, but to watchfulness, preparation, decision, and manly action when the time comes."

"In the hour of danger, when our enemies are said to be near at hand, let every man stand firm to his post. No cowardly stampedes and sudden flights from danger. Cowards are generally great braggarts, making all sorts of 'fuss and splutter' until the rumored approach of the enemy, and then they turn out to be great runners. For all such dastards we have the most supreme contempt. We have heard of men being spotted! Ay, we'll see who the brave souls are who merit spots! Brave men never run,—cowards, always!

"It is an easy matter for a few leaders to get a country into difficulties, but a very hard matter to get themselves and the country out of difficulties. A child can fire a house, which a whole community of men may not be able to rescue from the flames. Such is the present deplorable state and wretched fate of our now ruined, but once grand and magnificent, country. A few ambitious leaders have brought ruin upon us all, and the people quietly submit. After all that has been said of man, godlike man, what is he, but a compound of stupidity, treachery, ignorance, knavery, and cowardice, which are the principal constituents that compose the *theological pill of total depravity!*

"We can scarcely realize the fact that a nation of professing Christians are straining every nerve and making every possible preparation to cut each other's throats and tear out one another's hearts! Shame!

shame upon the boasted wisdom, philanthropy, patriotism, and Christianity of the American people!

"Reason is dethroned,—a nation is in confusion,—and our whole country is being plunged into anarchy and ruin. Truly may it be said that we are at our *wits' end.* Our only trust and hope are in God. Let us look to him, trusting in his almighty power and infinite wisdom and mercy to bring salvation out of ruin, and order out of confusion.

"It is madness and folly for Virginia to provoke a collision with the Federal Government. Let all this bravado be hushed into silence, and let the people act with dignity, system, and determination.

"When we retrospect the pleasures of past years with warm-hearted Christian friends and brethren, the many holy privileges we have enjoyed, and now think of the present condition of things around us, and look into the dark, mysterious future, at the saddening and gloomy prospects ahead, our philosophy is well-nigh overcome, and we feel that we could weep tears of blood, could tears save our country from eternal ruin."

GENERAL REMARKS.

"*Danger at any moment and everywhere.*"—We feared servile insurrections more than all the "army of the North." And we feel confident that before the close of this war, should it continue two or three years longer, the most fearful enemy with which the Southern people will have to contend will be the colored population of the South. Scenes, we fear, will be acted out which will horrify the souls of the bravest men. We tremble at the terrible reflection of what may be the fate of thousands of poor, unprotected females. While the country is filled with armed troops, the slaves are awed into partial obedience. In communities, however, where thousands of them have been *crowded* together for "safe-keeping," and the most of the white men gone, and as most of them will either be killed, or die in the army with disease, then the slaves will seize their opportunity and *scowl* at the commands of their rulers, who for the most part will be females, boys, and old men; and then to attempt to *coerce* them into submission will be a fearful and hazardous undertaking. And let it be remembered, moreover, that the strength of the white men at the South is constantly being diminished, while that of the black population is constantly on the increase.

"*No danger.*"—To influence men to enlist for the war, secessionists at one time would cry, "War! war! war!" and then, again, they would denounce men as "fools" and "traitors" who dared to tell them that war was inevitable, and that there was danger at *any moment* and *everywhere.* They would create a panic and keep it up sufficiently long to effect their *devilish* purposes, and then try to calm the terrified feelings of the people by affirming to them that there would be no war. To justify them in their conclusions and assertions that there would be no war, they would advance "arguments" such as the following:—

"Virginia has seceded;" "The whole South is a unit;" "Every border State will certainly secede;" "The old Federal Government will *break down;*" "Lincoln has already shown the *white feather;*" "The Yankee Government will *cave in;*" "The North will be *forced* to grant whatever the Southern Confederacy may demand;" "All that is necessary is for men to enlist, and let the North see what an array of armed troops can be mustered into service, and then the North will become panic-stricken and yield to all the demands of the South, and the whole difficulty will be settled without any, or but very little, war," &c. &c.

The game of deception which was practised upon the people of Virginia and the South was deep, dark, and iniquitous as *hell* itself. We saw this, and knew it to be the fact: hence the warning character of our editorials. We had been admonished for weeks either to change the character of our editorials, or to discontinue the publication of the "Banner." We would frequently prepare editorials with great care, and give them to the compositors, and, after being half in type, and sometimes entirely so, news would come and circumstances would occur which rendered it prudent, and absolutely necessary for our own safety, to suppress whole articles. It was a constant practice to write and re-write, to change and re-change and alter our editorials, as the young men in our office can testify.

We saw and felt that the liberty of the press, the liberty of speech, and the rights of freemen were all wrested from us, and that the withdrawal of patronage would ultimately force us to discontinue the publication of the "Banner;" and we determined, after the publication of the number of May 9, 1861, to close our office. We did so, and dismissed all our hands. We left our office with a heavy heart, determined never to resume the publication of our paper until the glorious "Stars and Stripes" should wave over us, which, we confidently hoped, would not be a great while. The reader cannot fail to observe, from the character of our editorials, that we *grazed the brink of damnation* as near as possible to escape *tumbling in.*

All the other printing-offices in Fredericksburg—four in number—continued to do an excellent business, as we were informed. On some occasions, as we were told, the editors received as much as five hundred dollars for one Government advertisement. Sometimes persons would tauntingly say to us, "A'n't you sorry you stopped your paper?" "If you had continued the 'Banner,' you could now make your jack." "What a pity you stopped it!" "Oh, I am so sorry for you!" &c. &c.,—when, at the same time, their hearts were as destitute of true sympathy for us as a cinder thrown heaven-high from the bottom of a burning volcano. Oh, what an amount of human *depravity* and *damnable hypocrisy secession* has developed! We could not conscientiously advocate the cause of traitors and treason, and we preferred being *crushed* by them rather than to join in with them to help crush our blessed country. We were entirely broken up in business of all kinds, and preferred to suffer rather than to hold any office in the Southern Confederacy, even if we could have obtained one by making the application. But such, however, were our Union proclivities and objectionable antecedents in opposing secession that we presume we could not have obtained an office even if we had asked for one. Thrown out of business, we remained an *anxious* observer of passing events until the arrival of the Union troops and the surrender of Fredericksburg, on the 18th of April, 1862. It was just one year from the time the Virginia Convention passed the ordinance of secession up to the time the civil authorities of Fredericksburg surrendered the town to the military authorities of the United States. To us it was a year of gloom and melancholy, of deep-toned sorrow and severe oppression; but it is lost in past eternity and gone forever, and may God in mercy grant that we may never again realize mental afflictions so severe!

Oh, the horrors of secession! Surely no *sane* man who has ever tasted the bitter fruits of secession will advocate an evil so destructive to all the blessings of this life and so pernicious to a progress in the divine life. Dear reader, if you are the least contaminated with the ruinous heresy secession, we entreat you, as one who has experienced its blighting effects and who is yet suffering its bitter fruits, to renounce it, and abandon the accursed thing forever. Oh, the horrors of secession!

The conspiracy is unveiled. The South is sacrificed on the unhallowed altar of aspiring demagogues and ambitious tyrants, in a death-struggle for the spoils of Government and to establish a permanent negro-oligarchy on the downfall of liberty and the ruin of the American Republic. But here, reader, we let the curtain fall. The conspiracy is unveiled: the South is sacrificed.

PART II.

In the number of the "Christian Banner" of May 9, 1862, we wrote the following *editorials*, which we publish as a continuation of the course of the "Banner," and as a historical record of events which transpired during the stay of the Federal army in the town of Fredericksburg, all of which will, no doubt, be more or less interesting to the reader. We shall make such notes of explanation from time to time as we may deem pertinent and proper.

CHAPTER I.

A singular coincidence in the history of the "Christian Banner" is, that we suspended the publication of it the 9th of May, 1861, and resumed its publication on the 9th of May, 1862. The following is a short article which we published in the first number, after the arrival of the Federal troops in Fredericksburg:—

"CHRISTIAN BANNER.

"May 9, 1861, is the date of the last number of the 'Christian Banner' up to the present time. To-day,

May 9, 1862,—just one year to a day,—we again unfurl its sheet to the breeze. When we closed our office twelve months ago, the *secession flag*—the emblem of all *folly*—was waving over our city. To-day the *American flag*—the 'Stars and Stripes,' the proud emblem of a nation's greatness, the *flag* which our fathers won through blood and death, the *flag* which our fathers loved, the *flag* which all nations honor, the *flag* under which we were born and have lived forty-five years save one—now floats proudly over us. Long may it wave 'over the land of the free and the home of the brave!' May it wave over *us*, *our* children, *our* grandchildren, and great-great-grand-children, down to the latest posterity, till Gabriel's trump shall sound and *old* Time shall end! Then good-bye, *old time-honored flag!* heaven is a better place than America.

"We resume the publication of the 'Christian Banner' because we feel it our duty to do all the possible good we can for our country and fellow-citizens. If we can only accomplish a single *mite* of good, our reward will be sure. We resume its publication because there is no other paper now published in our town nor all the surrounding country. Washington City and Richmond are the nearest points to us where any paper is published. The community needs a paper. Whether the people will patronize the 'Banner' or not, we cannot tell. As we used to do in olden times, so shall we continue to do in the future; and that is, to write just as nearly what we please as circumstances will allow. One thing is *certain* and *unmistakable;* and that is, we shall exert our undivided and untiring influence and efforts to get our fellow-citizens to become *reconciled* and *return to the Union.* This is our *only* hope of any peace or happiness in the future.'

CHAPTER II.

"THE CRISIS ON US."

FOOLS belch out nonsense and play the part of furious braggarts, spurning the admonitions of the wise and prudent. The maddening storm gathers blackness and darkness, and the deafening thunders burst over their heads, and the vivid lightnings play at their feet, before they can see and feel the danger, or admit the propriety or necessity of seeking a place of refuge and security. Thus it is with thousands of poor deluded souls at the present time. The storm has been gathering for more than twelve long months, and the cry has constantly been, "There is no danger;" yet, when men dared to say that danger threatened them in the future, they were *spotted,* regarded as traitors, and *eyed* as *suspicious characters,* who "ought to be reported to the military authorities, arrested, and sent to Richmond to be tried, condemned, and executed for treason against the *Southern Confederacy.*" The leaders in this terrible revolution have cried, "Peace and safety," when sudden destruction was at our very doors. If the leaders in this awful tragedy have knowingly and wilfully deceived the people, then they merit the unmitigated *anathemas* of all heaven and earth, through all time and eternity; if they have done it ignorantly, then they should be held up as brainless objects of pity, scorn, and contempt, to the whole civilized world, as blazing beacons to all stupid, unprincipled, political adventurers through all coming time.

Who is so skeptical or stultified as to deny any longer the fact that the terribly awful anticipated crisis is actually upon us? Politicians *swindled* the people out of their rights, made *slaves* of them, and then promised to lead them to *independence, freedom, prosperity, glory, honor,* and *national immortality. Have they done it?* The wide world answers, *no!* Where is our *independence? freedom?* prosperity? glory? honor? national immortality? *Ay,* where are the brave, heroic leaders themselves? Politicians turned generals, and generals turned cowards, or have proven themselves totally incompetent to accomplish the mighty work they promised to perform.

Not a single promise which the politicians made to the people has been met. In the science of political manœuvring and swindling they were accomplished proficients, but when they girded on the sword and went out to battle they proved themselves the veriest of dolts. With but few exceptions, what have they done? They have fallen back from place to place, and made so many surrenders that there are now but few more important points in the whole "Southern Confederacy" to yield.

When our army fell back from Centreville and Fairfax Court-House to Manassas Junction, this was "a strategic move," indicating great military skill, to draw the enemy from his stronghold. And, subsequently, when it fell back from Manassas Junction to Rappahannock Station, this was another grand device of military strategy. "Our generals know what they are doing. All is safe in their hands." Again, when our army fell back from Evansport, and from the whole line of the Potomac, to Fredericksburg, this was another "brilliant move of military strategy." Here a bold stand was to be made, and Fredericksburg was to be defended to the very last and at all hazards. And, finally, on the ever-memorable morning of the 18th of April, 1862, when by military authority our bridges were burned, and the vessels of poor *seamen* were wrapped in flames, and the *brave, heroic general fled for his life,* carrying with him his whole army, leaving helpless citizens, unarmed men, defenceless women and children, to an unknown and uncared-for destiny, this was another magnificently grand, military "strategic move."

Great God! Are men to be always deluded in this manner, forever following an *ignis-fatuus*, to be dragged into the vortex of irretrievable ruin, and, as they plunge headlong into the black whirlpool of destruction unless they shout hosannas to the *demon phantom* which caused their ruin, a thousand voices exclaim, "They are traitors, madmen, and ought to be damned!"

Our generals have fled and carried the army with them; and by this act they declare that they could not protect us. If they could, why did they not stay and do it? They have left us to our own fate; and it now becomes us as, wise and prudent men, to act the part of freemen, and take care of ourselves as best we can.

CHAPTER III.

HEART-RENDING THOUGHT.

HUNDREDS of wives and thousands of children, whose husbands and fathers have been forced into the war, are left wholly dependent on their own exertions for the scanty means of a wretched existence. What must be the mental agonies of those husbands and fathers when they reflect on the helpless and unknown condition of their wives and dear little children, who are far away, and no possible chance of seeing them, it may be, until the war shall have ended, and perhaps never again in this life? And what must be the painful reflections of these wives and mothers when they think of their dear husbands, and with sorrowing hearts and weeping eyes gaze on their poor little children, the whole responsibility of whose subsistence depends upon them? Wives are left worse than widows, and children worse than orphans. Who but fathers and mothers can feel the deep, heart-felt afflictions of those parents who have sons far from home in the army, and—*poor boys!*—it may be are actually suffering for food and raiment, and may-be wounded, sick, dying, or dead, and no affectionate hand to administer relief in a dying hour, and not even a slab to tell the stranger who they *were*, or *where they lie?* And all this affliction and sorrow, pain and death, produced to gratify the unhallowed and wicked ambition of unprincipled, aspiring demagogues!

CHAPTER IV.

SECESSION LIKE THE DEVIL.

It is said that the devil was a liar from the beginning. If he were a liar from the beginning, he was a liar in the days of Jesus Christ, is a liar still, and will continue to be till the end of time. He lied to Eve in paradise, and she, influenced by his falsehood, sinned, and ruined the world. If the lies were all written in a book which the devil has told, the world itself would hardly be able to contain it. To say nothing more at present of the old devil, the father of lies, let us scan a few of the lies of the *secession devil.*

1. That the Federal Government could be broken up, the Union dissolved, the old United States divided and two separate Governments formed out of them, without war and bloodshed.

2. That if, by any possible chance, war should happen, it would commence between the Black Republicans and conservative men of the North, and would probably end there.

3. That New York, Pennsylvania, Rhode Island, and Delaware would certainly unite their destinies with the South.

4. That Maryland, Virginia, Kentucky, Tennessee, and Missouri were all bound to secede, and would certainly go with the Gulf States. This was a *fixed fact.*

5. That if, in the event of any possible contingency, there should be war, the South had men, munitions,

and ample means of all kinds to prosecute it to a successful and glorious issue.

6. That the North had neither fighting-men, money, nor means to commence and prosecute a war.

7. That cotton was king, his throne was in the Gulf States, his empire the world, and that all the *little* kings and queens of the earth were bound to fall down and worship him.

8. That the vexed question of African slavery would be hushed into eternal silence, and the institution of slavery settled upon a firm and immovable basis.

9. That slave territory would be enlarged, and slave property would advance one hundred per cent.

10. That England and France, and consequently all other civilized nations of the world, would certainly acknowledge the independence of the Southern Confederacy. This was, also, a *fixed fact,* bound to be done of necessity.

11. That England and France would certainly raise the blockade; their interest would compel them to do it.

12. That the Southern Confederacy would be the greatest Government in the world, and the citizens the most free, independent, wealthy, prosperous, and happy people on earth.

All these, and many others, were the promises secession made to the Southern people. That they are all false, needs no argument: developed facts prove them so. By these fair promises the people of the South were deceived. They were swindled out of all their rights, as the sequel of this mournful tragedy will prove. Yes! for less than one mess of pottage the whole South sold her birthright, has become bankrupt, and the whole people plunged into a sea of sorrow, affliction, and death, the breadth and depth of which none but the all-penetrating eye of Omniscience can ever fathom. And yet, because we will not fall down and worship this *demon-phantom*, we must be *spotted*, and by ignorant, bigoted partisans branded as an enemy and traitor to the South. We are no enemy of the South; we are no traitor to the South. No. We love the South, and always have loved her; and because we love and always have loved the South, *we always have, and do despise secession.*

We have always known, and ever maintained, that the only security the South and Southern institutions had, was contained in the provisions of the Federal Constitution. We are no traitor to the South. We indignantly spurn the base imputation, and pronounce it an unmitigated secession falsehood.

The traitors and enemies of the South are the secession leaders of the South. Where are the men who *fired up the Southern heart and precipitated* this once glorious, independent, prosperous, and happy country into the present terrible revolution? Yes: where are they? Are they in the camp, with their knapsacks on their backs and muskets on their shoulders? Are they found lying side-by-side with the poor privates on the cold, wet ground? Are they performing the duties of poor private soldiers, exposed to all the dangers of camp-life, for the pitiful sum of eleven dollars per month? No. Their patriotism never pointed in that direction. With all their boasted patriotism and love of the South, they never intended to make such sacrifices to save her. Where are they? We answer, in Senate, Congress, and legislative halls, decreeing conscription acts by which to force and drag men from their homes, from their wives and children, and drive them into camp to fight and die, while they themselves are living in magnificent splendor, enjoying all the luxuries of life, and wreathing their own brows with laurels which they vainly imagine will be as imperishable as the records of eternity.

Those men who affect to despise traitors, and are so very suspicious of the loyalty of others, take special good care to secure to *themselves*, their *children*, their *near relations* and *dear friends*, all the *fat* offices and honorable positions, both in the State and in the army.

They are so patriotic, and love themselves so well, that they wish to monopolize the whole, lest in the scuffle for the spoils—the loaves and fishes—others should get a part. This is the mathematical measurement, the length, breadth, depth, and height, of the patriotism of thousands who are so vociferous in exclaiming against the disloyalty of *true patriots, gentlemen,* and *Christians.*

Unprincipled politicians and ignorant, fanatical religionists, North and South, have caused all the sorrows, afflictions, and troubles of war which now fill the country. In the *Abolitionists* of the North and the *fire-eaters* of the South, extremes have met, and the work of ruin is done. *Abolitionism* and *secession combined* to effect the overthrow of our Government, the downfall of our country. Great God! what a fearful retribution awaits them in the awful future!

CHAPTER V.

WHY DETHRONE REASON?

Why is it that men will suffer passion and prejudice to dethrone reason? Let us consider for a moment our present deplorable condition. Our generals and army have left us to the mercy of chance. Congress have broken up in a state of terrified confusion, and have gone to seek their own safety far from the seat of war, on their cotton, sugar, and rice plantations; the citizens of Richmond have become panic-stricken, and are leaving the city; the military and civil authorities are making preparations to burn the tobacco and public stores of the army, which have not been and cannot be sent away. These are facts, we presume, which are questioned by no one.

Why is it that at this important crisis, when the lives of our dear sons and so many of our fellow-citizens are trembling on the very brink of eternity, the very men—the leaders in this awful tragedy—fly before the advancing enemy? Why do they not stand and face the danger? Because conscience has made cowards of them. They feel the guilt,—they dread the penalty,—and fly to save their own worthless carcasses from being captured. And yet our dear children, neighbors, and friends must stay, and fight and die to protect the persons and property of the guilty leaders who have fired up the Southern heart and inveigled them into ruin. Are parents willing to see their own dear children butchered and slaughtered like wild beasts of the field, to gratify the unhallowed ambition of cowards, tyrants, and traitors? Can and will freemen submit to such an outrage? *No:* surely they will not. Then let us *demand* our children; let us call them home, and let Jeff Davis and his *clique* go to the devil, where they ought to have been long ago.

Clique.—By *clique* we mean the Cabinet and the ringleaders who were associated with Jeff Davis in his conspiracy against the Republic. We guess thousands will wish he had been at the devil long before this war commenced, both before and after it shall have ended.

CHAPTER VI.

REFLECTIONS.

SADNESS fills our heart, and tear-drops fill our eyes, when we look back on the past, scan the present, and take a peep into the dark, mysterious future. Memory brings up all the hallowed associations of the past, and forces a contrast with the present, while sorrow fills the soul, and we are made to exclaim, "O God, what is man, that thou shouldst regard him, or the son of man, that thou shouldst visit him?"

But two years ago, what a happy people we were, in the full enjoyment of all blessings, earthly and divine, that an honest and grateful people could have desired. Our fields were everywhere cultivated, and yielded abundant harvest. Men were happy in the peaceful possession of their homes, their political, social, civil, and religious rights. Freedom of thought, freedom of speech, freedom of the press, and freedom of action were the pride and boast of every American citizen. Every man could think what he pleased, speak what he pleased, write what he pleased, do what he pleased, go where he pleased, and come when he pleased, and *no one dared* to oppose, unless he acted in violation of the civil laws of his country.

Families were happy. Husbands and wives, parents and children, brothers and sisters, were happy in their quiet, peaceful homes. Homesteads, churches, and the groves were vocal with the praises of God. The millennium, or a thousand years' reign of Christ upon the earth with the faithful, was strongly anticipated by many. A nation's heart beat with joy and gladness inexpressible. We *were* a happy people,—a nation blessed above all the nations of the earth. No, never, since God conducted his own chosen Israel into the land of Canaan, has any people or nation of the whole earth been blessed as have been the American people.

How changed are all things now! Many of our finest farms are uncultivated,—fences are destroyed, and the fields are made desolate and have become the camping-ground of soldiers. The *tap* of the drum, the martial music of bands, the tents of the warrior, now fall upon our ear and meet our eye at almost every point. Men fly from their homes as from deadly poison, leaving all their interests to chance and blind fatality. Political, social, civil, and religious rights are no longer respected. Freedom of opinion, speech, the press, and action is no longer the pride and boast of freemen. Men are now afraid to express their opinions, simply because they are no longer freemen. The freedom of speech, the freedom of the press, the freedom of action, are all suppressed; and men who once boasted of their freedom and bravery now quail and writhe under the lash of military despotism. How are the mighty fallen, and the strong made to tremble! This is no fiction. Stern realities stare us full in the face, and we must meet them, whether we wish to do so or not.

Families are no longer happy. Husbands are torn from their wives, fathers from their children, and sons from their fathers, mothers, brothers, sisters, and homes. The once peaceful, quiet, and happy homes of thousands are either forsaken and left desolate, or changed into habitations of weeping, mourning, and deep lamentation. The homesteads and churches of thousands, and the groves, are no longer vocal with the praises of God. The millennium, or reign of Christ a thousand years with his people on earth, is no longer immediately anticipated. A nation's heart is made to bleed.

CHAPTER VII.

A WORD OF ADMONITION TO THE CITIZENS OF FREDERICKSBURG.

THE pall of death seems to have fallen on our entire community, embracing all classes within its encircling folds. If the destroying angel had passed over our city and had smitten the first-born of every family, a more gloomy appearance of things could hardly be presented. Places of business, with few exceptions, are everywhere closed up, and men walk about the streets as if in constant expectation of hearing the last shrill note of Gabriel's awful trump. Many private residences are closed and forsaken, and families have deserted their quiet, peaceful homes, to become refugees and sufferers among strangers in other parts of our country.

Horticulture, to a great extent, is neglected; while all are reposing in a state of idleness and inexplicable suspense, wondering *when*, and *where*, and *how* the scene will end. An indescribable panic has seized all classes of our once brave, happy, industrious, and prosperous people. What *must* be the end of all this? There can be but one answer to this question if things continue thus, and that is, starvation and death will be the inevitable result.

Hence we would say to one and all of our fellow-citizens, go to work! Up and at it! Attend more strictly to business than ever, because there is greater need than there has ever been at any former period of our lives. What is the use for men to become disheartened, and give up the ghost, and die before the time comes? If men refuse to work, nothing can be produced; and if nothing be produced, people must starve.

Gazing at soldiers, listening to martial music, and following the army about will never make the "pot boil." The duty and business of soldiers is one thing, and the duty and business of citizens is another thing. Soldiers consume, and citizens produce; if, therefore, the citizens neglect to produce, both citizens and soldiers must ultimately starve. Soldiers, however, have this decided advantage over citizens: the former are fed and clothed from the public crib, while the latter have to look after their own food and raiment. Armies *must* and *will be* supported, provided the produce is to be had, and citizens can only get the excess after armies are supplied. This fact, of itself, is sufficient to rouse every one to action, and stimulate all to do their utmost. Then we would admonish all, old and young, male and female, high and low, rich and poor, bond and free, to go to work, and work for life, or famine and death will be the result.

CHAPTER VIII.

THE CONFEDERATE ARMY LEAVES FREDERICKSBURG.

ON the morning of the 18th of April, 1862, the Confederate Army evacuated the town of Fredericksburg, leaving the citizens to share whatever fate might chance to befall them. Never, perhaps, did any army leave a place with greater expedition than did our army leave the venerable old town of Fredericksburg. Before leaving, however, they set fire to Falmouth, Scott's, and the railroad bridges; also to the following vessels:—

Steamer *Virginia,* Captain Fairbank; steamer *Saint Nicholas,* Captain Lewis, of the Confederate Army; schooner *May,* owned by McConkey, Parr & Co., Baltimore City, Md., and *Henry Armstrong,* valued at

$4500; schooner *Ada*, owned by Samuel G. Miles, of Baltimore City, Md., valued at $3500; schooner *Northern Light*, Captain Thomas Pritchett, Lancaster county, Va., valued at $2000; *Reindeer*, Captain Job Moore, Middlesex county, Va., valued at $1500; *Decapolis*, Captain John Evans, Fredericksburg, Va., valued at $700; *Mary Pierce*, owned by R. W. Adams and L. B. Eddens, Fredericksburg, Va., valued at $5500; *Helen*, Captain Solomon Philips, Essex county, Va., valued at $2000; *William T. Valliant*, Captain B. George, Lancaster county, Va., valued at $1500; *Anglo-Saxon*, owned by Segar & Purkins, Middlesex county, Va., valued at $1600; *Dazzling Orb*, Captain A. Jenkins, Fredericksburg, Va., valued at $600; *Puteola*, owned by A. Williams and B. Walker, Lancaster county, Va., valued at $1500; *James Henry*, owned by Captains Mullin and Dickinson, Richmond county, Va., valued at $400; *J. Wagner*, Captain Toleman, Lancaster county, Va., valued at $2250; *Active*, Captain Henry Taylor, Richmond county, Va., valued at $2000; *Sea-Breeze*, owned by Miles, of Baltimore, Crabb & Scrimger, of Richmond county, Va., valued at $2000; *Mary Miller*, owned by C. Burgess, of Northumberland county, Va., and Miller, of Middlesex county, Va., valued at $4000; *Nancy Sprewell*, owned by E. Mann, of North Carolina, valued at $2500; *Lucy Penn*, owned by Seirs, of Gloucester county, Va., valued at $1600; *Hiawatha*, owned by Mr. Garland, Richmond county, Va., valued at $2500; sloop *Amethyst*, Captain Charles Gutridge, Fredericksburg, Va., valued at $900.

Including the value of the steamer *Virginia* and the *Saint Nicholas*, it will be discovered that more than one hundred and twenty-five thousand dollars' worth of vessels was destroyed, to say nothing about the vast amount of grain and other property consumed in them, all of which will, probably, prove in the end a total loss to the owners.

Admitting the fact that the burning of the bridges was "a military necessity,"—which we very much question,—we utterly ignore the idea that the burning of the vessels was; and, while *no good* to the Southern Confederacy, and but little if any injury to the enemy, could possibly result from an act so outrageously cruel, it has reduced at least some of the owners of the vessels to a state of almost total bankruptcy. Some of these men have labored and toiled for years, and by rigid economy had succeeded in accumulating sufficient amounts to purchase vessels, and their *all* of earthly goods was invested in them, and in a single hour they behold the hard earnings of many years reduced to ashes. What a pity! What a shame!

In connection with the burning of the bridges and vessels, we would state that from fifteen to twenty thousand dollars' worth of cotton was also burnt, which might have been saved, had not such a terrible panic seized the managers of the cars.

We witnessed the burning of the bridges and vessels, and, truly, the scene was one of melancholy sublimity. May we never again witness such reckless, wanton, wicked destruction of property! On the 18th day of April, 1861, the Virginia Convention passed the ordinance of secession, and on the 18th of April, 1862, the Federal authorities took possession of Fredericksburg.

CHAPTER IX.

FEDERAL TROOPS TAKE POSSESSION OF FREDERICKSBURG.

Pursuant to orders of Brigadier-General Patrick, on Wednesday, the 7th of May, 1862, the Southern Tier Rifles, 23d New York Volunteers, Colonel H. C. Hoffman commanding, took up its line of march from camp near Falmouth, for the occupation of Fredericksburg, arriving in the city at nine o'clock A.M. Such respectful regard was paid to the sensitiveness of the inhabitants of our town as to dispense with the martial music usual upon such occasions, the regiment marching silently to its quarters, with fine and soldierly bearing. Companies were immediately detailed and despatched to outposts guarding the various approaches to the town.

The officers of this regiment, field, staff, and line, are gentlemen of the highest respectability and of dignified and courteous demeanor; and such has been the respectful deportment of this entire command as to elicit the most unbounded admiration and confidence of all the inhabitants of our town.

By order of Colonel Hoffman, Sergeant-Major Devoe and Color-Corporal Crocker flung the time-honored flag—the good old "Stars and Stripes"—to the breeze at head-quarters, opposite the railroad-depot, immediately upon their occupation. This regiment, we learn, has been chosen for the occupation of the town on account of its high character for respectability and rigid discipline; and, from what we have seen, we are confident a more judicious selection could not be made. Witnessing, as we do, the preservation of all personal rights and privileges, the protection of private property, and the unrestricted conduct and continuance of the accustomed business pursuits and avocations of our citizens, we cannot but conclude that this war is waged by the General Government upon principles infinitely transcending in mercy and generous magnanimity all others which the world has ever known, and of which history affords no precedent or parallel.

CHAPTER X.

FEDERAL TROOPS LANDING ON THE WHARF OF FREDERICKSBURG.

THE Federal troops effected a landing on the wharf of Fredericksburg on Friday evening, the 2d day of May, 1862, exactly two weeks to a day from the evacuation of the town by the Confederate forces. The bridge of canal-boats being completed, Major-General King and staff, consisting of Captain Robinson, Lieutenants Wood and Benkardt, Brigadier-General Patrick and staff, crossed over the bridge from the Stafford to the Fredericksburg landing, and rode through the principal streets, taking a survey of matters and things in general, and of the good old town in particular. Immediately in rear of the generals, Company D, 23d Regiment New York Volunteers, Captain L. Todd,

Lieutenants Colby and Jones, crossed over and occupied the large warehouse of A. K. Phillips, Esq., after which pickets were immediately stationed at different points through the city.

CHAPTER XI.

In the number of the "Christian Banner" of May 17, 1862, we published the following editorials:—

"REBELLION AND STUBBORNNESS.

"Holy writ says, and says nothing more true, that 'Rebellion is as the sin of witchcraft, and stubbornness is as iniquity and idolatry.' Saint Paul says, 'Let every soul be subject unto the higher powers. For there is no power but of God; the powers that be are ordained of God. Whosoever, therefore, resisteth the power resisteth the ordinance of God; and they that resist shall receive to themselves damnation.'

"This is the language of inspiration. What does it mean? Let us see.

"Dr. MacKnight says, 'The government of every State, whether it be monarchical, aristocratical, democratical, or mixed, is as really of divine appointment as the government of the Jews was, though none but the Jewish form was of divine legislation. God having designed mankind to live in society, he has, by the frame of their nature, and by the reason of things, authorized government to be exercised in every country. At the same time, having appointed no particular form to any nation but to the Jews, nor named any particular person or family to exercise the power of government, he has left it to the people to choose what form is most agreeable to themselves, and to commit the exercise of the supreme power to what persons they think fit. And, therefore, whatever form of government hath been chosen or is established in any country hath the divine sanction; and the persons who, by the choice, or even by the peaceable submission, of the governed, have the reins of government in their hands, are the lawful sovereigns of that country, and have all the rights and prerogatives belonging to sovereignty vested in their persons.

"'Wherefore, since *the power* of which the apostle speaks is the form of government, and not the rulers of a country, the subjection to the higher powers enjoined is not an unlimited passive obedience to rulers in things sinful, but an obedience to the wholesome laws enacted for the good of the community by common consent, or by those who, according to the constitution of the State, have the power of enacting laws. To these good laws the people are to give obedience, without examining by what title the magistrates who execute these laws hold their power, and even without considering whether the religion professed by the magistrates be true or false. For the same reason, the opposition to and resistance of the power forbidden is an opposition to and resistance of the established government, by disobeying the wholesome laws of the State, or by attempting to overthrow the government, from a factious disposition, or from ill will to the persons in power, or from an ambitious desire to possess the government ourselves.'

"The Constitution of the Federal Government is one of the ablest documents in the world, and contains the purest and best form of government with which any people have ever been blessed since the direct legislation of Heaven over the Jews in the land of Canaan.

"By the wholesome provisions embraced in this Constitution, our fathers, grandfathers, great-grandfathers, and we, their descendants, have been and were protected in our persons, and rights of all kinds, and were prosperous and happy,—enjoying all the blessings heart could wish,—until an *ill-natured faction* attempted the overthrow of this Government.

"The idea that a set of ambitious, disappointed politicians could destroy the Constitution framed by the clearest heads and purest hearts the world has ever known since the days of the apostles of Jesus Christ, or make such improvements on it as virtually to annihilate it, is an instance of political egotism without a parallel in the history of the world. It is absolutely as ridiculous as if a school-boy, who has just learned to decline a *Greek noun* or to conjugate a *Latin verb*, should attempt to improve on the beauties and elegancies of Homer or Virgil. The effort was made, however, and the result has proven a failure,—the ruin of all!

"We say that a *faction* of ill-natured politicians attempted to *usurp* the reins of government,—resisting the constituted authorities both of God and the people, —and, having resisted, they 'shall receive to themselves damnation,' or destruction. Are they not already politically damned? When this war shall have ended, will there be a single prestige of their former glory? When thousands of women and millions of children shall wake up to the astonishing reality that they are widows and orphans, left homeless, penniless, friendless, and thrown upon the cold charity of a heartless, bankrupt country, and shall ask, Who and what did this? and the volume of history shall be unfolded to their astonished vision, then will the *anathemas* of millions be heaped upon the very names and ashes of the leaders in this horribly wicked revolution.

"A faction of politicians, whose *motto* was, *rule* or *ruin*, met in secret convention, concocted all their plans, determined at all hazards to carry them into effect, *created* and *signed* an ordinance of secession, and then told their people, and published to the world, that the State had seceded. And for what cause was all this done? 'Not because Abraham Lincoln was elected to the Presidency of the United States;' not because of the passage of the 'personal liberty bills.' No; but because they had desired, and had been endeavoring for more than thirty years, to overthrow the Federal Government,—to dissolve the blessed Union, cemented by the sweat and blood of our ancestors,—in order to establish a Government in harmony with their own ambitious views, and in which they could rule and govern.

"The border States were to be *dragged* into the same political whirlpool of destruction. How was this to be done? By political intrigue. By a right-down swindle. At least, this was the way Virginia was carried out of the Union. Let us see.

"The Legislature of Virginia called a convention. Union and secession candidates were brought out before the people. Union candidates were elected by an overwhelming majority. They were elected with the perfect understanding that they were to take into consideration the policy or impolicy of passing an ordinance of secession; and the final result of their deliberations was to be referred back to the people. That convention met in Richmond; and it is useless to say how long it remained in session before an ordinance of secession was passed. Every outside pressure possible was brought to bear upon it. The Legislature of Virginia was in session during the whole time; and, if not all, a large majority of the members of the Legislature were rampant secessionists. And, finally, a secret secession convention of *select, simon-pure* secessionists was called, with which the *people* of Virginia had nothing to do,—not being allowed even the privilege of knowing why and for what it was called. In the mean time, an orator from Virginia visited Charleston, South Carolina; and the object of that mission our readers must divine. Secessionists began to despair as to the result of the Virginia Convention. At length, however, the news flew over the telegraph-wires that Fort Sumter had fallen. Cannons were fired. Speeches were made all over the town. Loud huzzas rent the air, and the 'tiger groans,' like the hollow mutterings of *devils damned* coming up from the lowest depths of perdition, sounded the death-knell of Virginia in our ears. All was over. Now, any man who dared to speak a word in favor of the Union was a *black-hearted traitor to Virginia and the South,* a downright *Abolitionist,* a *Lincolnite,* and ought to be *driven* out of the country or *hung.*

"If our memory serves us correctly, the news of the downfall of Fort Sumter reached Fredericksburg on Saturday evening, the 13th of April, 1861; and on the following Tuesday, the 16th of April, 1861, the secret secession convention met in Richmond, and on Wednesday, the 17th of April, 1861, the Virginia Convention went into secret session, and on Thursday, the 18th of April, 1861, the Virginia Convention passed the ordinance of secession, which sealed the fate, the downfall, of the greatest State in the Union.

"The action of the convention was yet to come before the people. All were urged to go to the polls and vote, and present a bold front to the North, and thus prevent war and secure peace. Those who had been Union men, if they voted the secession ticket and professed conversion to the *glorious* doctrine of secession, were to be marked as hypocrites. If they remained at home and refused to vote, they were *traitors*, and should be *spotted; a seal* of *black reprobation* was to be *stamped* on them and on their children through all coming time. If they voted for the Union, they were Abolitionists, and ought to be driven out of Virginia, and out of the whole South, or hung with a 'grape-vine.'

"It was likewise urged that, because the vote in the convention was almost unanimous,—there being only an insignificant minority of about six or seven votes, four of whom voted against the ordinance, and one, perhaps, was sick, one or two being absent who would have voted for secession if they had been present,—therefore the entire people of the State ought, by all means, to vote for the ratification of the action of the convention. But when the injunction of secrecy was removed from the doings of that convention in June following, and the facts were developed, there were upwards of *forty-five* members who never did vote for the ordinance of secession at all. And yet we were told that it was almost a unanimous vote. This was a political swindle.

"Nor was this all. The convention, instead of adjourning and letting the people at once decide the question for themselves, sent Congressmen to Montgomery, Alabama, and *tied* Virginia on to the Southern Confederacy before the people of the State had voted on the question at all. This called forth the following remarks from our pen, which appeared in the 'Christian Banner' of May 2, 1861, next to the last number we published:—

"'Is it not an alarming usurpation of authority that the Virginia Convention should have appointed gentlemen to the Congress of the Confederate States at all? Was this the purpose for which the Virginia Convention was called? We did not so understand it. Is it not an alarming usurpation of power that the Virginia Convention should unite the destiny of the *Old Dominion* with the Confederate States of America, before the vote of the citizens of the State is taken on the question? Are a million of freemen to be bartered and sold, and handed over to other authorities without being consulted, and without their knowledge or consent, by a convention of men elected by the people to transact other and different matters? If we understood the subject, the convention was called together to decide on the policy of passing an ordinance of secession or non-secession; after which the action of the convention was to be referred back to the *sovereign people* for their ratification or rejection. The whole matter is prearranged and virtually *fixed*, and then the people are called on to vote on all the subjects together. If this be the beginning of our *new order* of things, what will the end be?'

"These are facts which every citizen of intelligence in this community knows to be true. And because we exposed the system of wicked swindling, the political cheat imposed upon the people, we were admonished to 'beware how and what we wrote.' We had been treated with indignity, and insulted beyond measure, more than a month before this, when, in justice to ourself and to the Union men in Fredericksburg, we spoke at a public meeting in the court-house, where a powerful effort was made to raise a mob and break up the meeting. The conduct of our opponents on that occasion beggars all description; and while we were addressing our fellow-citizens, and warning them of the awful dangers ahead if Virginia should secede, some one in the crowd threw an egg at us; but, knowing and feeling that we were pleading for the interest of our fellow-citizens and for the salvation of our country, we silently endured the insult, treating it with contempt. All this happened more than a month before Virginia seceded. In the mean time, before the day of election arrived, when the action of the convention was to come before the people for their approval or disapproval, thousands on thousands of troops from the seceded States came pouring into Virginia and were stationed in most of the cities and towns in the State. Fredericksburg was literally filled with them.

"The day of election came, and we had determined not to vote, nor go to the court-house at all. During the day, however, one of our prominent citizens, and an able *jurist,* called on us, and invited us out of our office, to tell us, frankly, candidly, and most sincerely as a *true friend*, that, unless we went and voted for the ratification of the action of the convention, our standing, influence, and all our prospects even for living in the community, were *blighted and blasted forever*, and we would be called a *traitor*, and a *tory*, and that in years to come it would be thrown up to our children, &c. &c., as it was in the old Revolutionary War; and therefore, 'for the sake of your churches, all of which are in the South,—for the sake of your friends, of whom you have many,—for the sake of your children, and children's children, in years to come,—and for your own sake, standing, and influence, and very existence, in Virginia and the South,' &c. &c.,—'go and vote.' Knowing that our vote could effect nothing either the one way or the other, so far as the destiny of Virginia was concerned, late in the evening we went to the court-house, and stated to the commissioners that we were no *convert to secession*, that we *despised secession*, but that we were in Virginia, and would go with Virginia, and that if they considered *this* a *vote* they could take it. Immediately they called out our name, and cried out, 'Ratification.'

"Since the day of election for the ratification of Virginia's secession, what have we either said or done to cause any one, however stupid, to think that we had changed our views on the subject of secession? Have we delivered any secession speeches? No. Have we prayed any secession prayers? God knows we have not! Have we argued the cause of secession? No. Have we asked for any office, or for *any situation of any kind*, in the Southern Confederacy? No, we have not. Have we not uniformly said to all persons, at all times, and in all places, at home and abroad, on the streets, in the stores, and everywhere and always, that we *despised* secession, and that because we felt a devotion for the South which no blind secessionist could feel, therefore we opposed secession?

"What have we done? We have been slanderously reported as having held secret Union meetings for the purpose of plotting treason against the Southern Confederacy. This is infamously false. We have been treated with indignity, and attempts have been made by certain characters to insult us, who were themselves beneath contempt. We have been meanly and basely slandered both at home and abroad, simply because we used our best efforts to save the South from ruin. And now we are threatened with a rope, if ever the time comes and an opportunity is offered.

"What have we done? We opened a private boarding-house last winter, as a matter of necessity, to keep from starvation. We treated the poor soldiers the very best we could: we did this because we were sorry for them; we did it for their sake,—for the sake of their parents and friends; we did it for the sake of their wives and children, many of them being men of families; we did it for the sake of humanity and our common Christianity; and we feel sorry that we were not able to do more for them and better by them than what we did. This is our inconsistency; this our disloyalty to the South; this our treason. This is what we have done.

"What has secession done for Virginia and the South? It has inaugurated civil war; it has filled the South with the wildest anarchy and confusion; it has desolated our cities, towns, and villages; it has laid waste the most beautiful, wealthy, and prosperous portions of our State; it has built hospitals, and filled them with the wounded, sick, and dying; it has made widows and orphans by hundreds of thousands; it has opened a fountain of sorrow, affliction, woe, and death without a parallel in the history of the world; it has reduced the wealthy to a state of comparative poverty, and made the poor still poorer; it has brought Canada not only to our doors, but into our very midst. The Confederate States seceded from the Union to 'get their rights,' and the negroes are seceding from their masters to 'enjoy their right,' and the desolating work of secession is still going on. We are doing what we can to arrest it in its onward and ruinous course.

"But 'rebellion is as the sin of witchcraft, and stubbornness is as iniquity and idolatry.' There are those who still seem determined to resist to their own ruin, and, if possible, to the ruin of all others. What, we ask, will life be worth after our dear children, our neighbors, friends, and relatives, are all killed, our country left in ruins, and all reduced to a state of want and abject poverty? Our fellow-citizens may scorn us, persecute us, and curse us now; but in after-years, when the whole affair shall have been wound up, and the great excitement of secession and war shall have passed away, and men shall begin to think, then a reaction will take place, and posterity will do us justice. May God, in his infinite mercy and eternal goodness, save us from these awful calamities, and that right early!

"We have written the above article, because we learn that it is being reported through town that, before the

Federals arrived in Fredericksburg, we were one of the most *rampant secessionists* in all the country, but that as soon as they came we turned right over to their side. This is the reason why we have stated in the above article some few of the many revolting facts and circumstances connected with the political swindle in forcing Virginia out of the Union. If we can secure paper and ink, by the help of God and our fellow-citizens, we shall write many things which we trust will be of service to the people. Read, and think!"

CHAPTER XII.

In the number of the "Christian Banner" of May 27, 1862, we published the following editorials:—

"SUBMISSION.

"This word *submission* has for nearly the last two years produced a greater terror over the Southern people than any other word to be found in the English language, or in any language in the world. *Submission!* Submission to whom? Submission to what? 'Submission to old Abe Lincoln!' 'Submission to Black Republican *rule!*' 'Submission to the Lincoln Government!'

"Argue rationally, logically, philosophically, and according to the plainest rules of common sense with secessionists, and the best and profoundest argument one will ever hear them advance to justify themselves in their reckless course of ruin is simply this:—'What!

submit to old Abe Lincoln?' 'Submit to be ruled and governed by an old Abolition rail-splitter!' 'Submit to Black Republican rule!' 'Never! never! never!' 'We'll die, every man of us, first.' This was an irrefragable argument. No one in all the schools of common-sense philosophy could be found wise enough to confute it.

"Who had to submit to Lincoln? What government had Lincoln? What power had he more than was guaranteed to him by the Constitution, as Chief Magistrate of the United States? None whatever. If all the States had remained quietly and peaceably in the Union, Lincoln could not have inaugurated a civil war upon the South. This was a constitutional impossibility. The Federal Government never inaugurated war upon the South. South Carolina and the seceded States inaugurated civil war upon the Federal Government, or upon the Government of the United States. This is a fact which will go down in history to the latest generation of American citizens.

"But let us examine and see *who are the submissionists*. The *people* of South Carolina *submitted* to Messrs. Rhett, Keitt, Boyce & Co. Mississippi submitted to South Carolina. Alabama submitted to South Carolina and Mississippi. Georgia and Florida submitted to these three, and Louisiana and Texas submitted to these five cotton States, making seven; and these seven cotton States seceded, not by the popular vote of the people of these States, but by conventions; and these several conventions appointed delegates to meet at Montgomery, Alabama, for the purpose of forming a 'Provisional Government;' and this convention nominated and elected Jeff Davis, of Mississippi, President, and Stephens, of Georgia, Vice-President. The *people* had to submit in silence to all this.

"This convention then set to work and mutilated the Constitution of the United States, and, with their *improvements, amendments,* and *mutilations,* called it the 'Constitution of the Confederate States of America,' and forced it upon the people of these several States, and they had to *submit.* Then this Montgomery Convention empowered the conventions of the seven revolted cotton States to appoint members to form a Congress for the purpose of enacting laws by which to move and work the grand machinery of this new order of things. All this was done independently of the popular voice of the people of these States. There was no *submission* in all this, was there? Were there no Union men in all these seven cotton States, while these things were being acted out? What did they do? What could they do but *submit* to the arbitrary will and yield submission to the military power of this *self-constituted body?*

"Has not Virginia yielded in humble *submission,* through the intrigue of her leaders, to the confederacy of the seven cotton States? Yes: through the treachery of her State Legislature and State Convention, Virginia was forced out of the Union on the 18th (as they say) of April, 1861, and was immediately *tied* on to the *seven cotton-States Confederacy,* and Richmond city, Virginia, was determined on as the capital of the Southern Confederacy, and Jeff Davis and his army were urged to hasten on to Richmond and into Virginia to act as a kind of terror to the 'Union-shriekers,' 'submissionists,' 'traitors,' and 'Black Republicans' of Virginia, on the day of voting for the ratification of the ordinance of secession, which took place on the 23d day of May, 1861, more than one month from the time of the passage of the ordinance of secession. And on the day of election, as we have stated in our editorials of a former number of the 'Banner,' all the principal cities, towns, and villages in Virginia were literally filled with soldiers. And not only so, but civil war was inaugurated in Virginia before the day of election for the ratification or non-ratification of the acts of the convention. Gosport Navy-Yard was seized, and the Arsenal at Harper's Ferry was burned, before the day of election. All this was planned and executed for the purpose of forcing Virginia into *submission* to *secession rule, intrigue,* and *treachery.* So that at least a majority of some sixty or seventy thousand voters in the State of Virginia had at last to bow at the *point* of the *bayonet* in humble *submission* to the will, purpose, determination, and domination of a few leaders in the cotton States, 'away down South in Dixie.'

"This is submission, with a tyrant's rod and a vengeance. And all who were opposed to secession have been forced to *submit,* because a military despotism has been hanging over them ever since; and this is *freedom,* —*independence!*

"*Submission!* Are not the very men who indignantly spurned the idea of submission to the constituted authorities of their country now submitting to the greatest imaginable indignities from their own servants? Masters have set the ungodly example of non-submission to the 'higher powers, that be ordained of God,' and their servants have caught the *cue,* and swear that they will no longer *submit* to the *rule* of their masters. Why do masters submit to the reckless insubordination of their slaves? For the same reason that Union men, twelve months ago, had to submit to the will and dictation of secessionists:—simply because they can't help themselves; and hence anarchy reigns rampant everywhere, and among all classes, all over the country. Great God! to what a *queer* state of affairs our country is reduced. Secessionists will not submit to be governed by the 'Constitution of the United States,' and Union men will not submit to be governed by the Constitution of the 'Confederate States;' and servants refuse to be governed by the legal authority of their masters. Indeed, this is a terrible state of insubordination. We knew from the beginning that secession would inevitably produce this state of things; and therefore we opposed it. And because we did and do oppose it, we are branded as an enemy to the South. How blindly, how wickedly false!

"In proof that Virginia was forced out of the Union by the acts of the civil and military leaders of secession, we need no stronger evidence than the suppression of the publication of the popular vote of the citizens of Virginia. Who can tell the number of votes actually polled by citizens of Virginia for the ratification of the ordinance of secession? This is a question of grave importance, which we submit to the leading secessionists of Virginia. Still, the people must submit. *This is submission.*

"Nor is this all. When the people of Virginia were called upon, this spring, to go into a *mock-election* for a President of the Southern Confederacy, they were told that it would be bad policy to have two candidates in this early stage of our Government, and, moreover, that war-times was no time to be discussing politics, and therefore all the voters of Virginia ought to go to the polls and vote for Jeff Davis. Who can tell what was the number of votes polled? The people of Virginia ought to know this. We were urged to go to the polls and vote; but we did not. Why should we? Had there been but ten votes cast in the whole State, or in the whole South, Jeff Davis would still have remained President of the Southern Confederacy.

"Virginians have to submit to all these things, and a thousand more, and that in silence, or be threatened with a drawn halter around their necks. This is submission to the *one-man power*,—the submission of whole States to a few contemptible, petty, tyrannical traitors. Yes, these secessionists won't submit to the regular, constituted authorities of their country, but they pompously and arrogantly dictate to others; and, unless all others bow in humble submission to them, they are to be hung, shot, quartered, tarred and feathered, and banished from their country. Good Lord deliver us!

"Once more. When the militia were called out, this spring, it is well known that they were unwilling to go into service, and, the Confederate Government fearing the consequences, Congress passed an act of *conscription*, by which they were all *forced* into service, except a few, who so managed their cards as to elude the clutches of the military bands that were sent prowling through the country to catch them up and hurry them into the army. There was no submission in this, was there? Yes, submission of the most oppressive and aggravating character!—submission to a military despotism!—submission, not to the Constitution of the United States, but *to secession.*

"Is it not strange that men will croak and croak about submission, and the degradation of submission, while they themselves are trying to browbeat and force all others to submit to their own lordly dictations, and while at the same time they are themselves submitting to the disobedience and insubordination of their own negroes? We say that Virginians have submitted long enough to the oppression and tyranny of petty despots, and it is now time for men who wish to be free to rise up and assert and maintain their rights.

"If the citizens of Virginia were unanimously in favor of secession, why do they go into the army with so much reluctance? If every Southern man is to be left dead on the battle-field unless the South obtain her independence, why is it that so many Southern men had to be forced into service by an act of conscription? And why is it that so many desert from the army? And why is it that men will lie in the woods day and night, and for weeks, to keep from being picked up by these military man-hunters and murderers? These are questions and facts which should be duly considered by the people of Virginia.

"And, finally, suppose the South should gain her independence: what will become of the poor old desolated Dominion, Virginia? Her sons dead, her territory laid waste, her cities, towns, and villages demolished, the navigation of her rivers obstructed, her vessels all burned and destroyed, her horses and stock of all kinds used up, killed up, and taken away, her farms left barren, her schools and colleges all broken up, her negroes all gone, her citizens all in debt, the whole State bankrupt,—all, all left in one common wreck and ruin! We would earnestly beseech and entreat our fellow-citizens to look into and think seriously on this terribly black picture before all is lost, and lost forever."

CHAPTER XIII.

In the number of the "Christian Banner" of May 27, 1862, we published the following editorial:—

"THREE UNION PRISONERS HUNG IN RICHMOND.

"We clip the following paragraph from an exchange:— 'Two weeks ago Jeff Davis had seven hundred and fifty loyal citizens of Virginia in his Castle Godwin and Carey Street prisons, in Richmond. Every hour was adding to the number, as it was but necessary for one to express a doubt of the immaculateness of the Confederate Government to be denounced, arrested, and sent down to Richmond. Three of these prisoners were recently taken out and hung without judge or jury.'

"The above may all be true, or it may not. There may be seven hundred and fifty loyal citizens of Virginia in prison in Richmond, or there may not. Three may have been hung without judge or jury, or they may not. Be all this as it may, we are convinced that many of the so-called friends of the Southern Confederacy have done great injury to the success of the Southern cause.

"It is, and has been, very annoying to gentlemen, good and loyal citizens, to have a set of brainless, irresponsible, worthless, wicked, lying men, and a class of God-forsaken old *viragoes*, tattling, lying, and misrepresenting them to strangers at every corner of the streets and in every circle into which their low position in society may admit them. That this has been the case is well known to many of the citizens in this town and in the surrounding country. And men, too, are engaged in this low, dirty, slanderous work, who boast of being the noble ones whose

> 'ancient though ignoble blood
> Has crept through scoundrels ever since the flood.'

Yes, these men have acted well their part in this infamous game of persecuting, proscribing, and ostracizing good and loyal citizens of Virginia.

"For example: who were the accusers of Major Charles Williams? Who were the judges by whom he was condemned? What was the crime of which he was accused? What was the magnitude of his guilt? Why do not his accusers come out openly and let the world know all about it? It is high treason for one to condemn secession: it is a crime for which he must be adjudged to imprisonment for months, and, may-be, for years. But it is no harm for a man to abuse and curse the purest form of human government the world has ever known. It is no harm to rise up against the regularly-constituted authorities of one's country and seek to overturn the Government which has protected him and all his sacred rights from his cradle to the present time. No: this is patriotic, this is secession-patriotism!

"To roam the country over and drag poor hard-working laborers out of their beds and tear them away from their heart-broken wives and helpless children at the dark and lonely hours of midnight, is manly, heroic, patriotic; and for such deeds of chivalry, another and another degree of knighthood should be conferred upon the worthless names of the cowardly, unprincipled scoundrels engaged in this fiendish work.

"Terrible threats have been and are constantly being made against some of the purest men and truest friends of the South that can be found in all our country.

"They are to be hung, shot, quartered, or forever banished from their homes and country, and infamy, lasting as time and eternity, is to be stamped on them and their children if secession succeeds and the Southern Confederacy triumphs.

"Suppose, however, that secession should fail, and all the States are at last forced to let the 'Stars and Stripes' float over them: what then will become of our persecutors? As we hope to obtain mercy, we will show mercy to them on the condition that they will never again try to overturn the Government of our country to establish little petty monarchies for themselves and their children. The wicked leaders ought to be punished commensurately with their crimes, and the common masses, who were ignorantly drawn into this awful sink of treason by the cunning of their leaders, should, upon true repentance and returning to their loyalty, be pardoned. This would be magnanimous, patriotic, Christian."

CHAPTER XIV.

In the number of the "Christian Banner" of May 27, 1862, we published the following editorials:—

"CORRECTION.

"Our attention has been called to an article in the 'New York Tribune,' in which the correspondent says, 'The Christian Banner' was suppressed *by order* of Jeff Davis. The editor's life has been threatened, *and his property destroyed.*

"We have italicized the words 'by order of Jeff Davis,' and 'his property destroyed,' because they were underscored when the paper was sent to us. We did not discontinue the publication of the 'Christian Banner' 'by order of Jeff Davis.' Had we continued to advocate the Union longer than we did, an *armed mob* would have suppressed it. This we knew, and of this we were admonished frequently and long before we did discontinue its publication. 'And his property destroyed.' Our property was not destroyed directly; our business, it is true, was all broken up, and we shall lose the most of our hard earnings for the last several years; yet our property was not destroyed by order of Jeff Davis.

"We make this correction, because we would not do injustice, if we knew it, to any human being on earth, not even to the devil himself, nor yet to the hideous monster secession.

"Secession is the concentration of *all curses*, social, civil, political, and religious. That we have been under the *ban* of secession proscription for the last twelve months is a well-known fact. That our *arrest* has been threatened time and again, we presume none will deny. That our *life* has been and still is *threatened*, is a fact equally well known. And what is our offence? Simply that we *love* the *South* and *hate secession*, and expose the villanies of the political scoundrels who have forced secession, with all its concomitant evils and horrors, upon us. Men may threaten our life now, and thirst for our blood, and talk of driving us and all other Union men out of Virginia and out of the whole South; but they had better look into the future a little; for in less time than *five* years *secession* will *stink* in the very nostrils of Virginians, and the leaders who have forced it upon us will receive the execrations of all good and intelligent citizens."

CHAPTER XV.

PRESIDENT LINCOLN AND HON. E. M. STANTON VISIT FREDERICKSBURG.

In the number of the "Christian Banner" of May 27, 1862, we published the following editorial:—

"President Lincoln and Hon. Edwin M. Stanton, Secretary of War, visited Fredericksburg on last Friday, the 23d instant (May). They rode in a carriage drawn by four fine iron-gray horses. They crossed the Rappahannock River on the canal-boat bridge, and passed up Princess Anne Street to the Farmer's Bank, the head-quarters of General Patrick, where the carriage stopped about five minutes, and then moved off, as we were informed, to visit some camp of soldiers out of the town. A large escort accompanied the distinguished visitors. There were no demonstrations of joy, however, from any of the citizens. If they were met by the Honorable Mayor and Common Council, we have not learned the fact.

"Last winter Jeff Davis, President of the Southern Confederacy, visited Fredericksburg, and but few demonstrations of joy were manifested on the occasion. The citizens of Fredericksburg seem to have very little partiality for Presidents. Thus pass away the glories of this world. On the 23d day of May, 1861, Virginia is said to have seceded; on the 23d day of May, 1862, President Lincoln visited Fredericksburg."

CHAPTER XVI.

In the number of the "Christian Banner" of May 20, 1862, we published the following editorial:—

"VIRGINIA THE BATTLE-FIELD.

"Is it not strange that Virginians are so totally blinded to their own interests as to have suffered themselves to be imposed upon as they have been by the shrewd political leaders of the Gulf States? Before this war commenced, we predicted that Virginia would be the great battle-field of this wicked revolution, and repeatedly said that, if the Gulf States had been geographically located as Virginia was, they would never have seceded. The people of the Gulf States knew that Virginia and all the *border States* would be a *bastion*, a mighty bulwark of defence, between themselves and the enemy. They had never supposed that the war would be carried into their own territories. No: this was not their calculation.

"When the Southern soldiers came into Virginia and to Fredericksburg last spring, twelve months ago, they said that they had come to defend the soil of Virginia. This we regarded as an insult to the intelligence of Virginians,—a solemn mockery. They came to meet the enemy on Virginia soil, to keep him off their own soil and out of their own territories. This we knew, and the leaders of this revolution in the cotton and sugar States knew the same thing; and yet it was considered treasonable for any one openly to express such an opinion. Let any one now take a calm survey of the territorial boundaries of Virginia, and then say that our predictions were not correct to the very letter!

"At least two-thirds of her beautiful territory are in the actual possession of the Federal Government, while the small portion of Eastern Virginia which is not yet invaded, and in the centre of which stand the capital of the State and the capital of the Confederate States, is completely *environed*, pent up between two powerful armies advancing on each other, and still there are those in our midst, professing to be wise, who say, 'We'll whip them off of every inch of Virginia soil, and make them *rue* the day they ever set their feet upon it.'

"If there were the shade of the shadow of a reason for such a conclusion as this, then these persons might talk and be listened to, and be respected by men of common sense. But, when we take into consideration the fact that the whole of the *border* of Eastern Virginia from the mountains to the Chesapeake Bay and round to Suffolk, including the cities and towns of Norfolk, Portsmouth, Williamsburg, Yorktown, Hampton, Fortress Monroe, Alexandria, Fredericksburg, and Suffolk, (to say nothing of Winchester, and the whole territory of Northwestern and the mountain-regions of Virginia,) are all in the actual possession of the. Federal army, what foundation is there upon which any *sane* man can possibly build the shadow of a hope for the retaking, reholding, and repossessing 'every inch of Virginia territory'?

"It was confidently affirmed by the professedly *knowing ones* in our community, until within a few weeks, that the Federal army *never* would nor could get into Fredericksburg; and, if men dared to express a contrary opinion, they were *ruled* out of *treasonable* and '*decent* society,' as traitors, Abolitionists, and black-hearted submissionists.

"We have always argued that it is much easier to keep an armed enemy out of our house, than to give him possession and afterwards whip him out and keep him out. Twelve months ago, the Confederate army was fresh and buoyant with the hope of driving *submissionists* and all Yankees out of Virginia and of keeping them off her territory. If the Southern army, with Beauregard, Lee, Johnson, Floyd, Wise, and a host of others to lead it on, with all their munitions of war, commissary stores, strong fortifications, railroads, &c. &c., were not able to keep the enemy from advancing into the interior of our State, how can they expect, or even hope, now, since they have destroyed railroads, burned railroad-bridges, demolished towns, committed to the flames millions of dollars' worth of commissary stores, spiked and abandoned hundreds of their best and largest cannons, evacuated and forsaken their strong fortifications, committed to the flames millions of dollars' worth of cotton, and wellnigh all their navy, and, finally, with an army of *conscript* soldiers, to drive the Federal troops off every inch of Virginia territory, retake, repossess, and rehold it? The idea is absurd! And when we try to get our fellow-citizens to reason on the subject, and lay facts before them which are as plain as Heaven's own light, we are insulted and treated with the utmost indignity and contempt.

"With what heart can men fight who have been *forced*, literally *dragged* from their business, their homes, their wives and children, their fathers and mothers, their brothers and sisters, their friends, and all that is dear to them, to go away down South to fight and to defend the negroes and cotton and sugar plantations of those wicked politicians who have forced this common ruin upon us all, while they themselves are living at their ease, rolling in splendor and luxury at home, and would consider themselves degraded by association with the poor soldier with his knapsack on his back and his musket on his shoulder, and would scorn to permit him to sit and eat at their elegantly-furnished and sumptuous tables?

"Think of the many precious lives that have been lost in Western Virginia, on the plains of Manassas, at Yorktown, at Williamsburg; think of the bloody battle that is to be fought near Richmond, together with the great anticipated battle or battles that will take place in a few days at some point between Fredericksburg and Richmond. (This battle was fought in Culpepper county, and at Bull Run, or in that vicinity.) How many precious, undying souls are to be dashed in a moment into eternity, and perhaps without any preparation to meet their final Judge! And, still, preachers, and communicants at the altar of the peaceful Jesus, parents, fathers and mothers, wives, brothers and sisters, condemn the man who dares to expose the wickedness of the leaders and tries to save their husbands and sons from ruin. The Lord have mercy upon the wicked stupidity of mortals!

"'Tis strange that things are so; but so they are, and it seems that there are certain cliques and parties which are determined that things shall thus go on, until our whole State is desolated and our children and friends are all sacrificed.

"Look at the desolation of all the counties between the Rappahannock and Potomac Rivers,—at the condition of the country from Hampton to Richmond,—at the condition of the country from Fredericksburg to the Blue Ridge; and what will be the condition of the country from Fredericksburg to Richmond, when this war shall have closed? Desolation and one common ruin meet the eye of the beholder at every point. Nevertheless, in the face of all these facts, there are those who talk and enter into wild speculations as to the course to be pursued, and what *must* be done, and what *shall* be done; and, unless all others submit to their dictations and mandates, they are ruled out as traitors, Abolitionists, *submissionists*, and are marked, spotted, proscribed, ostracized, as men who ought to be driven out of the country, or hung, and who will be, when the time comes.

"In conclusion, we venture the prediction *that every foot of territory embraced within the boundary-lines of Virginia when she seceded will again be brought back into the Union.*

"This is only a question of time. Mark the prediction!"

CHAPTER XVII.

In the number of the "Christian Banner" of May 31, 1862, we published the following editorial:—

"AFRICAN SLAVERY.

"The fact can be no longer disguised: let this war result as it may, African slavery in Virginia is already virtually swept from her territory. If she would lay down her arms and return to the Union, her citizens might receive some remuneration for their servants from the Government, if the State would adopt a system of gradual emancipation. But, unless this action is taken by Virginia, and that speedily, the slave population of the State will, in a few years, under the most favorable circumstances which can possibly be conceived, all be free. It requires no prophetic eye to see that this will be inevitable.

30

"In fact, if the war should continue in Virginia twelve months or two years longer, there will be scarcely a slave in the whole State. Nor is this all. There will be but very few of the sons of Virginia left, to read and relate the history of her woes, after the war shall have closed.

"Is it possible that Virginians are so utterly blinded and prejudiced as to be willing to sacrifice their children, their whole State, and every thing that is near and dear to a true patriot, for no holier purpose than to try to establish a *negro-oligarchy* in the Gulf States? And are the poorer classes of the people so profoundly ignorant as not to see that the establishment of such a government would inevitably and forever seal their own religious, social, and political degradation?

"Great God! What *white* man, what freeman, what American citizen, can tamely, meanly, and cowardly submit to become the dupe of a system so shockingly revolting to all the finer and nobler instincts of free-born American citizens?

"We are sorry that matters are brought to this issue. But we faithfully warned our fellow-citizens of the fearful results of secession, and they laughed at our admonitions, and classed us with Abolitionists, *submissionists*, and traitors. We now solemnly ask the question, who are right in this matter? Secessionists said that *secession* would establish African slavery on a sure and immovable foundation,—that slave property in Virginia would advance at least one hundred per cent. We said that the day Virginia seceded, slavery in Virginia was virtually abolished. Let facts decide who were and are the true friends of Virginia and the South,—secessionists, or the 'Christian Banner' and the Union men of the South. And still, with all these facts staring them full in the face, men affect to treat us with scorn and contempt, and threaten us with terrible punishment, simply because we tried to save them from ruin, and because they have lived to prove themselves false prophets and the scourge of Virginia and the whole South.

"The idea that the owners will receive pay for all their servants who make their escape from the seceded States during the war, is supremely absurd. Who will pay for them? The Federal Government? Not one dollar! The Southern Confederacy? This is absurd. The fact is, those who have lost or who may hereafter lose their servants may just prepare themselves for the very worst."

CHAPTER XVIII.

In the number of the "Christian Banner" of June 7, 1862, we published the following editorials:—

"COERCION.

"When the secessionists commenced their wild career of madness, they most solemnly protested against the principle of coercion. They affected to deeply deplore the breaking up of the country and the downfall of our Government, but most earnestly and constantly deprecated coercion. No sooner was it ascertained, however, that forty-five counties in Western Virginia had determined to remain in the Union, than secessionists ignored their own doctrine, and resolved to *coerce* these counties out of the Union and force them into the Southern Confederacy. Generals Lee, Floyd, Wise, and others were sent to *coerce* them into submission to the Confederate Government; with what success, however, is well known to the American people.

"If South Carolina, or *seven* States, had the legitimate right to secede from the Federal Government, contrary to the wishes and interests of all the other States in the Union, by a parity of reasoning, had not the counties in Western Virginia the legitimate right to secede from the remaining portion of the territory of Virginia? The Federal Government is composed of all the States and Territories in the Union, and Virginia is composed of all the counties embraced within her geographical boundaries; hence, if one State or seven States had the constitutional right unconditionally to secede from the Federal Government, any one county or any number of counties in any State has the constitutional right unconditionally to secede from that State.

"The example being set, and the precedent approved and established, the whole country at once becomes disintegrated, and the Southern Confederacy has not the shadow of security for her permanency and duration, even if she should gain her independence. The only homogeneous institution existing in Virginia and the Gulf States calculated to bind and keep them together is the institution of African slavery. That Virginia will sooner or later become a free State cannot certainly be any longer questioned by any one capable of observation and reasoning upon the plainest common-sense principles. Facts are now constantly being developed which must convince the most obtuse and prejudiced mind that Virginia will certainly become a free State.

"Secession was the death-stroke to slavery in Virginia; and men may bite their lips and make their threats, and abuse Union men, as they may, they can never make the world believe but what they themselves have brought the ruin upon their own heads. They have done it. Every cause must and will produce its legitimate effect. Secession produced revolution and civil war; and revolution and civil war will produce the abolition of African slavery at least, and certainly, in Virginia, and we confidently believe that it will finally produce it throughout the whole South. It may exist nominally in the Gulf States for a number of years, but the end must and will come. This by the way.

"Did not secessionists ignore their own principles when they tried to force their army into the State of Maryland for the avowed purpose of coercing her out of the Union and of forcing her into the Southern Confederacy? Did they not ignore their own principles when they tried to coerce Kentucky and Missouri out of the Union, and actually declared to the world that both these States had seceded and had joined the Southern Confederacy? Strange consistency! No, reader: the fact is this.

"A party of leaders seize the public arms and arm themselves to the very teeth, and, thus armed, force or coerce the unarmed masses of the people to submit to their lordly behests. And when the properly-constituted authorities of the country attempt to carry out the laws, according to the Constitution and according to their sworn obligations, these leaders raise the

30*

hue and cry, 'There must be no coercion:' when to force or coerce all others is the constant, systematic labor and course of their lives. Secession leaders are the men who inaugurated the system of coercion, and they are determined to keep it up until they coerce and force out and kill out every poor man in the Southern Confederacy, to save themselves from infamy and death."

CHAPTER XIX.

"COLORED POPULATION OF FREDERICKSBURG.

"THE colored population of Fredericksburg for the most part are strolling about town, looking on at the wonders of creation, careless and indifferent as to the future, and seem to be perfectly happy. We learn that some of them who have left their owners have rented rooms and set up for themselves. Being set free, as they think, they are going to get rich and grow fat. Deplorable state of anarchy and confusion!

"What a contrast, between the feelings of the colored and white population of Fredericksburg!—the former, to all human appearance, perfectly happy; the latter with painful, bleeding hearts, with all the anxiety and deep-toned feelings that can possibly press upon the hearts of parents, wives, children, brothers, sisters, relatives, and friends crushed to earth. Terrible thought!—our country ruined, our children, relatives, and friends butchered and slaughtered up worse than beeves in a slaughter-pen, and all on account of the negroes! Yes, all on account of the negroes. This is a fact. God Almighty knows it, and the world knows it. Can it be possible that men are willing to sacrifice their country, their children, and all earthly happiness for the negro? Oh, what blindness! what madness!"—*Christian Banner, June* 7, 1862.

CHAPTER XX.

In the number of the "Christian Banner" of June 14, 1862, we published the following editorials:—

"NEGRO LOYALTY.

"The stampede of contrabands continues unabated. On Sunday, Monday, and Tuesday last we suppose that hundreds came into town seeking the land of freedom. Curiosity induced us to ask some of them from what sections they came, to whom they belonged, for what cause they had left their masters, where they purposed going, and what they intended to do. Some had come from Caroline county, some from Spottsylvania, others from Louisa, &c. &c. Some had 'bad masters,' others 'wanted to be free,' and one woman said she had left her master 'to get *shet* of trouble.' Some were going to the 'Norf,' and others wanted to see their 'kinsfolks in town,' while others wanted 'to get work anywhere' they could. And here they are, strolling through the town and country, unprotected, uncared for, homeless, penniless, and friendless, not knowing where to go, what to do, nor what is to become of them.

"Before Virginia seceded, and for some time afterwards, the impression seemed to be general and popular among secessionists that the negroes would all prove loyal, that they would take up arms, and, if necessary, die for their masters; that the slave-population of the South was one great and reliable element by which the Southern Confederacy was to prove successful.

"We never had any confidence in the loyalty of negroes to their masters, as a general rule. There may be a few isolated exceptions, but in the winding up of this war it will be found that these exceptions are few and far between. We faithfully and constantly warned our fellow-citizens of the danger and certainty of bringing Canada not only to our doors, but into our very midst. Secessionists laughed at our admonitions, and reproached us as being one of the crazy ones of the Lincolnite submissionists who left 'their slime behind them as they walk the streets of Fredericksburg.' They foolishly talked of the law of retaliation; that 'if the Yankees take our negroes we will take their horses, cows, and hogs,' &c. &c. Such were the absurd ideas of oratorical, logical, philosophical secessionists.

"We went further still, and warned our fellow-citizens that, if matters were carried to extremes, the black man would lift his arm against the white man, and that the time would come when the farther white men could get from the negroes the safer and better they would feel. We warned secessionists of all these and many other evils which would necessarily result from their course of action, for all which we received nothing in return from them but continual reproaches.

"And now we warn our fellow-citizens of greater evils than any that have yet befallen us, and would implore them, for their own sakes, and for the sake of helpless women and children, who in many instances, and especially in the country, are entirely unprotected, to act with all the wisdom, prudence, and discretion of which they are possibly capable. Will they do so, or will they not? Stubbornness, rashness, and madness can effect nothing now but one common slaughter. Facts and circumstances which occur every hour in our midst must certainly convince all of the utter disloyalty of the slave population of our country. Let us, therefore, *beware* as to the future. A word to the wise is sufficient; but fools can never be profited but by the bitterest experience. The loss of the value in property of the negroes is nothing in comparison to the horrible evils which may yet visit our distressed countrymen. *Beware! Beware!*"

CHAPTER XXI.

"THEN AND NOW.

"EIGHTEEN months ago the leaders of secession strained every nerve, and moved every power of earth of which they were capable, to carry out their deep-laid plans of treason against the *South* and the Federal Government. Vociferous orators, of whom there were many and of various intellectual gradations, foamed, raved, and ranted, denouncing the 'Flag' of the Union as an execrated thing, only fit to trail in the dust and to be trampled under foot, swearing that the accursed thing should never wave over them again, and that unless Virginia seceded there would be a great stampede of her noblest sons down South; that they would never live under the Lincoln Government; that they would 'root for their living among the rocks and dens and caverns of the mountains and woods,' before they would ever submit to 'Black Republican rule;' they would 'face the cannon's mouth, and wade in blood up to their necks;' Jeff Davis was their President, around his standard they would rally, and under his banner they would march. The 'Flag' of the Union, the Constitution, the incoming Administration, and the Federal Government, were constantly and most unqualifiedly denounced in the strongest possible terms by them. They denounced men who advocated the cause of the Union as traitors to the South,—Black Republicans, cowardly submissionists, mean Abolition Lincolnites, who left their 'slime behind them as they walked the streets of Fredericksburg.' They resorted to every measure of political *Jesuitism* to inveigle everybody into the secession noose, knowing that if they could once get them committed they could easily produce strangulation and choke them politically to death. These are facts, and the people in this community know them to be facts, and we suppose that no one is reckless enough to deny them. This is the way things were *then.*

"*Now* we are told that Fredericksburg is a unit on the odious doctrine or *idea* of secession; that there *may* be a *few Union-shriekers,* but they are men of no reputation, having no standing in the community; that they are the very dregs of society, and therefore are not worthy of being considered as any opposition whatever to the secession party.

"By these means the rampant secessionists are trying *now* to brow-beat and keep the friends of the Union in *servile* subjection to themselves and to their influence. Threats are being made of driving Union men out of town, of hanging them, shooting them, &c. &c., when the Confederate army returns to Fredericksburg. In this way, 'we, the nobility,' expect to keep down, smother, and crush out the *latent* Union feeling that is still smouldering in the bosoms of the true, patriotic, Union men of Fredericksburg.

"Will freemen ignobly submit to such vile aspersions, insults, and indignities from men who can claim no higher superiority over them than that they possess a larger number of negroes, finer dwelling-houses, and more acres of land? Will freemen *forever cower* before a *negro-aristocracy?* Will they always succumb to the *winks* and *blinks* of a set of designing, unprincipled, political pettifoggers? Will *freemen* forever remain in a state of passive obedience to the *will* and *dictates* of a set of old, broken-down, aristocratic fogies? We trust in God that the time will come, and is not far distant, when *respectability* and *position* in society will not be based upon *negroism,* but upon *true merit and genuine worth.*"—*Christian Banner, June* 14, 1862.

CHAPTER XXII.

"THE GREAT BATTLES NEAR RICHMOND.

"According to all accounts received of the great battles near Richmond, Va., on the 1st, 2d, &c. instant, the carnage was great and the loss of life was terrible on both sides. The most fertile imagination can never fully picture the horrors of that scene. Thousands upon thousands of the dead, dying, and wounded lay commingled upon the battle-field. All ranks and conditions, from generals down to the humblest private, the rich and poor, the high and low, the learned and unlearned, find a common level on the battle-ground. But the sad story of sorrow and suffering ends not there. A nation's eye is turned to that fatal spot, and a nation's heart is made to bleed. Wives are made widows, children are made orphans, and parents are deprived of the hope and stay of life in their declining years. Truly has the territory of Virginia become a common battle-field, and her sacred soil a common burying-ground. *All, all* to gratify the unholy ambition of ungodly, disappointed demagogues!" —*Christian Banner, June* 14, 1862.

CHAPTER XXIII.

"GETTING OUR RIGHTS.

"MANY of the humble poor who never owned a negro in all their lives, and perhaps never would, if they were to live to be one hundred years old, were the loudest in huzzaing at the downfall of their country, and the most vociferous in clamoring for 'our rights,' while the great struggle between the Unionists and secessionists was raging in Fredericksburg and in Virginia eighteen months ago. We were forcibly reminded of this the other day, when, walking down street, we happened to fall in with a man who remarked, 'Times are awful hard: poor people can't get any work to do. They can't get any thing to live on. What do you think of it?' We simply remarked, 'We are getting our rights,' and passed on. 'We want our rights; we must have our rights; we will fight for our rights!' was the cry at every corner of the streets,—when no one had troubled their rights in any respect whatever, and they were protected by the Government in every right they could claim or ever had.

"The leaders harangued the people,—told them of a thousand imaginary rights which were perilled,—that secession was the only security for holding on to their rights,—that secession would multiply their rights a hundredfold; and, verily, the poor, ignorant people thought it was all true, and, thus duped by their wicked, infernal leaders, they were swindled out of and surrendered up all the rights they ever had or could possibly claim. Now they see it and feel it. They are now getting their rights."—*Christian Banner, June* 14, 1862.

CHAPTER XXIV.

GOD WILL PROSPER THE RIGHT.

"BEFORE the inauguration of the present war, and long after it had commenced, we were repeatedly told that, if the Southern Confederacy were right, she would certainly succeed; but if she were wrong, the Federal party would triumph: that God would prosper the party that was in the right. If, therefore, the Federal Government should succeed, are these same persons willing to return to the Union and prove loyal to the Federal Government? If they are not and do not, then they will ignore the confidence which they professed to have in God, and will, to all intents and purposes, prove themselves to be *infidels,* as well as traitors to the South and to their country. To whom, then, can they look for mercy or help? European powers will not, in our humble opinion, recognize them; 'King Cotton' has proved impotent to save them; and if they continue to spurn the Federal Government, where can they go, and what will they do?

"These are questions which demand the serious consideration of all thinking people in the Southern Confederacy, and of all secessionists out of it."—*Christian Banner, June* 14, 1862.

CHAPTER XXV.

"A NEW ERA WILL DAWN UPON THE OLD DOMINION.

"THE present war is going to produce a general upheaving, turning-over, and a complete revolution, of all things in Fredericksburg and throughout the whole State of Virginia,—in society, institutions, politics, morals, literature, science, agriculture, mechanics, manufactures, and religion: so that within at least ten years after the conclusion of this ungodly war the whole appearance of things in Fredericksburg and all Virginia will be completely changed from what it was when the war began. A new era will dawn upon the Old Dominion, and she will ultimately become one of the most wealthy, intellectual, and densely populated States in the whole Union. We may not live to see it, but others will."—*Christian Banner, June* 14, 1862.

CHAPTER XXVI.

IN the number of the "Christian Banner" of June 18, 1862, we published the following editorial:—

"THE PRESENT ASPECT OF AFFAIRS.

"What can Virginians promise themselves under the present aspect of affairs, unless they renounce their rebellion, return to the Union, and become loyal to the Federal Government? Agricultural operations to a great extent, are neglected, and in many sections of Virginia where, a year past, thousands of bushels of wheat and corn, &c. &c., were raised, nothing at all is now being produced. Negroes are leaving from almost every part of the State,—which seriously diminishes the amount of labor hitherto bestowed on agriculture. Thousands on thousands of the laboring-class of the white male population of the State have been *forced* into the army, and their small farms are, consequently, neglected; and even in sections where there are no armies the state of excitement is such, and the scarcity of labor is so great, that comparatively little produce can, possibly, be raised in the State; while very nearly the whole army of the Southern Confederacy is encamped within the territory of Virginia, and must be supported.

"The money currency of the Southern Confederacy is comparatively valueless outside of the lines of the Confederate army. Suppose that soldiers in the Southern army who have families within the lines of the Federal army could send the money they receive to their families: it would answer no valuable purpose whatever, because they cannot purchase such articles with it as they need. It is well known that Southern soldiers are paid off in Southern money, and that, too, for the most part, in Confederate notes. Therefore, these notes, even if suffering families and destitute persons could obtain them, would profit them little outside of the Southern Confederacy. It requires no argument to prove the correctness of this remark: facts prove it to be true beyond contradiction.

"In Fredericksburg, for example, there are thousands upon thousands of dollars' worth of Confederate notes; and yet the holders of these notes cannot use them for any valuable purpose, because Federal merchants in Fredericksburg refuse to take them, for the simple reason that they can make no valuable disposition of them at the North. The question then naturally arises, what is to become of families who are destitute of the necessaries of life, having no means to obtain them, and whose husbands and sons, being in the army, are not able to provide for them?

"Under *ordinary* circumstances, this would be a rather unpleasant picture to contemplate; but, under present circumstances, the aspect of affairs is absolutely alarming. Just let any one reflect for a single moment, and common sense must teach him that the poor families of soldiers who are in the Confederate army are in a most terribly awful condition. Very nearly the whole country which has been forsaken by the Confederate army is left bare and desolate. Stock, and all kinds of provisions, to a very considerable extent, were taken for the support of the army. In many sections of the country, fencing has been totally destroyed, horses, oxen, and wagons have been pressed into service, and thousands of women and children have been left destitute, with no one to attend to farming-operations. What is to become of these families of forsaken, destitute women and children? Under the most favorable circumstances in which we can possibly view this subject, these families must suffer. It cannot be otherwise. And even if they had the means with which to purchase, the goods are not in the country to be had for any price or for any kind of currency. This is no fancy sketch. Stern realities speak in tones of thunder, warning men everywhere to return to their God, their country, and their duty before famine and death prove their ruin.

"True, this is a fearful picture to men of wealth, as well as to the poorer classes. Say they, 'We have sold our goods and our produce, and most of our money consists of Confederate notes, and our negroes are leaving us, and we cannot use our money, and we are making nothing and doing nothing; and, unless the South succeeds and gains her independence, we shall lose all we have, and will be reduced to a state of comparative poverty,—to which we *cannot submit. The South will—the South must—conquer.*'

"The fact is, the South can never conquer. It is trifling with the feelings of an injured and outraged people to talk about 'the darkest hour being just before day.' There never has, in our humble opinion, been but one dark hour to the South; and that hour began when the 'flag' of our country was insulted at Charleston, South Carolina, on the 12th day of April, 1861; and that dark hour will never end until the South lays down her arms and returns again into the Union. The longer she holds out, the darker and darker the hour will become, until it shall condense into Egyptian darkness, that can and will be *felt.*

"What chance is there for the bursting out of light on the Southern Confederacy? Let us see.

"The whole fighting population of the South, by the *conscription* law, has been forced into the Southern army. When, therefore, the Confederate army which is now in the field shall have been diminished by fighting and disease to an inconsiderable number, where will the men come from to reorganize another Southern army? The men are not in the South: therefore the South can never raise another considerable army. The most of the Southern army is now cooped up in and around Richmond, and evidently the greater part of the Confederate force is in Virginia. How can that army be sustained there during the summer, fall, and the next winter,—even supposing Richmond cannot be taken by the Federal forces? Where are all the supplies to come from to support two hundred and fifty thousand soldiers, and all the horses,—to say nothing about the citizens, and the thousands of negroes that have been sent from different parts of Virginia to Richmond for protection? Suppose they have corn and flour in abundance to last them for so long a period, (which we very much question:) where and how can they obtain meat, salt, and clothing for such a vast number of men? The soldiers, citizens, and negroes must all have something to eat and wear, or else they must starve. The horses and oxen must all be fed, or they will die. The blockade is complete, and resources for supplies are nearly all cut off. How then, we ask, can the great army in Richmond be sustained for ten or twelve months longer, unless supplies can be obtained elsewhere than from Virginia and from the South? It cannot be! The truth is, every hour the South continues in arms, the worse it will be for her; and time will prove it so.

"Suppose that another terrific battle should be fought at Richmond, and that McClellan's whole army should be demolished: would the United States Government give up the contest and acknowledge the independence of the South? We do not believe a word of it. Soon another army would be organized, and the war would still go on, and would be prosecuted with greater vigor than ever. A grand and signal defeat of the Federal army would only prolong the war, and especially in Virginia.

"Secession is as much like the devil as the devil is like himself: the more you try to compromise it, the more devil it is. This is the character of secession,—always has been, now is, and so it will be to the end of time."—*Christian Banner.*

"The average number of contrabands constantly coming into Fredericksburg we would suppose to be at least two hundred per day; and the number seems to be rapidly on the increase. This is emancipation with a vengeance! At this rate, how long will it take Virginia to become a free State? Let the leaders of secession answer the question. For this they worked by day and night; for this they *lied* with all their might; and now, verily, they are reaping the reward of their labor."—*Christian Banner, June* 18, 1862.

"If certain characters (secessionists, we mean, and some few others, if you please) could be bought for their *legitimate* worth and sold for their own imaginary worth, heavens! what grand speculations could be made! What do you think of that, reader?"—*Christian Banner, June* 18, 1862.

CHAPTER XXVII.

"NEGRO STAMPEDE.

"THE stampede of negroes continues with increased numbers. On last Thursday, one hundred and fifty crossed over to the north side of the Rappahannock River. They are going, going, and will all soon be gone! What do secession orators say *now?* Why do they not make speeches now, delineating the beauties, glories, and excellencies of secession? Where is the 'immovable foundation,' on which 'African slavery' is 'based'? It is sliding away by degrees, and is becoming wonderfully small and weak.

"The leaders of secession are the men who 'ought to feel ashamed to hold up their heads as they walk the streets of Fredericksburg,' beholding their disloyal servants running at will. They are the men who feel and know, and their consciences force them to mentally exclaim, 'This is the work of our own hands; these are the blasted, withered fruits of our own unparalleled folly. We sowed the wind, and are reaping the whirlwind. We are the true enemies of ourselves, the enemies of our fellow-citizens, of the South, of our country, and the enemies of our God.'

"Yes, all this is the work of the *demon* secession; and secessionists feel it, and know it, and are drinking the cup of bitterness to its very *dregs.*"—*Christian Banner, June* 24, 1862.

CHAPTER XXVIII.

"RING-LEADERS OF SECESSION.

"THE ringleaders in this secession rebellion will, when the tragical scenes shall have closed, become a proverb, a byword, and a hissing among all the nations of the civilized world. They shall be scattered to the four corners of the earth, and, like the old, hard hearted Jews, shall be politically sold to their enemies for bondmen, and no man shall buy them.

"Then it will be seen and acknowledged that the whole plot was conceived in *iniquity*, was conducted by a systematic course of *villany*, and ended in irretrievable *infamy*. This is what we predicted when the rebellion began, and it is what we have believed ever since. And as certainly as every cause produces its legitimate effect, so it will come to pass. Union men have nothing to fear in the distant future. History and posterity will do them and their cause justice. Then it will also be seen that the Union men of the South were the only true friends of the South."—*Christian Banner, June* 24, 1862.

CHAPTER XXIX.

In the number of the "Christian Banner" of June 26, 1862, we published the following editorials:—

"SUBJECTS FOR REFLECTION.

"Superstition and credulity have acted well their part in working out the ruin of Virginia and the whole South. Many of the clergymen of the South, long before the inauguration of the present war, were actively engaged in sowing the seeds of discord and contention and in firing up the Southern heart to deeds of daring rebellion against the Federal Government. That they handled this subject cautiously and ingeniously, yet, but too effectually, facts prove beyond contradiction.

"Certain preachers *itinerated* all through the State of Virginia, delineating the 'glories of Southern Methodism,' and hurling unmitigated *anathemas* against the 'Northern Methodists' particularly, and the 'Northern people' generally. They took 'the field,' politicians-like, and went from county to county, from village to village, from town to town, from city to city, and from one community to another, discussing the merits of African slavery, and begging money to endow their sectarian, Southern-Methodistic, pro-slavery colleges. Slavery! Slavery! Slavery! and Money! Money! Money! were the all-absorbing topics. Persons who happened not to be of their peculiar *cast* of mind, and who refused to *chime* in with them, were placed under the *ban* of public censure, so far as their influence extended. To listen to the pompous utterances of these little divinity, self-conceited, clerical coxcombs, one would infer that they firmly believed themselves to be the divinely-appointed guardians of the South and of the whole Southern people, and that no one was interested in the whole matter but themselves. They acquired popularity and found favor in the South because of the peculiar denominational title which they assumed to take to themselves: 'The Southern Methodist Church;' 'The Methodist Episcopal Church, South.' They seemed to think that the name 'Southern Methodist' was sufficient to place one above suspicion of being an Abolitionist, or of having any Northern proclivities whatever.

"Their strong argument was, God was with them: God had blessed their labors; God had added thousands and thousands to their numbers; and their very fanaticism and extravagance were passed off as emanations of the eternal divinity, or direct influences of the 'Holy Ghost.'

"The hearts and minds of the Southern people being fired up by these *divines*, and by *politicians* acting in concert with them, it was an easy matter for them, when the war began, to attribute every seeming success to the direct interposition of Almighty God, and to induce the people to believe it. Hence, when the attack was made on Fort Sumter, and after the battle had been fought and no one was killed, the cry was, 'God is with us;' 'God is fighting our battles for us;' 'God directs the bullets.' After the fight at Acquia Creek, last spring was twelve months ago, and 'nobody got killed,' the cry was, 'God is fighting our battles.'

"When portions of the Federal fleet stranded last year on the Carolina coasts, 'God had raised the winds and sent the storms for the express purpose of destroying the Yankee vessels.' After the Federal troops had rebuilt the railroad-bridge across the Rappahannock River at Fredericksburg, and the freshet came and washed it away, 'God sent the freshet to destroy the bridge.' 'Such doings can't prosper.' 'God will put a stop to it.' Again the bridge was rebuilt, and had been used only a day or two, when there came another freshet, at an unusual season of the year, and swept it away again. 'Surely this is the work of God.' 'Don't you see?' 'Didn't we tell you so?' 'It can't prosper.' 'God is above the devil, thank the Lord.'

"Now, let us examine this subject a little. If God was *specially* with either party in the beginning of this unholy war, and favored that party because it *was in the right,* why has he at any time suffered reverses to befall that party? Has he not the wisdom to see, and the power to accomplish all his purposes? Surely he has! Why then is he constantly changing his purposes,—to-day with the Confederates, helping them, and to-morrow with the Federals, lending them a helping hand! Really, we think it high time for the people to put a stop to all this nonsense about God being with this, that, or the other party, fighting their battles for them, &c. &c. We consider it nothing more nor less than horrid blasphemy to make God Almighty a party to the wickedness of mortals.

"If God raises the winds and sends the storms to wreck the Federal vessels, why does he not make a clean sweep of it, and sink them all at once, and have done with it? If he sends the rains to raise the rivers to wash away their bridges, why does he not send the lightning and storm and kill them all in a body, and sweep them from the face of the earth in an instant? Does he lack the power? If not, why this piecemeal work? If Heaven be actually and specially engaged in fighting for the Southern Confederacy, why is all this running away of the *darkies?* Could not

Providence put it into the minds and hearts of them all to remain at home and continue to work for their owners?

"The truth is, designing men have imposed upon the credulity of the ignorant and unsuspecting so long that they think they can *gag* and *cram* any and every absurdity down their throats, however ridiculous, and the *common people*, the masses, are bound to receive and swallow it all, as coming directly from the high and holy fountain of divine inspiration. There is a fearful responsibility resting on preachers, editors, politicians, and others in this fearful tragedy, the due weight of which has never been felt by them. But a day of terrible reckoning is at hand, when men shall call upon the rocks and mountains to fall upon them and hide them from impending wrath; but it will then be too late.

"That good *may* ultimately come out of this war, and order spring out of confusion, we do not question. The political, ecclesiastical, and moral world have all become so abominably corrupt that war may be absolutely necessary to purify the elements. Men must be humbled for their sins and rebellion against Heaven. God permits men and nations to quarrel and fight, and to take one another's lives, and to destroy each other; but this is not the will of God. God is a God of love, peace, and order, and not a God of wrath, of confusion, of battles, blood, and carnage.

"If an individual violate any one of the fixed laws of nature, he *must* and *will* suffer the penalty annexed to that law. If nations violate the laws of nature, humanity, and justice, they too must suffer for their crimes. This is cause and effect, and the effect can never finally cease until the cause is removed which produces it.

"Let men, then, cease to prate about Divine Providence, about God's being with this, that, or the other party. The fact is, God is *with* and *for* but one party, and that is the good and right party, and that which is pure and holy and right and just God will bless and prosper, and nothing more; and for men whose minds and hearts are filled with vindictiveness, and every discordant and *devilish* passion, to prate about divine interposition, is folly, is wicked, is blasphemy.

"The elements in the political, religious, social, and moral world are all in commotion, and the whole order of things is undergoing a complete revolution; old things are passing away, and all things are becoming new; a great struggle is going on between the spirit of despotism on the one hand, and freedom on the other, between mind and institutionalism; the great question is, shall despotism and institutionalism triumph over freedom and mind, or shall freedom and mind conquer despotism and institutionalism? This is the great, grand, and sublime problem now being solved. Let us, therefore, patiently wait the result; in the mean time, however, let us discharge our duty to God, to our country, and to our fellow-man, and trust to Heaven for mercy in the future. Reader, think on these things."

CHAPTER XXX.

"PRACTICAL SECESSIONISTS.

"On Wednesday (yesterday) one hundred and thirty contrabands left Fredericksburg, and crossed the Rappahannock River, going northward; and this (Thursday) morning forty-four others, who came in town last night, were sent in the same direction. The whole of these one hundred and seventy-four contrabands are practical secessionists. Secession is taking to itself wings and flying away. This is *secession,*—practical *secession,*—the movable foundation, the flying, rolling basis of African slavery. What do secessionists—*white* secessionists, we mean—think of this?"—*Christian Banner of June* 26, 1862.

CHAPTER XXXI.

In the number of the "Christian Banner" of July 2, 1862, we published the following editorials:—

"THROW OFF THE VEIL.

"That African slavery is the direct cause which has produced the present wicked civil war, cannot be longer disguised. Is there a solitary man in our whole community, who has any claims to intelligence whatever, who can longer deny the fact? No; not one.

"Suppose the 'Southern Confederacy' should gain her independence, and should establish a permanent government based upon African slavery,—as it certainly would be: what would become of the poor white population in such a government? The condition of the poor whites would be infinitely worse than that of the negroes themselves. The negroes would be cared for by their owners, housed, fed, clothed, attended in sickness, and decently buried when dead, if owned by good, humane masters.

"The rich, being independent of the labor of the poor white population, except so far as overseers and housekeepers are concerned, would have no respect nor sympathy for the poor laboring white class of the people whatever. It requires no argument to prove this fact. It is a lesson which the laboring poor have learned long ago, in all slave-holding communities. And even the labor of poor white mechanics is already reduced to an insignificant figure in the South. Already there are in the South thousands upon thousands of negro carpenters, shoemakers, blacksmiths, brick-masons, plasterers, &c. &c. All this labor comes into direct competition with the labor of poor white mechanics. They know it, they feel it, they quarrel about it; and still they wish and are trying to establish it permanently, thus fastening the curse upon themselves, and entailing it on their children through all time to come, by fighting to establish a negro-oligarchy!

"Colored labor costs the slave-owners nothing more than the board and tax of the laborers (after the laborers are once paid for); and the board is of the cheapest kind, and the tax but a small trifle. Hence slave-owners can have work executed much cheaper than white men can possibly do it. Therefore, when slave labor comes into competition with the labor of poor white men, how can the poor white laboring-classes support their families, pay all contingent expenses, and educate their children so as to give them a position in society and a rank with rich slave-holders' children? They cannot do it; it is impossible.

"Nor is this all. It is a fact well known that wealthy citizens in the South, instead of patronizing their own mechanics, as a general rule, send to the North to purchase articles which would be manufactured at home if the manufacturers were encouraged. As long as this state of things continues, the poor will remain poor, and their children must of necessity be brought up in comparative ignorance, which, according to the opinion of some men, is just as it ought to be; because, say they, 'poor people's children have no need of education.' Why have they no need of education? Because, if the masses were educated, they would no longer become the vassals of political tricksters, aspiring demagogues, and ecclesiastical knaves. Our country would be safe in the hands of an intelligent and virtuous *people;* and this, aspirants know and dread, and hence their aversion and deep-rooted prejudice to popular education.

"We have always been pro-slavery in our feelings,—more, however, on account of the negroes themselves than of any permanent, solid good they are to their owners. Our opinion has ever been that to change the relation which servants hold to their masters would be a great evil to the former; because, semi-civilized and semi-christianized as most of them are, and being uneducated, they are incapable of self-government. It seems to us, however, that the time has actually come when important changes are to be made and new relations are to be formed. And, while we deeply and truly sympathize for the condition of the colored population of our country, we sympathize for our country more. And *now,* since our country is thrown into one end of the *balance,* and negroes into the other end, and the issue is being forced upon us, and the question is being asked us, which we will take, our country, or negroes, or our country without slavery, or slavery without our country, we answer, emphatically and uncompromisingly, OUR COUNTRY FOREVER!

"We say that changes are being made and new relations are being formed. Servants are everywhere leaving their masters and flocking within the lines of the Federal troops. That they do this thing willingly, cannot be denied. It is an act of their own free volition. True, it is said that the 'Yankees are stealing our negroes.' For the sake of argument, let us suppose that the 'Yankees' have stolen all the negroes who have left their owners in the town of Fredericksburg. The negroes are constantly flocking into Fredericksburg from the extreme borders of Essex, Hanover, King and Queen, Louisa, Caroline, Culpepper, Orange, Madison, Albemarle, and all the counties in the northern neck of Virginia, and from all parts of Spottsylvania county. Did the 'Yankees' go to all these different localities and 'steal away the negroes'? No: the negroes *voluntarily* leave their homes and come to Fredericksburg. What does all this argue? The problem is practically and literally demonstrated that the slaves of Virginia have an idea of *freedom* and a wish to obtain it, and are determined *to be free.* This is the only rational conclusion at which any sensible, logical mind can arrive. That they are determined *to be free,* and will certainly be free, is only a question of time. If, therefore, it is their wish and determination to be free, it is by their own voluntary act; and if evil shall come to them by this act, let it fall upon their own heads. That the condition of many of the present generation will ever be bettered, we do not believe; while, on the other hand, we do not think that the condition of some of them can be very much worsted. Where they are going, and what ultimate destiny or locality awaits them in the future, we cannot tell. This is a grave question, and one which will demand the profoundest legislation of the nation. That provisions, however, will be made for them by the Government, we do not entertain a doubt.

"Look at the deplorable condition to which our country, our children, our neighbors, and fellow-citizens, are all reduced on account of the *negro*, and then let any true-hearted patriot, humane father or mother, who have the natural sympathies and affections of parents or patriots, say what estimate they can ever hereafter place upon the *institution* of African slavery.

"The question of African slavery has been made a pretext for secession; has broken up our Government, has inaugurated civil war, has desolated our country, has drenched our land in blood, has bleached the lofty hills and beautiful plains of our country with the bones of our children, brothers, fathers, friends, and neighbors, has made heart-broken widows of thousands, and penniless, starving orphans of millions, has *robed* a whole nation in the drapery of sorrow, lamentation, and woe; and the horrible work of destruction and death is still going on, while there are those who say, 'Let it go on, until the last man in the South is killed, rather than ever return again to the Union or seek the protection of the Government of the United States!' That is to say, 'Let the whole South be *baptized in blood;* let our children be slaughtered like cattle in the market; let every man in the South be killed; let our whole country sink to eternal ruin; but, for *God's sake, let us keep our negroes!'* This is the idea! Yes, Heaven knows that the *negro* is the *one* great, grand, and sublime idea with many of those who are constantly making terrible threats against good and loyal citizens and genuine patriots.

"If these *negro-idolizing* gentlemen were forced to shoulder their muskets, buckle on their knapsacks, eat hard bread and spoiled meat, lie on the wet, cold ground, be drenched in torrents of rain, go half clothed and half starved as thousands of the poor soldiers are, and then had to face the mouths of cannons, and charge bayonets, they would find it a very different work from standing about the corners of the streets in the cool shade, concocting plans by which to hang Union men and have them punished after the Federal troops 'are driven away.'

"We say, and thousands of others would say the same thing if they were allowed to speak, and could be heard, both *in* and *out* of the Southern army, 'Give us our country, our liberty, our freedom in the Union, under the time and heaven honored old Stars and Stripes, and *let* the negroes *go,—all* the negroes *go* to Africa, or any other place to which God and the Government may be kind enough to send them.' What mother is there, and what father is there but he who has the heart of a *demon*, and what wife is there, but would gladly give up their negroes to receive back to their embraces their sons and their husbands?

"If the Federal Government had inaugurated war for the purpose of freeing the negroes of the South, or for any other unjust cause whatever, then the South, the whole South, would comparatively have been a unit in repelling the injustice. But such is not the case.

"South Carolina inaugurated the war, and the United States Government has been and is still endeavoring to put down the ungodly rebellion and to restore peace and order once more in the country. And, under all the provoking circumstances, the lenity of the Federal Government towards the Southern people is absolutely without a parallel in the history of all wars, and of the whole wide world. The very mildness of the Government only provokes secessionists to greater insolence and contempt for the Union and the Government. We have been told that secessionists make their boasts that the Federal officers think more of them than they do of Union men. In fact, we have heard this remark ourself; and it has been told to us, as goading us for our Union sentiments, 'Oh, yes: the Yankees don't think half as much of you *Union men* as they do of secessionists.' As if we professed to be Union men because of what 'the Yankees' might think of us! Secessionists seem to presume upon their *dignity* to *awe* the Federal army into submission to their own will and pleasure. That leading secessionists in our community are daily becoming more and more bitter and vindictive towards Union men, and more and more hostile to the Federal Government, is questioned by no impartial observer.

"We deeply deplore the present ungodly state of affairs, and do most devoutly wish and earnestly pray that men would reason on the subject as they should do, because this dignified stubbornness and haughty rebellion can never be productive of any good. Let men throw off the veil and take a common-sense view of matters and things as they actually exist. All have got to come into measures, sooner or later, and the sooner the better for all parties interested, and especially for Virginians: therefore, throw off the veil."

CHAPTER XXXII.

"WON'T PATRONIZE YOU.

"A citizen of Fredericksburg said to one of our town mechanics the other day, 'I won't patronize you, because you are a Unionist,'—when, in fact, he never had patronized him to the amount of ten cents in his life!

"This is like the patronage of a great many *boasters*. They will never patronize a man who refuses to read through their own smoky glasses, and who will not sneeze every time they take snuff. The more *patronage* honest men receive from such characters, the poorer, in a general way, they become. They take every thing they can get, and never pay for any thing they take. We simply give this as a specimen of the spirit of secessionists generally."—*Christian Banner, July* 29, 1862.

CHAPTER XXXIII.

In the number of the "Christian Banner" of July 5, 1862, we published the following editorial:—

"SLANDERS REFUTED.—LOOK AT THE OTHER SIDE.

"We understand that certain characters in town are reporting to the Federal officers and soldiers that we were a rank, rampant secessionist before the Federal troops came to Fredericksburg, but as soon as they came we turned right over to the other side.

"This is an *infamous lie,* number one! Let any man come to us and tell us so.

"Secondly, that we took the oath of allegiance to the Southern Confederacy.

"This is a double-and-twisted, *infamous lie,* number two.

"Thirdly, that we are a real genuine Yankee, from the State of Massachusetts.

"This is a *diabolical lie,* number three.

"If we were a rank, rampant secessionist before the Federal troops came to Fredericksburg, why did certain slanderous, infamous characters try to have us arrested last fall and winter because we were accused of holding secret Union meetings? We then indignantly hurled back the infamous slander into the face of the nefarious liars, and denounced the whole as being secession falsehoods. We have never held a Union meeting in the town of Fredericksburg, nor anywhere else, since the ever-memorable night we held a public Union meeting in the court-house in the town of Fredericksburg, when a set of unprincipled secession scoundrels tried to break it up, and, while we were addressing our fellow-citizens and warning them of the evils which they are now suffering, some finished scoundrel threw an egg at us, which, failing to reach us, hit a young man on the head who was seated in our front. Because we denied the libellous charge of holding 'secret Union meetings,' and avowed our devotion to the South, as we have always done and still glory in doing, therefore we were 'a rank, rampant secessionist before the Yankees came to town.' We humbly trust in God that the time is not far distant when we can once more hold public Union meetings in the town of Fredericksburg, and then we will make a revelation of facts which will astonish secessionists themselves.

"If we were 'a rank, rampant secessionist' before 'the Yankees' came to Fredericksburg, why was it reported throughout the State of Virginia last winter that we were arrested and sent to Richmond for treason against old Jeff Davis and the Southern [*Conspiracy*] Confederacy?

"If we were 'a rank, rampant secessionist' before 'the Yankees came to Fredericksburg,' why did some one in Cary's regiment, the day they passed our door on Main Street as they were on their way to North Carolina last winter, cry out, '*God damn old Hunnicutt! Let's drive him and old Miller, and all the damned party of them, before us to Richmond*'? How can these same individuals, who used their utmost endeavors to have us arrested last winter and this spring because of our 'Union proclivities,' now have the unblushing impudence to say that we were one of the most 'hot-headed, rank, rampant secessionists in all the country'?

"As to the report of our taking the oath of allegiance to Jeff Davis and the Southern Confederacy, the idea is so supremely ridiculous that it needs no comment. No human being upon the face of the broad earth ever asked us to take any such accursed oath.

"As to the report of our being 'a Yankee from Massachusetts,' it so happened in the order of events that we were born exactly in the other extreme,—in South Carolina,—and, with all her faults, we love her still; and, were it not for the political trickery and imposition of her leaders, South Carolina would be in the Union to-day.

"'But why did we not come out and write and speak in this way last year, when the Southern soldiers were in town?' Ay, that's the question. Let us turn over a new leaf, and see what is on the other side of the page.

"Why did the editor of the 'Democratic Recorder' leave Fredericksburg in such great haste the morning the Federal troops arrived in Falmouth? Why was not the publication of the 'Democratic Recorder' continued after the arrival of the Federal army?

"Why were the Fredericksburg 'News' and the Virginia 'Herald' discontinued?

"Why do not secession flags float over the town of Fredericksburg now?

"Have all the secessionists left Fredericksburg? No, indeed. Why, then, do they not hoist their colors?

"Why have all the ministers of the gospel in Fredericksburg ceased to offer up publicly in their congregations holy prayers for Jeff Davis, the 'chief magistrate' of the 'glorious Southern Confederacy'?

"Have editors, ministers, and all the citizens turned Union-shriekers, submissionists, and Abolitionists since 'the Yankees came to town'? Why, then, do they not go on and write and act and speak as they did last year? Ay, reader, they have no aspirations for a Northern prison. Nor had we any particular desire last year to be cooped up in a damp, dirty Southern dungeon. 'Turn and turn about is fair play,' is an old adage. Circumstances prevented us from writing and speaking as we wished to do last year; and circumstances prevent secessionists from writing and speaking as they wish to do this year. It simply proves that we are all creatures of circumstances and must act accordingly."

CHAPTER XXXIV.

In the number of the "Christian Banner" of July 14, 1862, we published the following editorials:—

"LET REASON AND COMMON SENSE HAVE FAIR PLAY.

"It is folly to reason and argue with men who are governed by prejudice and passion. This class of persons cannot be profited by any arguments used to convince them, simply because they are determined not to be convinced. There is another class, however, who are not wholly abandoned to prejudice and passion and who are not entirely given over to judicial blindness; and to this latter class we wish to make a few remarks, earnestly hoping to be able to influence them in their future course of action. If by any possible argument we shall be able to induce them to return to their former allegiance to their country, our highest wish will be attained. To this class, then, we appeal.

"Do not facts fully justify us in saying that secession is a political swindle, and that Virginians have been swindled out of every right which they held dear and sacred? Has not this been accomplished, too, by every grade of intellect, from Senators down to fifteen-shilling lawyers and *penny* political editors? Did not these political tricksters say that if Virginia seceded she would be the greatest State in the whole Southern Confederacy? that her wealth would increase abundantly, and in the shortest conceivable time? that slave property would advance at least fifty per cent.? that millions of capital would flow into all the towns and cities of Virginia, and that they would soon become large and populous? that she would soon become a great manufacturing State, and would be to the other States of the Southern Confederacy what the North had always been to the whole South? that there would be 'peaceable secession'? that there was no danger of war of any magnitude? that the 'Yankees' loved the *immortal dollar* too well to involve themselves in the expenses of war? that the North had not the means to prosecute a successful war against the South? that, in the event of war, one Southern man could whip five 'Yankees'? that 'Yankees' neither knew how to fight, nor had the 'spunk' to fight even if they knew how? that the Southern army would take Washington City, 'rescue downtrodden Maryland,' and go on to Philadelphia and make it a war of invasion against the North, and not a defensive war? that if there should, by any possible contingency, be war at all, it would be one of short duration? that the interest and sympathy of England and France were with the South, and that those Governments would certainly acknowledge the independence of the Southern Confederacy? that cotton was *king*, and would rule and govern the European powers, and the 'North into the bargain'? that when volunteers were called for, the promise to many of them was that they were not to leave their own sections of the country, and certainly should not be sent out of their State? that negroes would prove loyal to their masters, and would be one of the most effective elements in prosecuting the war? that they would cultivate the farms, and raise an abundance of produce, while the white men would carry on the war?

"And, since the war has been progressing, has not the promise always been that the 'Yankees' shall be driven off every foot of Virginia territory? Has it not been said that every defeat and retreat of the Southern armies was only a strategic move to draw the enemy out of his strongholds? that Southern forts and cities were impregnable to the assaults of the enemy, and could never be taken? And, since they have been taken, has not the promise been made to the remaining citizens of the Southern Confederacy that they will all soon be retaken by the Confederate forces? And still the cry is, 'The South will soon whip the North, and make the North submit to just such terms as the South may demand; and then Union men in the South will be dealt with as traitors, and all their effects will be confiscated.'

"By such threats, Union men in the South are still held in awe, and fear to avow their honest sentiments, because of the threatened vials of wrath which are to be poured out, without any mixture of mercy, upon their devoted heads.

"We might extend our remarks on this subject much further; but we pause to inquire if all these things have come to pass. And now, kind reader, we entreat you to lay all prejudice aside and look facts and realities full in the face, and then answer candidly if you have not been most shamefully and wickedly imposed upon by stump-speakers, speech-makers, and political aspirants of every grade of intellect.

"Since Virginia seceded, in what has she become great, except in that she has become the great battle-field of all the Southern States, and her territory a great common burial-ground? Truly may it be said that Virginia is the great valley of dead men's bones. In what has she increased in wealth in so short a period, but in thousands of armed soldiers, in the desolation of her farms, and sorrow, woe, and afflictions on all her inhabitants? Has slave property advanced fifty per cent. in value? Is the institution of slavery placed on a sure and immovable foundation? Have not slaves become valueless, and is not the institution virtually abolished? Have millions of wealth flowed into the towns and cities of Virginia, and have they become populous? Is there any probability that this will soon be the case? Are they not deserted in many instances by native citizens, and filled with legions of armed soldiers? Is there any reasonable prospect that Virginia will ever become a great manufacturing State by her own native-born citizens, and that she will be to the other Confederate States what the North has always been to the South? Instead of 'peaceable secession,' has there not been war, and that, too, of the most fearful magnitude and of the most malignant character? Is not the war still raging most terribly, so that no one can tell *when* and *where* and *how* the awful scene will end? Have the 'Yankees' proved that they loved the *immortal dollar* too well to involve themselves in the expenses of war,—a long-protracted war? Has the North failed in men or means to prosecute 'a war'? Has it been demonstrated throughout tne war, thus far, that 'one Southern man can whip five Yankees,'—that the Yankees do not know how to fight, and that they have no 'pluck' to fight? Has the Southern army taken Washington City, rescued 'poor down-trodden Maryland,' and marched into Philadelphia, making it a war of invasion on the North? Has the war been one of short duration,—only three, six, or nine months, or a year? Are the interests and sympathies of England and France with the South, and have these Governments acknowledged the independence of the Southern Confederacy? Has cotton proved to be universal king, ruling the European powers, and the North 'into the bargain'? Have not many of the volunteers who first enlisted in Virginia been called away from their own sections of the country and sent out of the State? and when the twelve months for which they enlisted had expired, were they not *all forced*, by an act of the Confederate Congress, to remain in the army? Have negroes proved loyal to their masters, and are they likely to prove themselves to be one of the most effective elements in prosecuting the war? Are they cultivating the farms of their owners, and raising an abundance of produce to carry on the war? Have the 'Yankees' been 'driven off every foot of Virginia soil'? If every defeat and retreat is only a strategic move to draw the enemy out of his strongholds, why are the defeats so frequent and the retreats so far? Have Southern forts and cities proved to be impregnable to the assaults of the enemy? How many of the Southern forts, towns, and cities which have been taken by the Federal army have ever been recaptured and held by the Southern troops?

"Look at all these facts, intelligent reader, and then tell us how long it will take the South, according to the progress which she has made for the last eighteen months, to whip out the North and make the Government of the United States submit to just such terms 'as the South may demand.' With all these solemn facts and stern realities staring men full in the face, still there are those who persist in saying that 'the Southern army will soon retake all the Southern towns, cities, forts, and localities which are now being occupied by the Federal troops.' True, some of them may be recaptured and held for a short time; but what will the retaking of them advantage the citizens? Will it not be attended with great loss of private property, and perhaps at the expense of the lives of many of the citizens themselves? What, then, can be gained by a continued, pertinacious rebellion against the Government of the United States? Nothing, absolutely nothing, is to be gained, but every thing to be lost.

"Again: were we not told by secessionists that, 'whenever' and 'wherever' the 'vandals' got possession of any of the Southern towns, cities, localities, &c. &c., they insulted and outraged Southern ladies, offering to them every vulgar indignity of which debased and corrupt humanity is capable?—that their mission was one of robbery, plunder, insult, and general carnage, and that they laid waste every thing before them in their onward move? Yes; secessionists said that the Union troops did all these things.

"Have they done these things in Fredericksburg? Have they disturbed any citizen, male or female, in his or her daily, legal avocation? No, not one. What lady has been insulted or outraged by the Union troops since their arrival in the city? Has not the 'Flag of the Union' been constantly insulted and the Federal Government abused by citizens ever since the town has been occupied by the Federal troops? And, notwithstanding all this, has not the property of secessionists—and those, too, of the bitterest stamp—been guarded and protected by the Union soldiers? Has there ever within the memory of the oldest citizens been better order uniformly maintained in the town of Fredericksburg than there has been since its occupation by the Union army? Was there ever such lenity in time of war extended to any people in the world's history as has been exhibited towards the people of Fredericksburg? Yet, astonishing to say, the very kindness of the Federal authorities seems but to increase the stubbornness and deepen the hatred of many of the citizens.

"'But they steal our negroes; and that's just what they came down here to do.' Indeed! Did Government send out an army to station guards around men's houses, farms, and negro-quarters, to keep the servants from running away from their owners, and to catch them and carry them back to their masters? Is it not strange that a people who say that they *despise* the Union, *detest* the Federal Government, and declare that they have taken themselves from under its safe and kind protection, should complain because that Government does not keep their slaves from running away, and, after they do run away, complain because the soldiers do not run after them, catch them, and return them to their masters? Is not this insubordination and running away of negroes one of the legitimate results of secession? Were not the people faithfully warned of all these evils long before they came to pass? Secessionists have done it all; these are the direct evils of their own wicked doings: they have no right to complain; they did it.

"Nor is this all. If the people continue in a state of vindictive rebellion against the Federal Government, they have not yet realized half the bitter fruits and terrible evils that are in store for them. Hence we do most earnestly entreat our fellow-citizens to lay aside their hostile feelings to the Government and take their stand with loyal citizens, and then they can confidently claim, and will certainly obtain, protection under the time-honored 'Flag of the Union.'

"To continue in a state of unconditional, uncompromising rebellion cannot possibly better the condition of any one. It will never make Confederate notes equal to *specie*. It will never bring back a single servant who has left his master, nor will it prevent others from running away. It will not diminish the number of our children, relatives, friends, and neighbors who are being slain in battle or are dying in distant hospitals. On the contrary, the longer this ungodly rebellion continues, the greater will be the number of slaves that will make their escape, and their value will constantly diminish. The less valuable Confederate notes become,—if they *can* sink below their present value,—the more and more of our sons and friends will fall either by the sword or by disease, the more and more will our country be desolated, and the more destitute the great masses of the people will become, until one common ruin will swallow up the whole.

"Where is the regard the leaders in this rebellion have shown the poor destitute women and children whom they have left forsaken, uncared-for, and unprotected at the mercy of the 'vandals'? If they believed what they themselves said in relation to the conduct of the Union troops, they have manifested but little sympathy, and still *less respect,* for the wives and daughters and sisters of the men whom they have caused to be dragged from their homes, thus depriving helpless females and children of that protection which God and nature designed they should have. We cannot believe that many of the leaders in this unrighteous rebellion have any sympathy for the great mass of the 'common people;' and yet the people seem bent and determined on believing in them, and following them to the very last extremity and consummation of ruin. 'The South will whip the North,'—will drive every one of the 'Yankees off Southern soil;' 'the Southern army will soon pass through Fredericksburg on its way to Washington City,'—will carry the war into 'Africa,' or into Pennsylvania, and onward and northward, until all *Yankeedom* is subdued and brought under the power of the 'South;' 'Confederate notes will soon be equal to gold and silver;' 'we will make the North pay the very highest kind of prices for all our negroes they have stolen;' 'we will make the Yankees pay the whole of the war-debt;' 'England and France will step in and settle up matters very soon now,' &c. &c.

"How can men who profess to be intelligent, longer remain the dupes of folly so extravagant and of nonsense so consummate? Surely the people—*all* the people—have heard, seen, and felt enough of secession and its *damning* results to convince them that it is the grandest cheat, the blackest swindle, and the most diabolical deception that has ever been wickedly imposed upon any people since God made the world. The seduction of old Eve and Adam by the devil is not a circumstance to secession. The devil seduced only one poor, uneducated woman, and she seduced only one poor, uneducated man; and the beauty of it was, they had no 'niggers' to lose,—the *issue* between the devil and the woman being simply about an apple; the 'nigger' question was not introduced. But secession has seduced and destroyed millions, many of whom are highly educated; Senators, Congressmen, orators, editors, politicians, statesmen, poets, divines, doctors of divinity, doctors of medicine, lawyers, and even the *common class*,—the ignorant, uneducated '*poor white people*,'—have all been seduced by secession, and they have lost and will lose their 'niggers' into the bargain.

"Intelligent reader, think on these things; and may God in mercy grant that you may view secession in all its loathsome aspects, and that you may fly from it as from a deadly poison. *Let reason and common sense have fair play.*"

CHAPTER XXXV.

"SECESSION.

"SECESSION is a finished compound of all the discordant, disorganizing, diabolical, and damning elements which can possibly afflict and curse poor, suffering humanity. Only in *hell* there can be no secession, because *there devils damned firm concord hold.*

"*Secession* hoists the flood-gate through which flows

every conceivable curse that can visit mortals. It says to *Diabolus*, the prince of devils, '*Punch* up your emissaries; drive them on to do their work of finished ruin; now is the time; do not let the favorable opportunity slip; the work of death and general and effectual ruin must now be accomplished.'

"It says to the leaders in this infernal rebellion that they shall all have crowns and thrones,—if nowhere else, *in hell: better to reign in hell than serve in heaven.* That they must never rest satisfied until *negroism* is established on a foundation as immovable as the everlasting rocks of Gibraltar, and the last vestige of *freedom* is swept from Southern soil, and *Breckinridge locofocoism* seated on a 'topless' throne. That they have lost the *reins* of the Federal Government, and, consequently, all the 'spoils'—the 'loaves and fishes'—of the Government. That the spoils of Government have all fallen into Yankee hands, and their only hope now is to fight on, and on, and on, and establish a kingdom for Jeff Davis and his dignified and important satellites; and that they shall all be chiefs, or aristocrats of the highest importance. That, unless they succeed, they will all lose their dignified positions, their fat offices, and all the 'spoils' and 'loaves and fishes' of the Confederate Government, together with all their negroes, and perhaps their own necks into the bargain.

"It says to the disloyal clergy, 'Remember, the people think that you are called and sent of God to preach; and verily they believe the *lie*, because you have told it to them, and they are therefore now prepared to receive as messages coming from heaven any teachings or declarations which you may please to impose upon them. Pray long, loud, and fervent prayers for Jeff

Davis and all the arch-traitors of this great rebellion, and then preach treason against the Government, and expatiate eloquently to the people about the "God of battles" and the "everlasting nigger." Never rest from your work of destruction until every vestige of power and all the rights and privileges of the sovereign people are wrested from them, and American freedom is forever abolished. Tell the people that the "God of battles" is in for traitors and treason, and that he will lead them to certain victory, and will crown them with glory and honor as imperishable as the records of eternity.

'"Say to the people that this rebellion must succeed; that God has promised to be with Jeff Davis and his band of conspirators until this "great Southern empire" is permanently established, and Breckinridge *locofocoism* and *negroism* shall sweep over the land, bearing down all opposition. Be earnest and solemn, and, withal, affect a great deal of piety, so that the people may believe without a doubt, and *know assuredly*, that you are called and sent of God to preach Breckinridge *locofocoism* and *negroism* to them, and that they must receive and obey your divine teachings at the peril of their salvation. In all your discourses be positive, dogmatic, dictatorial, and very denunciatory against the "old Union," "Yankees," and especially against "Union men and submissionists." In all your exordiums and perorations be sure and remember the institutions of *slavery* and *freedom:* exalt the *former* to *heaven,* and *sink* the latter to *hell.* This will fire up the hearts of the people, and will make them wrathy, and then they will fight like tigers and devils. Punch up the people; do your duty as preachers "called and sent of God" to preach treason and the overthrow of the Government, and make all the people do their duty. Be sure and always stick up to your text: do not forget your text: keep it constantly before the people. *Negroism* and *locofocoism* is the text. Stick up to it, and punch up the dear people; and verily you shall receive your reward, either in time or eternity,—in heaven or *low down in hell.* But, at all hazards, do not forget the "nigger."'

"It says to death, 'Come, do your work; do not leave a single husband of the weeping wives of all these poor soldiers; do not leave a father of all the suffering, starving children throughout the country; make widows and orphans of them all; make a clean sweep of it; finish your work, and do it thoroughly. Do not spare a single son to return home to gladden the hearts of fathers and mothers crushed to earth.'

"It says to military tyrants, 'Burn up and destroy all produce of every kind in your onward march; leave neither cotton to clothe the naked, nor bread and meat to feed the hungry, starving poor. Do not let conscience disturb you, nor the imploring and sufferings and distresses of women and children move your sympathies. All these things are military necessities; this is war, and these are war-times: so roll ahead.'

"It says to servants, 'Your time has come at last; the long-looked-for and long-wished-for day of jubilee has dawned; the long, dark night of bondage is rapidly being swallowed up in past eternity. Arise and burst off and cast forever from you the manacles of despotism. Now is your time: gather up all you can carry along with you, and be off; put out at once; do not tarry; make no delay. Beware! Delays are dangerous. *Off, off*, to the city of refuge, to the land of freedom, at once!'

"It says to merchants and speculators generally, 'Now is your time to make money and get rich: so pitch right into the *grease-tub;* roll up your sleeves and pitch in; bring *up out* of your cellars, and *down out* of your garrets, all your *old* unfashionable moth-eaten goods and adulterated liquors: stick on the profits thick and heavy. If the people complain at having to give fifty cents and a dollar per yard for six-cent calico, old and out of fashion at that,—if farmers *mouth* and grumble because they are forced to pay from ten to sixty dollars for a sack of salt,—and if poor soldiers curse and swear because they are *coerced* to pay from five to fifteen dollars per gallon for *rot-gut* whiskey, which would vomit *devils damned*, if they were fools enough to drink it,—tell them all about the blockade; that in war-times people always have to pay from ten to twenty times more for articles than in times of peace; swear that you can barely live by the small profits laid on your *old* wares; and if they ask *when* and *where* and *how* you obtained them, tell them that, a *few* days ago, right from the *North*, a party *ran* the blockade, and that you were "devilish lucky" to get them at any price; tell a thousand *lies*, and stick up to them; never back down: you will never have such another chance to stick it on to the "poor devils." And all the time you are selling to them, talk eloquently about the glorious Southern Confederacy; what a rich and independent people you will all be when the South gains her independence; that the war will soon end; the "vandals" will all be driven back to *Yankeedom*, and all the Virginia traitors and "Southern Yankees" shall be hung or driven out of the South; old Lincoln will have to pay all the people the highest prices in gold and silver for the negroes whom he and his *minions* have stolen, and all the other losses they have sustained by the war. Roll out the *lies* smoothly and eloquently, just like oil dripping from a feather; cheer up their spirits, fire up their hearts, and they will more cheerfully pay the prices for your goods. Tell them how much you love the South,—what terrible sacrifices you are making for the people of the South. Be sure and stick on the profits. Seeing your zeal for the "glorious cause" and your love for the South, they will never once suspect your damnable rascality. Let all the merchants combine, and have uniform prices for all their goods of every kind and quality, and let them perfectly harmonize as to the amount of profit to be laid on, and let there be no competition in the market, and then, when the people come to buy, let them seem perfectly indifferent about selling. Remember, you have now got the people in your power. Press them, crush them, skin them, strip them; all things are fair in war, you know; and if at any time you should feel a little squirming about the tender part of your consciences, if you have any, go to church on Sunday the next following after feeling these squirming sensations, and when the preachers pray to the "God of battles," thunder, blood, and carnage, for old Jeff Davis and his "infernal" clique, do you say, *Amen! amen!* and be sure and speak out your *amens* loud enough to be heard by the preachers and church-dignitaries, and all will be easy, and you will be perfectly hardened to pitch right in again, fresh and early, on the next morning. Lay on the profits. Do not forget that. The profits are what must be looked after now. Make money now, and give your conscience credit till the judgment-day of the great God.'

"It says to *gamblers*, '*Hang* upon the army; follow up the army; live among the poor soldiers: many, and, indeed, most of them, are "green-horns" in the diabolical science of gambling; watch them; keep your eye on them, and, whenever you find they have money, throw out the bait. Do not let them suspect you; be very friendly, social, and familiar; if possible, *treat* them, and let them drink freely, and when you get them in the right mood, go in for a *game*, no matter what, so you get the poor fellows' money. If you do not get it, somebody else will. *Cheat* them out of it; *lie* them out of it; *bully* them out of it; *scare* them out of it, and be sure and *get* it; *rake* up the money. You may never live to see another war, nor realize such another harvest for rogueing poor, unsuspecting, innocent men out of their money. "Make hay while the sun shines," is an old adage, but a mighty good one. Now is your time; and, if you cannot get money by gambling, go right in for counterfeiting; make money, and pass off your counterfeits to the soldiers: the army is the place; stick up close to the army, and whenever and wherever you meet a man out of the army, "poke" your counterfeits upon him: let no one escape whom you can rogue out of his money. Remember, this is the rule and law among rogues. Do not violate your principle, but be sure and get money; life itself, in war-times, is nothing to compare with money. Take the hint; you understand; get money!'

"It says to commissaries and quartermasters, and undertakers generally, 'You hold very important offices, occupy very tempting positions; fine opportunity for grand speculations, and no one can be injured. Make purchases from private citizens on your *own* responsibilities; pay your *own* individual money, purchase goods from individuals at the lowest possible prices, or get *agents* to do it for you, and when Government wants such goods,—no matter what, whether corn, oats, hay, flour, horses, mules, beeves, &c. &c.,—just have your *private, unknown agents* at hand, ready with the goods called for, and make Government pay the highest prices. Do you not see what a chance for wide and grand speculations? You can soon get rich, and "nobody hurt." Everybody is making all they can out of this great war; and you had better take chances while the game is being played, and get your part of the public plunder. It will be too late after the war is over. Pitch in; now is the time; do not delay; "make hay while the sun shines."'

"It says to *unsalaried* and *unpensioned* clergymen, and even to some with *small salaries* and pensions, 'Something has turned up, at last, worthy your profoundest consideration. A grand revolution is on foot. A powerful civil war is culminating. If you will be active, energetic, and persevering in preaching up war, discord, and anarchy, and give your whole influence to the work of enlisting poor fellows for the war, they will choose some of you for chaplains, others, it may be, for generals, colonels, majors, captains, lieutenants, adjutants, sergeants, corporals, fifers, or drummers, and thus you will all get fitted out with fat offices and high and honorable military positions; and this will be much more respectable and, withal, much more profitable than staying at home, lounging about, preaching to a few ignorant country-people. Roll up and pitch in. Make up your regiments and companies, get your commissions, secure your fat offices, and gain your respectable positions, before the number is made up and the door for admission is closed against you. Be quick. *Punch* up the young men. Do not delay. Now is your time!'

"And, finally, having *ejected* every principle and feeling of loyalty from the minds and hearts of the arch-traitors in this rebellion, and having stirred up all the discordant, disorganizing, carnal, ambitious, and devilish passions within them, and having influenced them to inaugurate war upon their country, and having dissolved society and involved the whole country in one general ruin, perched at last upon some lofty, towering pinnacle, the grim, ghastly monster beholds a nation in ruins laid, and chuckles at the *hellish* work it has done.

"Secession would break up and overturn all Governments, human and divine, dissolve society universally, scatter broadcast discord, confusion, anarchy, desolation, sorrow, affliction, woe, ruin, death, and bloodshed everywhere! Detestable monster! What philanthropist, patriot, parent, child, or Christian can ever offer an apology for a *creature* so hateful, loathsome, damnable as secession?"—*Christian Banner of July* 14, 1862 [somewhat enlarged].

CHAPTER XXXVI.

"TRUE TO ONE'S OWN SECTION OF COUNTRY.

"AMERICAN citizens can only be true friends to their own individual sections of country by being true friends to their whole country.

"If the country, as a whole, can be broken up and destroyed, then each and every part composing the whole may likewise be destroyed. If, therefore, the elements of destruction within the Federal Government be sufficiently strong to destroy that Government, then the elements of destruction within the Southern Confederacy are sufficiently strong to dash it into as many fragments as there are constituent parts. or States,—these States having been parts of the whole Federal Government.

"If the Union, the Federal Government, this nobly grand and toweringly sublime fabric reared by our ancestors, by men who possessed the purest hearts and clearest heads the world has ever known, cannot stand, what must be the fate, the ultimate destiny, of a confederacy built upon the disorganizing principles of secession,—the very etymological meaning of which word—*secession*—is to disorganize, rend, tear, divide, cut asunder, split up, and rush on to general destruction? Away, then, with this accursed, traitorous, damnable doctrine and idea that *secession* teaches, that because a man is a friend to his whole country, therefore he must be an enemy and a traitor to his own little peculiar section, State, or county! The idea is superlatively absurd."—*Christian Banner, July* 14, 1862.

CHAPTER XXXVII.

"LYING.

"NEVER, within the memory of the oldest man now living on earth, has there been an age of such general, malignant lying as the present. It seems that almost everybody has given up all kinds of business, and 'pitched' into a system of general, scientific lying. Men sit and stand about the corners of the streets, speculating upon what has been and what has never been, what is and what is not, what will be and what will never be, until their imaginative powers have become so very acute that they can metamorphose the God of love and mercy into a God of wrath and vengeance, a God of peace and order into a God of war and anarchy, the devil into an angel of light, sin and death into holiness and immortality, treason into loyalty, and rebellion against the authorities that be into the supreme duty man owes to his God.

"Every one has his own story, and dresses and fixes it up to suit his own taste, and then tells it to every one he chooses; and if a man of sense should think proper to controvert it, the narrator gets as savage as a 'meat-axe,' and swears his auditor is a fool for want of sense,—the very thing that makes all fools. If a premium were offered for *lying*, about this time, and the devil were anywhere about, he would stand no chance. He would blush and *skedaddle*. The fact is, men have become so much accustomed to hearing lies and telling lies that when they see or hear the truth it appals them; and, without investigation, they declare that he who tells the truth is either a knave, a fool, or a madman, or, at least, a man of no character or respectability."—*Christian Banner of July* 30, 1862.

CHAPTER XXXVIII.

In the number of the "Christian Banner" of July 30, 1862, we published the following editorial:—

"ARRESTS.—SLANDER REFUTED.

"On Tuesday night, the 23d instant, four prominent citizens of Fredericksburg were arrested by the authorities of the Federal Government, and on Thursday morning following two others were arrested, and all were sent North. Many rumors have been circulated relative to the causes which led to their arrest. Being ignorant of the facts in the case, of course we cannot say, certainly, for what cause they were arrested. We believe, however,' that the general impression is that they were arrested and are held as hostages for certain Union men who were arrested some months ago and are now confined as prisoners by the Confederate Government. From all the circumstances connected with the arrest of these gentlemen, we are inclined to the opinion that they were arrested and are held as hostages for these Union men, and that they will probably be held until the Union prisoners are released. Not having heard of any specific charges which have been brought against them, we are led to adopt this belief.

"Immediately on the arrest of these gentlemen, we were charged with having had some hand in the matter. In justice, therefore, to ourself, we feel it our duty to make a few remarks of general explanation, which we hope will be satisfactory to the parties and set the matter at rest forever. And, as we trust that this will be the last time that we shall be forced to bring this subject before our readers, we shall enter somewhat into details.

"In the number of the 'Christian Banner' of the 14th instant, we published the following paragraphs, which we republish in this number, that our readers may understand the subject fully. Here are the paragraphs. Read them.

" 'A *reliable* citizen of our town informed us, the other day, that he was told that *we* were running over the river every day to inform General King that one of the reverend clergymen of Fredericksburg had gone to Richmond. He said that he contradicted the report, because he did not believe it to be true. We pronounce the *report* a *base slander* and an *infamous lie.* We have never had the pleasure of forming the acquaintance of General King. We have never spoken a word to him in our life. We do not know him, even by sight, and, if we have ever seen him, we are ignorant of the fact.

"'We have never crossed the Rappahannock River but twice since the Federal army arrived in Falmouth. Once we went to General McDowell's head-quarters to get a pass to go to Baltimore; but we did not see the general, and failed to obtain a pass. Once we visited Falmouth, and on our way were introduced to General Gibbon at his tent, which was directly in our way to Falmouth. What business is it of ours, or why should we care, if every clergyman in town should go to Richmond and stay there forever?'

"We shall handle some of the *respectabilities* with 'gloves off,' if they don't mind how they talk about us. We may be 'flighty,' as one of the learned M.D.s has represented us at head-quarters, but we wish it to be distinctly understood that if we are too 'flighty' to make pills, we are too stubborn to swallow those compounded and retailed out to strangers for the purpose of blasting and *damning* the influence of the '*Christian Banner.*'

"*Respectabilities* must surely judge of the actions and doings of Union men by their own acts and doings. Because they try to defame and blast the reputation and influence of Union men, they seem to think that Union men are constantly engaged in the same dirty, filthy work. *Secession* is a hard road to travel: it leads directly to destruction, and many there be that walk therein.

"We had not heard, nor had we any knowledge of the fact, that Mr. Broaddus had gone to Richmond, until our friend informed us that the report was in circulation that we had informed General King that he had gone. It was commonly reported that a number of our citizens had gone to Richmond, and that any person could go who wished to go. Why, then, should we wish to inform General King that Mr. Broaddus had gone? We have enough to do to attend to our own business, without running with 'batches' of news to General King to instruct him in the discharge of his duties.

"We mean no disrespect to the clergymen of Fredericksburg when we ask, 'What business is it of ours, or why should we care, if every clergyman in town should go to Richmond and stay there forever?' We have nothing to do with the clergy, nor they with us. Their systems of religion and politics, and ours, are so very dissimilar that they can never approximate and harmonize. As to religion, they can go to heaven in their own way. We believe in the *doctrines* and *Christianity* of the *Bible.* If we fail to get to heaven, we shall not lay the blame on the clergy. If they should fail to get to heaven, it is to be hoped that they will not seek to charge their condemnation on us; for God knows we have long and faithfully warned them of their danger.

"When it comes to breaking up our country, however, this is another question. In preaching up their own political destruction, they drag us into the same whirlpool of perdition with themselves; and to this we do most seriously object. And we do argue that if they should prove as successful in working out their own eternal ruin as they have been in effecting their own temporal destruction and that of us all, they are gone and lost forever. And, while we wish it to be distinctly understood that we do not charge the sin of secession upon the clergy *only*, we do say that many of them have done their full share in this awful, *hellish* work.

"We returned from Washington on Saturday evening, and on the following Tuesday night four of the gentlemen were arrested; and before our paper went to press last week we learned that it was currently reported in town, and generally believed, that we had caused the arrest of those gentlemen. This being told to us by several of our prominent citizens, we wrote the following article, which we thought was quite sufficient to satisfy the minds of all. But we learn, however, that there are those who are still disposed to force the blame of the arrest of those gentlemen upon us. Read the article. We give it entire:—

'ANNOYANCES.

"A multitude of little things often annoy one more than one single charge of greater magnitude. We took occasion some time ago to make an explanation relative to certain reports against us, to the effect that we had visited General King and informed him that Dr. Broaddus had gone to Richmond, &c. &c. We disposed of the charge by denouncing it as a base slander and an infamous lie. We are now informed that the report is circulating generally through town, to our injury, that we went to the provost-marshal, Captain Mansfield, and informed him that Dr. Broaddus had gone to Richmond, and that Captain Mansfield, in reply, 'asked' us 'if' we 'had any business to attend to, and, if so, go and do it.' Now, we pronounce this a base slander and an infamous lie.

"And, now that we are forced and provoked to notice these infamous slanders which are being circulated to our injury, we will notice other reports which are in circulation, but for the truth of which we do not hold ourself responsible.

"It is reported that the citizens of Fredericksburg go to and return from Richmond at pleasure; that there is a regular mail kept up between Richmond and Fredericksburg; that a quantity of goods have been carried out of Fredericksburg supposed to be sent to Richmond; that the leading secessionists have made arrangements with the authorities of the Federal Government that Captain Mansfield shall be continued in the office of provost-marshal in Fredericksburg; that a scouting-party brought in from the country a Lynchburg newspaper giving an account of the great victory obtained by the Confederates over the Federal army near Richmond, and that the paper was given to Captain Mansfield, who sent immediately to Mayor Slaughter to come and *see the news;* that a gentleman living out of town said that he would 'drink slop' or 'dish-water forever' before he 'would buy any thing from the *damned Yankees*,' and this gentleman's property was then being guarded by Federal soldiers, and was afterwards continued to be guarded by the Union soldiers, and this was made known to Captain Mansfield, and the gentleman's property was continued to be guarded by the 'Yankees;' that there is not a Union man in Fredericksburg who is in confidence with Captain Mansfield, they believing that he has no sympathy for them, and of course they have none for him; that the secessionists control Captain Mansfield at pleasure, and that they boast of their influence over him; that his counsellors are the leading secessionists (the respectabilities) of Fredericksburg; that Captain Mansfield *is just the man for secessionists.*

"While we are on the subject of rumors, we will add that it is rumored over town that we went to Washington City last week to see President Lincoln and the authorities at the War Department, to get them to turn things 'upside-down' and to 'play the devil' generally with the secessionists of Fredericksburg. These are all secession lies. We went to Washington for no such purpose. We went on business of our own, and that of an entirely private character,—simply to get a little paper and some other articles which we were bound to have. We neither saw, nor went to see, President Lincoln, Secretary Stanton, nor any of the officials at Washington. Surely, secessionists watch us with a 'critic's eye.'

"While in Washington, at the National Hotel, a lieutenant in the Federal army informed us that Dr. Rose, of Falmouth, had told him that we were a perfect maniac. Then, upon the authority of Dr. Scott and Dr. Rose, we are 'flighty' and a 'maniac,' and, of course, we ought to be caged. If greater maniacs and more flighty persons than secessionists can be scared up this side of perdition, may all the heathen, civilized, Grecian, and Roman gods and goddesses pity them!

"We deeply regret the necessity of having to make these remarks; but slander after slander being heaped upon us, day after day and week after week, we are tired of it, and are determined, if possible, to put a stop to it. And now we say to one and all of our vile, cowardly, worthless slanderers, that any human being who says that we have at any time reported any citizen of Fredericksburg, or that we have reported any man, woman, or child, male or female, black or white, south of Mason and Dixon's line, at any of the head-quarters of the Federal army, either in Virginia, at Washington City, or elsewhere, or that we have ever written any letter or letters to any of the official authorities of the Federal Government, or to any private individual or individuals, implicating any human being, or that we have ever carried or sent any document or documents, or signed any document or documents, to be sent to the official authorities at Washington City, or elsewhere, implicating any human being on earth, *is an infamous liar.*

"There is a great fuss made over the arrest of secessionists; but when Union men were seized and hurried off to prison, nothing was said against the course of action pursued by the Confederate authorities. This was all right: there was no sympathy for the poor wives and children and friends of these Union men. Secessionists rejoiced at it, and said the physic was acting, was doing its work well, &c. &c. Secessionists can make their threats against Union men, and say what will be done with them when the Southern army returns to Fredericksburg,—that they shall be shot, or hung, and that they shall never live in this community, —and Union men must submit to all these threats and every vile indignity and insult that can be offered by every worthless poltroon that drags his vile polluted carcass through the streets of Fredericksburg, and Union men dare not open their mouths in self-defence, for fear of being murdered by the Confederate soldiers when they 'come back'!

"We feel truly sorry that these terrible calamities have come upon us; but we cannot help it. We sympathize with our fellow-citizens. We warned them of the danger, and entreated them to return to their former loyalty to the Government. But they spurned our counsel and treated us as an enemy, and still seem determined to rush headlong into irretrievable ruin and drag every soul after them who will be influenced by their ungodly example.

"In conclusion, we will just state that we have never been officious at any of the head-quarters of the Union troops since their arrival in Fredericksburg and its vicinity, never having visited them except when business absolutely called us there. We have attended closely to our own business, and have interrupted no one in attending to his. Our sentiments we have written and published in the columns of the 'Christian Banner,' and for doing this we hold ourself individually responsible. If to be a Union man, a friend to our whole country, be a disgrace, then we are disgraced, and we glory in it. If to advocate the cause of the Union, and to entreat our fellow-citizens to respect and observe the Constitution of the Federal Government, to the end that our own section, our own beloved South, may be saved from total destruction, be treason, then are we a traitor. But to whom, and to what, are we a traitor? A traitor to Jeff Davis and his accomplices in treason? A traitor to a man who was never a candidate for his office *before the people* of any State before the State of Virginia was tied on to the 'Southern Confederacy'? A traitor to an anticipated Government, known and acknowledged by no nation of people upon the face of the whole earth? A traitor to a set of leaders who swear that they will hang or drive out of their prospective kingdom or empire every man who is not a *simon-pure* unsuspicioned secessionist? A traitor to traitors! A traitor to treason! Heavens! the whole charge is a burlesque upon traitors and treason!"

CHAPTER XXXIX.

In the number of the "Christian Banner" of July 30, 1862, we received and copied into the columns of the "Christian Banner" the following extract from the "Richmond Dispatch" of the 23d of July, 1862, on which we made a short editorial, both of which we here insert. First the extract:—

"'MISDIRECTED PHILANTHROPY.

"'We noticed recently statements in Northern papers that Messrs. Marye and Slaughter, of Fredericksburg, had left that place to come to Richmond with the view of obtaining the release of the Federal Brigadier-General Reynolds, who was captured in one of the battles on the Chickahominy. They were said to have been induced to do this in gratitude for the liberal and considerate manner in which General Reynolds had governed their city while under his command. It was further alleged that the citizens of the town, entertaining the same feeling, urged the mission upon them.

"'It has been more lately stated by the same journals that the committee of two had returned, declaring their disgust with the Government at Richmond, all access to which was closed against them.

"'Now, we do not believe all that the Yankee papers have said on the subject; but we suppose at least so much is true as relates to the expedition of the gentlemen named to this place. They no doubt stated their case to the proper officers; and their appeal was, of course, rejected, as it ought to have been. Was not General Reynolds in arms against us? Did he not lead a brigade of cut-throats to take the lives of our brave soldiers, to subjugate us, and take possession of our property? Was he not taken in the field fighting against us? Why then is he to be entitled to the commiseration of the Fredericksburgers and to discharge from the custody of our authorities? If he is less a brute and more of a man than some of his colleagues, he cannot be excepted from the treatment due an enemy, though he may be less execrated. But he is in very bad company, and must take pot-luck with them. The people of Fredericksburg may run over with gratitude, but nobody will be lost in admiration of the good sense displayed in the commission to this city in behalf of the man who led so many Yankees to desolate our country.'

"From the above it will be seen that the authorities at Richmond have very little sympathy for General Reynolds, notwithstanding all his kindness to the citizens of Fredericksburg. Surely, if the leaders in the Confederate army were sincere, and believed that they were telling the truth, when they delineated all the crimes of abomination which the Union troops would perpetrate against women and citizens generally whenever and wherever they advanced into the country, they ought to feel thankful to God and to the Federal officers that the people in Fredericksburg have been dealt with so tenderly. But General Reynolds 'is in very bad company, and, if he is less a brute and more of a man than some of his colleagues, he must take pot-luck with them.' This is the gratitude of the officials at Richmond for all the kindness shown to the citizens of Fredericksburg by General Reynolds. Wonder what they would do with some of the other kind, sympathizing Federal officers if they had them in Richmond! They would have to take 'pot-luck' too, we guess."

CHAPTER. XL.

In the number of the "Christian Banner" of July 30, 1862, we published the following editorial:—

"OATH OF ALLEGIANCE.

"The late order of General Pope has fallen like a thunderbolt from a clear sky on the citizens of this community. As long as they were allowed to talk treason against the Federal Government and threaten vengeance against Union men with impunity, they thought matters were going on very nicely. But when it comes to swearing,—to taking the oath of allegiance to respect and support the Government which has protected them and all they possess from their cradles up to the time of this unprovoked rebellion,—they begin to look with wonder and astonishment. And this becomes the more terrible when they look at the dread penalty which is annexed to the oath if not respected by those who take it.

"We heartily wish that all our citizens could conscientiously take the oath and honestly observe it. But we learn that there are some who declare they cannot and will not take it. They say, 'It is hard for men to be forced from their homes.' Yes: this, we admit, is very hard; but then, on the other hand, it is very hard that a country like ours should be broken up by a set of unprincipled, aspiring demagogues. It is very hard that millions of soldiers should be forced to leave their quiet, peaceful homes, their wives and children, their fathers and mothers, and all the blessings and comforts of life at home, and peril their lives in camp, on the battle-field, and die far away from home, friends, and relatives, all on account of the diabolical ambition of a few wicked, God-forsaken usurpers. It is very hard that our country should be desolated, and all our privileges, social, religious, and political, should be destroyed, by a set of disappointed tyrants. It is very hard that our dear sons, whom we love as we do our own heart's blood, should be immolated upon the accursed altar of a band of ambitious traitors. All these things are hard,—yes, very hard; and yet the leaders who forced this state of things upon the country think it very hard that they should be subject to any inconveniences or losses during the whole rebellion.

"But men talk about 'property' in this matter. What true-hearted patriot would throw his country into one end of the *balance* and a few goods and chattels into the other end, and then hesitate a moment which to choose? Would not every true patriot exclaim, 'Our country forever!'

"'But suppose we take the oath to respect and support the Federal Government, and afterwards the Confederate army should return: then we shall lose all our property, and, it may be, our lives into the bargain.'

"Well, suppose you do not take the oath of allegiance: you will forfeit all your property by refusing to take the oath and by going outside of the Federal lines; and if the Confederates return all your property will be destroyed anyway, except, perhaps, the ground upon which your houses stand: hence, if you go against your country, you will certainly lose all your property, and may-be your lives into the bargain, and, worse than all, you may die fighting against your own dear, heaven-blessed country.

"By taking the oath of allegiance to the Constitution and support of the Federal Government, men may save their honor, their property, their lives, and their country. And, remember what we say, this is but the beginning of the evils that are yet to come upon us if we continue in a state of ungodly rebellion. Men may stand upon their affected dignity until they see their country crushed, but dignified and titled pride will fall into muddy waters before this rebellion ends. If there should be a doubt, therefore, in the mind of any one as to what course he should pursue, we would honestly, before God, say, Let our country have the benefit of that doubt. Our country first, our country last, and our country forever!"

CHAPTER XLI.

"PRIVILEGES ABUSED.—SUNDRIES.

"SINCE the occupation of Fredericksburg by the Federal troops, a quantity of goods have been brought to town, and vast quantities of them are said to have been sent on to Richmond. In consequence of which, the traffic, or speculations, have been suppressed by Government; and we learn that no more goods will be allowed to come to town, except supplies for the army. If this be true, we shall soon see and feel suffering times in Fredericksburg."—*Christian Banner, July* 30, 1862.

"PUBLIC NOTICE.

"For the last eighteen months we have been annoyed and constantly insulted by a set of worthless, impudent, low-lived, contemptible, lawless boys, who visit our door and often so disturb us and our company that it is impossible to enjoy any satisfaction with gentlemen who visit us. We have in one or two instances informed their parents, and all to no effect.

"We now, therefore, give these hopeful candidates of *hemp* and their parents public notice that if we are again interrupted or insulted by these said worthless scamps, they must take the consequences. We know the boys, and have got the proof."—*Christian Banner, August* 6, 1862.

These boys, we believe, were influenced to this course

of conduct by their *secesh* parents, because we were a Union man. Their conduct was absolutely intolerable both by day and by night, as many of our visitors can testify.

"The provisions embraced in the Constitution of the United States and the Fugitive Slave Law were the only securities and safeguards for the perpetuity of African slavery in the South. The seceded States, having repudiated the Constitution and the Government of the United States, have virtually abolished African slavery by their own acts."—*Christian Banner, July* 6, 1862.

CHAPTER XLII.

"GUERRILLA BANDS.

"'PARTISAN rangers,' says Secretary Randolph, 'require stricter discipline than other troops to make them efficient, and, without discipline, they become a terror to their friends and are contemptible in the eye of the enemy.'

"Who could have supposed, three years ago, that the citizens of America,—proud, happy, enlightened America—could ever have inaugurated a system of warfare so barbarous, savage, and cruel as this *guerrilla-band* system,—a system, too, clothed with all the pomp, dignity, and importance which the authorities of the Confederate States can bestow upon it?

"These bands are 'a terror to their friends,' simply because no one can regard them in any other light than legalized bands of highway-robbers, who would as soon take from friends as from foes. No man is safe in a community where these guerrilla bands are allowed to prowl through the country with impunity." —*Christian Banner, July* 6, 1862.

CHAPTER XLIII.

"EXAMINE THE LOGIC.

"VIRGINIANS were warned that *secession* was the broad, sure, and direct road to universal ruin. They are *now told* that to continue in a state of rebellion against the Federal Government will certainly complete the destruction and general ruin which are now going on all over the State; and still the men who warn them of their danger are regarded by secessionists as the worst enemies of Virginia, traitors to Virinia and to the South, who ought to be punished with death, and shall be when the time comes.

"Ministers of the gospel warn sinners to flee from the wrath to come. They declare to them that the wages of sin is death; that the way of transgressors is hard; that if they continue to rebel against the authority of Heaven they will certainly be lost forever. 'It is all nonsense,' say sinners: 'these preachers are all crazy: they are in league with his *satanic majesty*, and want us all to go to hell.'

"Just as certainly as that sinners will be lost who refuse to repent and yield obedience to the word of God and the laws of Heaven, just so certainly, in our opinion, will Virginia and Virginians be forever temporally ruined, unless they lay down the weapons of their rebellion against the Federal Government and speedily return to their former loyalty to the Constitution and Government of the United States. And because we thus warn our fellow-citizens of the awful calamities which must certainly visit them if they remain rebellious, they regard us as their worst enemy. Are we indeed an enemy to our countrymen because we tell them the truth?"—*Christian Banner, August* 6, 1862.

CHAPTER XLIV.

"'CAN'T DISGRACE OURSELVES AND OUR CHILDREN BY TAKING THE OATH OF ALLEGIANCE.'

"Is it not passing strange, and a most ridiculous idea, that men who have been protected by the Government of the United States, ever since they were born, in their persons, property, and every blessing, civil, political, social, and religious, which men can hold near and dear on earth, should now raise the canting cry, 'We can't take the oath of allegiance to the United States Government; it would disgrace us and our children forever.' 'Can't take the oath of allegiance to the Black Republican Abolition Government.' 'Can't take the oath of allegiance to old Abe Lincoln.'

"Men refuse to take the oath of allegiance to support

the best Government in the world,—and one, too, under the fostering care of which they have lived all their lives,—for fear by this act of being eternally disgraced and for fear of entailing infamy on their dear children! But they are not afraid of disgracing themselves and their dear children by taking the oath of allegiance to support an organized mob, the avowed design of which is to break up the Government and to establish a despotism more to be dreaded than death with all its horrors.

"'Can't take the oath of allegiance,' to support a Government acknowledged and respected by all the nations of the civilized world, but do not blush to swear allegiance to a prospective Government, which is neither acknowledged nor respected by any nation on earth, and perhaps never will be to the end of time.

"'Can't submit' to the administration of a man who was constitutionally elected by a large majority-vote of the American people, but are willing to submit to the administration of a man who received his appointment at the hands of a few *arch*-traitors to their own Government, which they had sworn to respect and defend.

"'Can't take the oath of allegiance to old Abe Lincoln:' this would disgrace them and their children in the estimation of all honorable men; but they can take the oath of allegiance to old Jeff Davis, which is honorable, and entitles them and their children to consideration and position among *all* the *respectabilities* and *all* the *first families* of all nations, kindreds, tongues, and people who live and dwell and move upon the face of the whole earth! What a pity it would be for *some men* and their *dear* children to *lower* their standing, position, and *respectability* in society and among all the *respectabilities* of all the respectable nations of the world, by taking the oath of allegiance to the Constitution of the United States!

"For American citizens, who profess to be patriots, to abandon the Constitution and the Federal Government for a prospective Government to be established by a set of traitors, is as ludicrous as for men professing to be Christians to swap the Bible for the theological works of Thomas Paine."—*Christian Banner, July* 6, 1862.

CHAPTER XLV.

"FREDERICKSBURG THREE YEARS AGO, AND FREDERICKSBURG NOW.

"How very different was Fredericksburg three years ago from Fredericksburg now! Who could have supposed that such great changes could have taken place in so short a period? Then she was a gay, fashionable, happy, and prosperous town; now she looks as though the angel of death had passed over her and smitten the first-born of every family in town. In half a century from this time, Fredericksburg will be a large manufacturing city, with five times the population she now has, or has ever had. Remember the prediction!"—*Christian Banner, August* 6, 1862.

CHAPTER XLVI.

"VIRGINIANS, PREPARE FOR THE WORST!

"'Tis hard for those who have labored and toiled for years in order to accumulate the necessaries of life, and who by the most rigid economy, and in many instances by the greatest self-denial, have secured a competency of this world's goods to sustain them in the decline of life and old age, to have it all swept from them, as it were, in a single day. But such is the present state of things. And, what is most provoking, the innocent in this *infernal rebellion*, in many instances, will suffer equally with the guilty parties, if not more.

"The action of a few leaders in the cotton States has involved Virginia in universal and inextricable ruin. The great wealth of Virginia, and especially of Eastern Virginia, consisted principally in her slave population. This portion of her wealth is irrecoverably lost. To think of ever recovering the slaves that have escaped, or shall hereafter make their escape, is absurd. And equally fallacious is the idea that the rebellious owners will ever receive any pay for them. They are gone,—and from their former masters they are gone forever! That the whole of the slave population in Eastern Virginia, with the exception of a few old, superannuated men and women, and a few children who have no fathers and mothers to aid them in making their escape, will ultimately leave, no *sane* man can doubt for a moment.

Then it is certain that by far the greatest portion of the wealth of Virginia is already lost! lost! lost!

"Real estate is the next species of property which is the most valuable in Virginia. To say nothing of the confiscation law, the landed estates in Virginia will, before the war ends, diminish at least one-half or one-third their original value. What will farms be worth without enclosures, houses, and even destitute of timber in many instances to rebuild them? The whole country desolated, houses torn down, fences destroyed, negroes gone, and most of the white male population either dead or wounded and disabled for life. This will be the condition, the destiny, of Virginia, when this war shall have closed; and no sensible man will controvert it.

"In connection with this subject, we would ask, what is the money worth which is now in circulation in Virginia? Confederate notes are worth nothing outside of the Confederate lines, and are worth nothing inside of the Confederate lines except for present purposes; and, let the success of the war be what it may, Confederate notes, as we have often said, can never be redeemed. This money will ultimately be a dead loss to individuals who have it on hand. Even Virginia money is greatly below *par* now; and what it will finally be worth is altogether a matter of wild speculation.

"In addition to all this, Virginia is now, to a considerable extent, maintaining both the Federal and Confederate armies. How long will it take two such armies—say a million and a half of men and horses—to eat Virginia out of house and home? All the produce which was raised last year, and all that is being raised the present year, will soon be eaten up and consumed, and but little preparations are being made for crops next year; and what, we ask, will become of the citizens of Virginia during the next eighteen months or two years? Terribly dark is the picture to contemplate; and, in addition to all this, there are many calamities more fearful than any yet named, and of which we tremble to think, and forbear to mention, but which will certainly befall us if this wicked rebellion continues. And we repeat that, in the face of all these things, many of our citizens continue fixed, firm, and steadfast in their course of rebellion,—determined, if possible, to break up the Government, annihilate the Republic, and establish the reign of anarchy, guerrilla despotism, and terror, all over the land. We do most devoutly pray that those of our fellow-citizens who are not given entirely over to judicial blindness, hardness of heart, and reprobacy of mind, will think more seriously, calmly, and dispassionately, and withal more sensibly, on this subject, and renounce and denounce this most unholy rebellion, and return to their duty as loyal citizens.

"We say, therefore, let Virginians prepare for the worst; for, under the most favorable circumstances in which this subject can possibly be contemplated, all hands must go to work. Males and females, young and old, those who have been rich, as well as the poor, all must henceforth go to work. Therefore, let all hands roll up their sleeves and pitch right in."—*Christian Banner, August* 6, 1862.

CHAPTER XLVII.

"WONDERFUL TO TELL.

"On last Saturday morning our attention was called to a crowd of contrabands, which by far surpassed any thing we have seen during the war. An elegant carriage, drawn by two splendid horses, came rolling into town, and halted in front of General Patrick's head-quarters. Being induced by curiosity to look into the interior of the carriage, we discovered that it was thoroughly filled with female contrabands and children. The women were sitting up, fanning themselves, and looking as *aristocratic* as if they belonged to the 'first families of Virginia,' and no doubt but what they had; but, alas! the primitive glory was rapidly departing, as it is from most of the proud, aristocratic first families of Virginia, that good old State, sacrificed on the unhallowed altar of would-be petty tyrants and contemptible demagogues. The whole retinue belonging to the carriage, including the driver and a companion seated by his side, numbered ten contrabands in all. We learned from the party that the carriage and horses belonged to Mr. ——, of Caroline county, who 'had' been their master, and who was at home when they left, and was, perhaps, asleep, as they *skedaddled* while it was yet dark.

"In company with the carriage-party there was an ox-cart, drawn by four large, fat oxen, filled with furniture, and about fifteen women and small children on top. There were others on horseback. In all, we learned that there were between twenty and thirty contrabands, all of whom had belonged to one man, as did also the carriage and horses, and cart and oxen, and all left the owner in one single night! The whole lot of negroes, carriage and horses, cart and oxen, three years ago would have commanded in actual cash, at the lowest calculation, twenty-five thousand dollars, and all gone in a single night!

"Virginians are being reduced to the most abject poverty. This, we must remind the reader, is a part and parcel of the *promised* glories of secession. Let the *wise* leaders in the damning work of secession *now* come forward before the *dear people*,—the *hard-working yeomanry* of Virginia,—and give an account of their stewardship. How the citizens of Virginia can longer tolerate these men, who must be either *fools* or *knaves*, or both, is one of the riddles of riddles to us, and one which we cannot solve, except upon the principle of the old Roman adage, 'Whom the gods intend to destroy they first make mad.' And still the *dear people* seem bent and determined on following their political and spiritual guides, even if they land them in temporal and eternal ruin.

"Great numbers of contrabands are flocking into town,—more for the last few days than usual, owing, we suppose, to the report that the Southern army is returning to town, and the negroes are trying to make their final exit before it arrives.

"What a change of things in Virginia! Negroes riding in fine carriages, while their masters and mistresses are left at home to cut the wood, milk the cows, 'tote' the water, cook the victuals, sweep the floors, and nurse the children! And still they shout hosannas to secession, to old Jeff Davis and the glorious Southern Confederacy! The reaction must come, it will come; and then woe be unto the leaders."—*Christian Banner, August* 16, 1862.

CHAPTER XLVIII.

"'I NEVER EXPECTED IT WOULD COME TO THIS.'

"A GENTLEMAN and a friend of ours from the country observed to us in our office the other day, in course of conversation on the gloomy appearance of affairs, that he 'had no idea things would turn out as they have,' when he was advocating secession and when he 'voted for it.' With a deep sigh, and a downcast look, he exclaimed, 'I never expected it would come to this.' 'No,' he added, 'I never expected this.' Thousands can say the same thing now. Why, then, hold on to the abominable doctrine of secession,—the abomination of desolation? Why not abandon the accursed evil, and at once take a decided stand in the ranks of loyal citizens?

"The leaders in this rebellion had no idea themselves that things would turn out as they have done. If men had honestly and without a doubt believed that secession would have caused the death of their dear children, the abolition of their slaves, and the general ruin of their country, would they, could they, have advocated and voted for secession? And would they have denounced those who were opposed to secession as traitors and Abolitionists, and have forced them to vote whether they wished to do so or not? Common sense says, No; every sympathy of humanity says, No. These same men are daily and hourly seeing and feeling the results of secession; and we now tell them plainly that the half has not been seen and felt unless they renounce their rebellion and return into the Union and do their duty as loyal citizens.

"Men see and feel the blasting, withering, and desolating effects of secession everywhere, and still they persist in saying, 'We'll soon whip them out; we'll have Washington soon; we'll get all our negroes back, or get well paid for them; we'll keep fighting on until the last man in the South is killed out; we'd rather see every thing in ashes, every soldier killed, the whole country annihilated, than ever to return again into the Union.'

"Was ever such folly and madness heard of, read of, or thought of, since God made man, as the folly and madness which spring from secession?

"'I never expected it would come to this.' Thousands can now say this, and they are saying it every day, We never expected 'it would come to this.' No: the champion leaders, the *arch*-traitors in this terrible rebellion are as much disappointed in their calculations and expectations as are the great body of the people whom they have deceived. They never expected things would take the course and produce the results which they have done. Virginians never expected to see their beautiful towns desolated, their farms laid waste, their property scattered like chaff before the wind, their slaves leaving them at will and marching off never to return again, their children sacrificed and butchered like sheep for the slaughter. They never expected that Virginia would become the battle-field and the burial-ground of a great national revolution. No: Virginians never expected any of these things.

"Six months ago, the secessionists in our town laughed at the idea that the Union troops would ever get to Fredericksburg. They never expected things would come to what they have; and it would have been dangerous for any one to have predicted the present state of affairs in town. They now see with their eyes and hear with their ears; but all seems to make little or no impression on their minds and hearts for the better. They see with their eyes, but cannot perceive; they hear with their ears, but cannot understand. They obstinately refuse to contemplate the ultimate result of things dispassionately and impartially. If this rebellion should continue twelve months or two or three years longer, the horrible scenes which will be acted out will be without a parallel in the history of the world. The simple circumstance of slaves leaving their owners will be regarded as an insignificant trifle compared with other things which will happen.

"The whole colored population of Virginia is becoming alarmingly demoralized; the spirit of insubordination and rebellion against the authority of their masters is constantly being demonstrated in our midst. This is obvious to all persons. There are but few white men in Virginia apart from the army, except old men and invalids. The most of the white male population of Virginia is in the Southern army. When, therefore, this spirit of rebellion in the colored population becomes fully rife, what will become of these old men and invalids? and, worse than all, what will become of helpless women and innocent children? The future is a picture terrible to contemplate, to avert which, every sensible man and woman in the whole country should exert his or her undivided and untiring influence. The half has neither been seen, heard, nor felt, if this rebellion continue twelve months or two or three years longer. Remember, fellow-citizens, what we say; and may the Lord grant you wisdom and understanding before it is finally too late!"—*Christian Banner, August* 13, 1862.

CHAPTER XLIX.

"RESPECTABILITY.

"ONE of our country friends informs us that he heard a prominent citizen of Fredericksburg, and a member of the *bar*, say that 'there are not more than four men of respectability in the town of Fredericksburg who are in favor of the Union' or of the Federal Government. The gentleman and the Union men of Fredericksburg may only differ on the simple question, What is respectability? Of course, all lawyers are men of *respectability*. They never twist, turn, nor change their political *status*, or position! The fixed and immutable laws of *nature* may change, but lawyers, *never!* They are always men of respectability! This is a fixed, undeniable fact: therefore it is useless to look for a Union man among them. All leading secessionists are men of unquestioned respectability: they never change their political principles, do they? They say they will rule or ruin; and they swear that they will stick up to their text, if they drag the whole world headlong to hell with themselves. Who can, henceforth and for evermore, question the respectability of lawyers and leading secessionists?"—*Christian Banner, July* 14, 1862.

CHAPTER L.

"POOR WHITES LOYAL.

"A CORRESPONDENT of the New York 'Herald' says,—

"'Out of one hundred and twenty citizens of Sperryville who have taken the oath of allegiance within the last two days, there are fifty who cannot write their names. The whites, as a rule, are loyal; and but few of them will be sent South.'

"What a glorious eulogy this correspondent passes on 'poor whites'! They, 'as a rule, are loyal.' The poor white classes are honest, loyal, and would do their duty were it not for the intrigue, deception, and damnable villany of designing men, who, taking advantage of the position which they occupy in society, impose upon the ignorance and credulity of the 'poor whites.'

"'The poor whites, as a rule, are loyal:' by inference, therefore, the rich, white respectabilities are traitors to their country. The men who have involved the poor, loyal whites in this awful rebellion are Senators, Congressmen, Legislators, members of conventions, lawyers, preachers, clerks, office-holders, and office-seekers, who, having no office, and finding and knowing it to be hard to roll and shine without means to uphold them in their extravagances, preached secession to the poor loyal whites, and, by fair promises, eloquent speeches, and terrible threats, involved them in ruin, with the vain hope of obtaining the rich spoils of Government and honorable positions for themselves.

"Why, then, should *men* who are trying to 'crush out treason and put down the rebellion,' as they call it, seek the counsel of the rich, treasonable respectabilities of 'rebeldom'? *Have wealth and position, though clothed in the long black robe of treason, such charms as to attract and allure into their influence epauletted loyalty?*"—*Christian Banner, August* 13, 1862.

CHAPTER LI.

"THE UNION AS IT WAS.

"'Let us have the Union as it was. Give us back the old Union, with all our rights and institutions, and we will be satisfied.'

"Are secessionists in earnest when they speak thus? Did they not have the Union, the old Union, the Union as it was, with all their rights, privileges, and institutions, religious, political, social, and domestic? They did; and still they were not satisfied. After millions of dollars have been spent, and hundreds of thousands of lives have been sacrificed,—after a nation has been baptized in blood, the innocent blood of its noblest sons,—after the peace and happiness of thirty millions of people have been destroyed,—after the pall of gloom and sorrow has enveloped the whole nation,—when sadness is depicted in every countenance, and every heart throbs with grief,—for the instigators and leaders in this awful tragedy to talk about getting back the old Union—the Union as it was—is an absurdity in thought.

"Disappointed in their ambitious and wicked attempt to break up the Government and to destroy the old Union, the Union as it was,—and failing to establish a negro-oligarchy upon the ruins of liberty and the downfall of a free and independent Government, they cry out, 'Give us the old Union,—the Union as it was,—and we will be content.'

"When the leaders in this wicked rebellion shall have restored to the Government every dollar that has been expended in putting down this rebellion, and shall have refunded to the people of the seceded States every dollar they have spent in carrying on this rebellion,—when they shall have restored to all the weeping widows and orphan children their murdered husbands and fathers,—when they shall have given back to heart-stricken parents all their sons who have fallen and shall yet fall in the battle-field and with disease occasioned by this unjust war,—in a word, when the guilt and stain of the last drop of innocent blood of all who have fallen in death, produced by this unholy war, shall have been wiped from their guilty souls, and when this whole country shall have been restored just as it was before this war began,—then, and not until then, may the leaders in this rebellion expect to get back the Union, the old Union, just as it was.

"The Union can never be restored just as it was.

This is an absolute impossibility. The dead can never be restored back to the living; the sorrows and afflictions of the injured living can never be healed; the demolished towns, villages, dwellings, and the desolated country, can never be restored just as they were before the war commenced. The thousands of slaves who have already escaped, and those who shall yet escape from their owners during this war, will never be returned to their masters. The kind feelings and friendly relations which existed between the people of the North and the people of the South before this war began, will not be restored, during the present generation at least. These things are all impossible: hence, to talk about getting back the Union,—the old Union,—the Union just as it was,—is folly, is nonsense, is absurd, is impossible."

CHAPTER LII.

ORDER IN FREDERICKSBURG DURING THE TIME THE TOWN WAS OCCUPIED BY OUR TROOPS.

Previous to the arrival of the Federal troops in the town of Fredericksburg and its vicinity, secessionists had reported that wherever the Union troops went, they committed all kinds of depredations and outrages on the property and persons of citizens. Hence the general panic among the people generally, and the female portion of the population particularly, at the advance of the Union troops on Fredericksburg in April, 1862. Instead, however, of the depredations and outrages being perpetrated which most of the citizens seemed to have anticipated, the officers appeared to do every thing reasonable and consistent with their position to conciliate the good feelings of the citizens. Private property was not only respected, but assiduously guarded by the troops, and men were encouraged to attend to their lawful, usual avocations. But we are sorry to say that the very kindness of the Federal troops seemed only to provoke the leading secessionists to feelings of greater vindictiveness than ever, if possible, against the officers, the soldiers, and the Federal Government, and certainly more so against the Union citizens of the town. The reader may judge of the order observed in the town of Fredericksburg from the following editorials which we published in the "Banner," and which if they had not been true would have been contradicted by all parties:—

"We have lived in Fredericksburg sixteen years, and have never witnessed our town more quiet, during the whole time, than it has been since the arrival of the Federal army. General Patrick is certainly a fine disciplinarian, and his men know how to deport themselves. We sincerely hope that quiet and good order will continue; and we confidently believe they will, so long as General Patrick and his command remain."—*Christian Banner, May* 27, 1862.

Owing to the insults which were offered to the Federal soldiers and the indignities which were heaped on the flag of the Union after the arrival of the Union troops at Fredericksburg, by way of a friendly hint we wrote the following:—

"Every cause must and will produce its legitimate effect: if, therefore, persons [citizens, we meant] do not wish to be insulted, they must not provoke insults. We make this remark by way of a friendly hint to all those persons who are seeking notoriety by offering insults to others, thereby rendering themselves supremely ridiculous in the estimation of all wise and prudent persons, both male and female."

"MILITARY GOVERNOR.—We regretted when we learned that General Patrick was going to leave town, there being such excellent order during his administration. We are happy to learn, however, that General John F. Reynolds is one among the very best of men, and a fine general, and therefore sincerely hope and confidently believe that the same good order will be maintained as has been heretofore. We most devoutly wish that all our citizens may co-operate in endeavoring to maintain good order in town. Mobs, even on a small scale, are very much to be deplored in any community of good citizens."—*Christian Banner, May* 31, 1862.

"We are happy to say that since General Reynolds has been in command in Fredericksburg the same good order has been maintained in town as was observed during the administration of General Patrick. Truly the citizens of Fredericksburg have abundant reason for gratulation in having two such accomplished generals to preside over them, taking care of their interests and saving them from insult and injury, from any and all sources, so far as their knowledge and jurisdiction extend. We hope that General Reynolds and staff may remain in their present position until the war in Virginia shall have closed, or until the civil shall take the place of military authority. And we do most earnestly trust that all our citizens, male and female, old and young, will co-operate with the military authorities in maintaining good order."—*Christian Banner, June* 7, 1862.

The following brief paragraph may explain the reason why we threw out the "friendly hint" of which mention is made in a foregoing paragraph:—

"UNION FLAG.

"Some of the fastidious female population of our town leave the side-walks and circle around into the streets, to avoid passing under the Union flag. We have heard it suggested, however, that none of the *ladies* belonging to the *élite class* of the community have manifested such stupidity. Of course, none but the *lower class*, the poor, uneducated, would be guilty of such folly. Here we drop the subject for the reader's reflection."—*Christian Banner, July* 20, 1862.

"MILITARY GOVERNOR.

"Major Livingston, recently military governor of this place, has been succeeded by Captain John Mansfield, provost-marshal of General King's division. Governor Livingston was peculiarly felicitous in his policy of administration, and accomplished a great deal of business during the short time he remained in office. Captain J. E. Cook, provost-marshal, was active, energetic, and persevering in ferreting out nuisances and curses to our town; and both Governor Livingston and Captain Cook merit the unqualified commendation of our citizens generally, for their indefatigable assiduity in maintaining good order in our town during the short period they held command.

"Captain John Mansfield, our present provost-marshal and military governor, has made a very considerable beginning in clearing the town of some of the curses yet remaining in the place, having already captured six cases and one barrel of liquors, which he has handed over, we presume, to the proper authorities. We confidently believe, from what we have seen, that Governor Mansfield will spare no labor in his endeavors to maintain good order in town, and sincerely hope that all our citizens will co-operate with him in his efforts to do so."—*Christian Banner, June* 24, 1862.

"General Patrick has returned to Fredericksburg, and, we learn, will be military governor of our town. It will be remembered that he was the first military governor of Fredericksburg after the surrender of the town to the Union troops; and his popularity is proverbial. We are gratified to learn that he will take command, and hope that he may be successful as formerly in maintaining good order in town."—*Christian Banner, July* 30, 1862.

Colonel H. Kingsbury was the last military governor of Fredericksburg. He was acting at the time the town was evacuated by General Burnside. Suffice it to say that Colonel H. Kingsbury *was a gentleman.*

We hoped and prayed that the mildness and kind

treatment of the officers and the good deportment of the soldiers of the United States army towards the secessionists and the citizens generally of Fredericksburg would win secessionists over to the cause of the Union. But they did not. Ephraim is joined to his idols: let him alone. And so it is with leading secessionists: they are given over to judicial blindness, they are joined to their *demon idol secession:* let them alone. The more you try to conciliate, harmonize, and compromise, the more determined they seem to be in their awful work of utter and general ruin. They construe the very kindness of their friends into *cowardice* and *treason* against Jeff Davis and the Southern Confederacy. Our heart's desire and prayer to God is that our countrymen, our brethren and kinsmen according to the flesh, may be saved.

We feel it to be our duty to make the above statements, in testimony of the course of conduct pursued towards the citizens of Fredericksburg by both officers and soldiers during the time the United States troops held command of that town. We have written the truth, the statements of any others to the contrary notwithstanding.

CHAPTER LIII.

"SLAVES SEEKING FREEDOM.

"SINCE the surrender of the town of Fredericksburg to the Federal authorities, hundreds of servants have left their masters and gone to seek the blessings of freedom. Thousands of them may find, when it is too late, that the anticipated blessings of freedom will result like the anticipated glories of secession. The one idea with them is freedom: all other blessings will follow as a matter of course. So it was with secessionists: just secede, and jump into paradise."—*Christian Banner, May* 9, 1862.

"GUERRILLA WARFARE.

"This is a kind of irregular mode of carrying on war by the constant attacks of independent bands. It was adopted in the North of Spain during the Peninsular War. Guerrilla warfare is nothing more nor less than a legalized system of plunder, highway-robbery, murder, and assassination, and none but humans *demonized* would inaugurate a mode of warfare so revolting to humanity, civilization, Christianity, and the honorable modes of warfare.

"We learn that some cowardly scoundrels are rendering themselves notoriously and eternally infamous, by sneaking through the country during the dark hours of night, and by violence taking men from their homes, their wives and children, and dragging them either into the army, or having them sent to Richmond for imprisonment, simply because they won't shout hosannas to secession. There is an hour of terrible retribution awaiting such characters."— *Christian Banner, May* 20, 1862.

"STAMPEDE OF SLAVES.

"Thousands of negroes in Virginia are taking leave of their owners, and are going they know not where.

Some say they are going 'Norf,' where they anticipate an admittance into the ante-chamber of heaven, there to remain till the doors of the New Jerusalem are thrown wide open, when the champions of Abolitionism will give them an introduction to the highest dignitaries of the unknown world.

"We most devoutly trust that Abolitionists will get their satisfaction of 'niggers.' Yes, they now have an unmistakable opportunity of developing their long-pent-up fountain of sympathy for the 'poor oppressed negroes of the South.' Let them now untie their purse-strings and scatter their money broadcast for the dear, darling idols of their hearts. What a pity that so many servants who have kind masters to feed, clothe, and look after their welfare, should be so foolish as to forsake all, to go in search of greater pleasures at the 'Norf'!

"It is precisely like the folly of secessionists. They had comfortable homes, and were enjoying every blessing that a free and intelligent people, it seems to us, could have wished. But they were not satisfied. Driven to madness by ambition to reign, rule, and govern all things and all people, they plunged themselves into ruin, and have *dragged* the whole country along with them. And still they rant and swear that they are right, notwithstanding thousands of fully-developed facts stare them in the face, rebuking them for their supreme folly and unparalleled wickedness. Never was the old Roman proverb more clearly illustrated than it is in the present case of the leaders of secessionists, that 'Whom the gods wish to destroy they first make mad.' And holy writ says, 'For this cause God shall send them strong delusions, that they may believe a *lie*, that they all may be damned.' "—*Christian Banner, May* 31, 1862.

"NORTHERN MEN SECESSIONISTS.

"Some of the most violently envenomed secessionists in our whole community, during the great struggle of 1860 and 1861, were Northern men. If the whole South had belonged to them, they could not have put on more important airs than they did. Southern men who feel a devotion to the South of which these men are incapable, have been the subjects of their taunts, sneers, and insults."—*Christian Banner, July* 30, 1862.

The following concise letter may explain to the reader some of our persecutions which were observed by the Union troops during their stay at Fredericksburg. How sincerely it was appreciated by us, the reader may well imagine when he reflects upon the many sore trials we had to endure, and the gloomy circumstances which constantly surrounded us:—

"[To the Editor of the 'Christian Banner.']

"CAMP RUFUS KING, VA.,
"OPPOSITE FREDERICKSBURG.

"MR. EDITOR:—I have just been looking at the latest issue of your valuable and patriotic little paper; and, amongst my thoughts, I was thinking of what you have come through since the so-called secession of the Southern States. But may God prosper you in your undertaking, and bring you safely through all your reverses and troubles.

"When this unholy war is ended, and peace restored, then can the citizens of Fredericksburg see their folly clearly, and that, in the end, all will be for the best.

"Let the citizens *talk* and *lie* of you as they may, your little paper shows your sentiments, and in the end you will be justified. Wherever we may go, our hope is that you may continue in your good work, and, by your diligence and perseverance, you may win back a great many to the Union.

"By a MEMBER OF COMPANY A,
"23D REG'T N.Y. S. V."

Christian Banner, July 30, 1862.

By whom the above letter was written, we have never been able to learn.

CHAPTER LIV.

UNION ELEMENT OF THE SOUTH.

THAT there is and always has been a strong Union element in the South, is beyond a doubt. This element, however, is kept latent, because, by force of circumstances, it cannot be developed without making victims of the loyal men, as they would be sacrificed on the unholy altar of treason and traitors if they were known to be Union men. "If this Union feeling exists," say some, "why is it not developed as the United States troops advance into the rebellious States?" Simply because Union men have not confidence in the ability of the Federal army to hold the territory which they take. For example: if the Union men in Fredericksburg could have known positively that the town never would have been evacuated by the Union troops, and that the Confederate army would never have returned there, then there would have been a much stronger Union element developed at once than there has been since. This we positively know to be correct.

It was reported by secessionists on the arrival of the Union troops at Fredericksburg, in April, 1862, that there were not more than one or two Union men in town,—that the whole community was a unit on secession; and this, as we were informed, was the impression constantly sought to be made on the minds of the Union troops by secessionists; when, in fact, nothing was more false. When General Burnside evacuated the town, there were more than fifty men who left Fredericksburg and its vicinity on account of their Union sentiments. A number of others, who were as true to the Union at heart, no doubt, as those who left, were, by force of circumstances, compelled to remain, but, not having committed themselves so thoroughly, hoped to be able to escape the penalties for treason against Jeff Davis and the Southern Confederacy; and we hope they have escaped punishment. We were truly sorry for them, and deeply regretted that they could not leave when we did.

Secessionists, knowing that they are above suspicion with their own party, and holding all the offices in towns and communities, are always first and foremost to impose themselves on the Federal troops when the latter advance into the territory of the rebellion. Whereas Union men, for fear of being suspicioned and reported by secessionists, act, as a general rule, with more reserve. And hence the first impressions that are made on the minds of the Union troops for the most part when they first enter a community, are made by secessionists, who declare that there is no "respectable Union" influence in the community. And afterwards, if loyal men express Union sentiments, Union troops think they are dissembling, and will perhaps give them the "cold shoulder," which disheartens the Union citizens and tends to crush out the loyal feelings which they have.

Especially are Union men intimidated when they see no difference made between themselves and the most violent secessionists by the officers of the Federal army, and hearing it repeated that the "Yankees don't think half as much of Union men as they do of secessionists," because they believe they are "hypocrites;" and, fearing that the Union soldiers will leave, and that the Confederates will return, they are awed into submission by the infernal rod of tyranny which is constantly being held over them by secessionists, who threaten what shall be done to them and with them "when the time comes." We are not guessing at things now, but writing what we believe and know to be facts. There are numbers of Union men all through the seceded States who are afraid to commit themselves, knowing the terrible consequences which would follow if they should be suspicioned, reported, and convicted by their secesh neighbors of disloyalty to Jeff Davis and the Southern Confederacy. The people know that they have been swindled out of all their rights and privileges, but they know, likewise, that they have no redress under present circumstances, and must therefore submit in silence to the many ten thousand wrongs which have been forced and heaped upon them. They scorn secession, and hate it *worse than they can hate the very devil himself.* But they can't help themselves. What can they do but submit?

The Union feeling in the South is very considerable, and should be sacredly respected and encouraged by the United States Government. Suppose this rebellion should not be put down, and that Jeff Davis should succeed in permanently establishing his empire: what will become of the Union men of the South and of the thousands of refugees who have been driven from their homes and families and forced to leave all their property, and every interest they have on earth, behind? Must they all become totally bankrupt, and return to live among a people to be insulted, persecuted, proscribed, and degraded, they and their children, forever? The thought is revolting. What then? Must they, by force of circumstances, seek new countries and begin the world anew with all the infirmities of age and helpless families? Surely this cannot be, unless justice has taken its everlasting flight from the abode of mortals.

But this is not all. Should the United States Government fail to crush out this rebellion, the whole country in process of time will become disintegrated and broken up, so that not only the Union men of the South, but the whole of the free States, will become the vassals of this great negro-oligarchy. Hence it becomes a question of dignified importance for the most serious and profound consideration of the people of the free States, as well as of the Union men and refugees of and from the South.

We, therefore, argue that with all true patriots and friends of liberty there should be but one party, until this gigantic and wicked rebellion is put down; and that party should be *the uncompromising Union party.* Let all other subjects and questions for the time-being be merged into this one *all*-absorbing consideration, the *salvation of the Union.* Let every lover of *freedom,* every friend to his country, and every friend to humanity say, *The Union must and shall be preserved.* If this be not done, then *America* will become *a land of slaves indeed.* Let the *negro question* in this great struggle be forgotten, and let the whole race be transported to Africa when the proper time comes, where they now ought to be, and from whence they should never have been brought. We can live, thank God, without negroes to wait upon us, but we cannot live without a country! With true patriots this is no war about the "infernal nigger." No: it is a war between *despotism* and *freedom,*—between *tyrants* who are seeking to overthrow the Republic and all the rights of freemen, and the *friends* of liberty, who are fighting and trying to save them. The question is not *whether negroes shall be made free, but whether free white men shall be made slaves! This is the question,* when fairly stated and correctly understood. Give us poverty, but give us freedom! Heap labor and toil upon us, but let them be made tolerable by the blessing of freedom. Strip us of all the *plunder* and *trash* of earth, but as long as heaven's own light shall shine upon our path, and the branches of the tree of *American liberty* shall wave over our head, securing to us the freedom of speech, the freedom of the press, and the freedom of action, we can endure all the ills of life. In a word, *give us liberty, or give us death.*

In conclusion, we would say to the *people* of the South, You confided in your political leaders and spiritual guides, and they abused your confidence. They deceived you, and their deception, consummated, has involved our country in civil war, has desolated Virginia, and sacrificed the South upon the accursed altar of their unhallowed ambition. If they did this thing ignorantly, they are no longer worthy of your confidence; and if they did it knowingly, they are less worthy of it: so that under no circumstances are they worthy of your regard. They *forced* upon you secession, revolution, and civil war. They promised you peace, and have given you war; they promised you plenty, and have given you destitution; they promised you independence and freedom, and have fastened upon you military despotism; they promised you a *permanent basis* for the security and perpetuity of your slave property, and have virtually emancipated all your slaves; they promised you prosperity and happiness, and have given you desolation, lamentation, and woe; they promised you national honor, and have forced upon you national degradation; they promised you day, and have given you night; they promised you light, and have given you darkness; they promised you bread, and have given you stones; they promised you fishes, and have given you scorpions; they promised you life, and have given you death. All these things have your leaders done. They have deceived you, swindled you out of your rights, your freedom, your property, and your happiness. Abandon them; be led by them no longer;

denounce secession as a deadly poison, and return to your former loyalty to your country. *Save the Union, and you save the South; destroy the Union, and you destroy the South.* Stand by the Union until you die,—not that you *love the South less, but the Union more.* League not with speculators, bankers, stock-holders, involved merchants, disappointed office-seekers, aspiring demagogues, ambitious tyrants, political tricksters, clerical knaves, and damnable traitors, to overthrow the Government, to destroy the Union, and to annihilate the South.

THE END.

www.ingramcontent.com/pod-product-compliance
Lightning Source LLC
LaVergne TN
LVHW021124110826
845150LV00005B/944

9781425551186